About the

Søren Kierkegaard (1813–1855) continues to exercise a wide influence on philosophy, theology, and literature. After a youth spent cultivating the lifestyle of a Romantic aesthete, he finished his studies at the University of Copenhagen with the dissertation "On the Concept of Irony." Many of his books were published under exotic pseudonyms and explored different dimensions of life outside Christianity. These include *The Concept of Anxiety*, *Either/Or: A Fragment of Life*, and *Fear and Trembling*. He also wrote a number of more directly devotional works, including *Works of Love* and the discourses collected in *Spiritual Writings*, but in the last years of his life attacked the established Church in a series of polemical leaflets.

About the Translator

George Pattison is Lady Margaret Professor of Divinity at the University of Oxford and a canon of Christ Church Cathedral, Oxford. He is the author of, among other books, *The Philosophy of Kierkegaard* (McGill-Queen's University Press, 2005), *Thinking about God in an Age of Technology* (Oxford University Press, 2005), *Kierkegaard, Religion and the Nineteenth-Century Crisis of Culture* (Cambridge University Press, 2002), and *Kierkegaard's Upbuilding Discourses: Philosophy, Theology, Literature* (Routledge, 2002).

SPIRITUAL
WRITINGS

Also by Søren Kierkegaard

AVAILABLE FROM HARPER PERENNIAL MODERN THOUGHT

The Present Age
(Translated by Alexander Dru)

Works of Love
(Translated by Howard and Edna Hong;
Foreword by George Pattison)

SPIRITUAL
WRITINGS

Gift, Creation, Love

Selections from the Upbuilding Discourses

Søren Kierkegaard

Selected, translated, and with an introduction by
GEORGE PATTISON

HARPER**PERENNIAL** ✖ MODERN**THOUGHT**

NEW YORK • LONDON • TORONTO • SYDNEY • NEW DELHI • AUCKLAND

HARPER**PERENNIAL** ● **x** MODERN**THOUGHT**

HarperCollins books may be purchased for educational, business, or sales promotional use. For information please write: Special Markets Department, HarperCollins Publishers, 10 East 53rd Street, New York, NY 10022.

FIRST EDITION

Designed by Justin Dodd

Library of Congress Cataloging-in-Publication Data is available upon request.

ISBN 978-0-06-187599-1

11 12 13 14   OV/RRD   10 9 8 7 6 5 4 3 2

For all those who read Kierkegaard in order to seek God
and who seek God in order to learn love

Contents

Part III
LOVE: AT THE FEET OF THE SAVIOR

Foreword

There is little doubt as to Kierkegaard's importance in the story of modern European thought. Once described as the leader of modernity's "awkward squad,"* he formulated a set of concepts and concerns that have been revisited many times in the more than one hundred and fifty years since his death. It has undoubtedly been at times of crisis—of which there have been not a few in this period—that he has especially come into his own, times when prevailing systems and worldviews have collapsed under the weight of modernity's complex and contradictory demands, and when culture, intellectual life, and religion have come to the brink of disintegration. If we wanted to pinpoint Kierkegaard's contribution to the history of modern ideas, then, it would be natural to look to such characteristically "Kierkegaardian" terms as melancholy, irony, anxiety, the absurd, the para-

---

* Julian Evans, "Leader of the Awkward Squad," *The Guardian*, November 20, 1993.

xi

dox, the leap of faith, the moment, and despair. Kierkegaard did not, of course, invent these terms, but he gave them new meanings and fresh currency, and his way of using them would be taken up into the philosophy of existence and the theology of crisis in the 1920s and pass from there into French existentialism and, later, postmodernism. But while this history of reception is not entirely unconnected to Kierkegaard, it represents only a part of what was going on in his authorship and—on his own account—not the most important part. In fact, we could go so far as to say that the Kierkegaard known to the history of modern ideas is, in an important sense, not Kierkegaard at all.

The main discussions of nearly all the terms listed above, along with many of the best-known images, stories, and dramatizations by which he brought the abstract terminology of postidealist philosophy to life, are found in works that he published under a series of strange pseudonyms and that, he repeatedly said, by no means represented his own point of view. And while it is also true to say that his journals played an important part in shaping our image of Kierkegaard, these have often been presented in selections that reveal an all too biased editorial hand—a comment that applies equally to selections in Danish, English, French, and German. Where, then, is Kierkegaard's true point of view to be found? He himself consistently claimed that it was not to be found in such pseudonymous works as *Either/Or*, *Fear and Trembling*, *Stages on Life's Way*, *Philosophical Fragments*, or *The Sickness unto Death* but in the religious writings he published under his own name and which he called "upbuilding" (or "edifying") discourses and, sometimes, "Christian" discourses.

What is the difference between these two groups of writings? It is not that the former deal with topics such as music, literature, seduction, and unhappy love affairs while the latter speak about prayer, worship, and other religious matters. Religion is already a prominent

theme in the pseudonymous works, whether in terms of the com-
fortable Biedermeier religiosity of Assessor Vilhelm in *Either/Or*, the
paradoxical faith of Johannes Climacus (the pseudonymous author of
Philosophical Fragments), or the extreme Christianity of Kierkegaard's
last pseudonym, Anti-Climacus, who professed a radical version of
Christianity that Kierkegaard declared himself unable to live up to.
So there is plenty of religion in the pseudonymous works, but even
when it is specifically called "Christianity," it is generally presented
by the pseudonyms in terms of a "thought experiment," as one possibility among others that the reader is invited to contemplate and play
with, but without regard to putting it into practice. This is very different in the case of Kierkegaard's discourses. These are modeled on
contemporary printed sermons, and, as such, they presume that the
reader is someone who is serious about living religiously. Readers are
repeatedly addressed as "You" and invited to give their own response
to what the author—or, as he often refers to himself, "the speaker"—
is proposing. Everything is to be tested against our life experience
and, if it fits, to be applied in life or, to use that characteristically
Kierkegaardian term, existence. The discourses are not thought ex-
periments but offer real input into real problems.

Yet they are not exactly like the sermons on which, in literary
terms, they model themselves. For, unlike a preacher, Kierkegaard
does not presume to stand in a relation of authority to his readers. He
cannot tell them what to believe or do, he can only seek to persuade
them or to recommend a new way of looking at their lives and the
challenges they face. So here, too, as in the pseudonymous works,
there is a kind of "indirect communication," a play of possibilities
that gives scope for imaginative invention and transformation—not
least, as we shall see, when Kierkegaard takes up the theme of the
lilies and the birds mentioned in the Sermon on the Mount and turns
them into teachers who lead their students into a world sometimes

resembling that of Hans Christian Andersen's fairy tales. The discourses are not plodding expositions of ready-made dogmas but have an almost conversational feel, sometimes serious, sometimes playful, but always seeking to open a dialogue with the reader, whose own response is anticipated and responded to.

Like many authors, including authors of prose fiction, Kierkegaard may be said to construct his reader, to assume a certain set of commitments and attitudes that he then engages and either challenges or helps the reader deepen and develop. But what if these are not our commitments and attitudes? What if you do not recognize yourself in Kierkegaard's imagined reader? After all, it is rather well known that fewer people today class themselves as Christian believers than in Kierkegaard's time, and many say they have no belief at all. Even among the believers, many of the ways in which Christianity is formulated and expressed today differ considerably from those familiar to the mid-nineteenth-century Danish Lutherans who were Kierkegaard's first readers. And today, there will also be many readers of Kierkegaard who, if they are religious, belong to religious traditions other than Christianity. If the lack of religious commitment in the pseudonymous works allows them to speak to our arguably post-Christian age, what about the discourses? How can those who do not share Kierkegaard's religious assumptions find a way into these avowedly religious works and benefit from them?

As a first step to answering this important question we should note that Kierkegaard typically uses one of two designations for these discourses. Sometimes he calls them "upbuilding" or "edifying" discourses and sometimes—only sometimes—specifically "*Christian*" discourses. Broadly speaking (there are exceptions), it is the earlier discourses that are described as "upbuilding," while the later ones are more frequently called "Christian." This progression corresponds to the development that Kierkegaard claimed was also to be seen in the

movement of the pseudonymous authorship, namely, a movement
from the rather diffuse aesthetic or ethical worldview of his contemporaries to a more decisively religious position and then on to a specifically Christian life of faith and discipleship. With regard to the
upbuilding discourses themselves, Kierkegaard's own pseudonymous
author Johannes Climacus wrote that they are not in fact Christian
in an emphatic sense, since they do not assume the authority either of
Christ or of Scripture—in fact, he claims, they do not even mention
Christ or deploy Christianity's distinctively paradoxical concepts. All
they assume, he implies, is that they are addressed to readers who are
ready to take seriously the possibility of religion. But how much (or
how little) does that involve?

The claim that the upbuilding discourses do not overlap with what
is distinctively Christian doesn't entirely stand up. While it is true
that Kierkegaard consistently avoids speaking as if he had any kind of
authority, even the early discourses draw attention to the authoritative
nature of apostolic teaching and put in play such doctrinal concepts
as the Fall—while Christ Himself makes an appearance in several of
them and is shown as offering liberation from situations of sin and
suffering. And yet—although this is something readers must test for
themselves—the tone is, in a way that is hard to define, very different from that of a sermon. Even where apostolic authority or Christ's
saving love are mentioned, the reader is not so much being instructed
to accept this as to consider how and why it might be important for
him or her to accept this authority or believe in this love. In fact, all
that is really assumed on the part of readers of the early discourses is
that they have become concerned about the meaning of their life in
the world and are prepared to listen seriously to the speaker's sugges-
tions as to where such concern is pointing them and how it is miscon-
ceived if it ends up in anxious self-absorption when its real function is
to help them find a deeper and more solid foundation for their lives.

The later discourses will, it is true, presume rather more than this. Several of them are written in the form of addresses given to those about to receive Communion at the penitential Friday Communion service that Kierkegaard especially liked to attend in Copenhagen's Church of Our Lady. But can these later discourses speak to those who do not believe that Jesus Christ is the Son of God who died to save them from their sins and whose body and blood are offered for them at the altar?

Many Christians will be able to take Kierkegaard at his word and will not imagine that there could be any better way of saying what needs to be said. But, I suggest, even those who do not share this faith can find great value in his discourses and even take comfort and encouragement from them if they read them in the larger context of Kierkegaard's program of existential questioning and personal deepening. And, as often in our pluralistic world, we must be ready for what philosophers might call "hermeneutical generosity," that is, the willingness to enter into worlds of thought and experience other than our own with the assumption that they will prove to be humanly important testimonies. In order to see how we might do this in the particular case of Kierkegaard's discourses, let us therefore take a step back and look at the overall view of life presented in them, with particular reference to those translated in this present collection.

GIFT, CREATION, LOVE

First, it may be useful to set out some of the, as it were, "technical" facts about the discourses assembled here. They are only a relatively small selection from the overall body of such writings produced by Kierkegaard over roughly a ten-year period. In each of the years 1843 and 1844, he published three sets of, respectively, two, three, and four upbuilding discourses, the printed remainders of which were bound together and sold as *Eighteen Upbuilding Discourses.** In 1845 there followed a volume of three short discourses, *Discourses on Imagined Occasions*, which dealt with confession, marriage, and death (none of which are included here). 1847 saw the publication of two substantial sets of discourses, *Upbuilding Discourses in Various Spirits* and *Works of Love*. *Upbuilding Discourses in Various Spirits* itself was divided into three parts, the first of which, "On the Occasion of Confession," was published separately in English under the title *Purity of Heart*. The theme of the lilies and the birds, found in the second part of *Upbuilding Discourses in Various Spirits*, is taken up again in the first part of Kierkegaard's 1848 collection *Christian Discourses.†* Thereafter, Kierkegaard published only smaller sets of one, two, or three discourses, the last in 1851, when he was thirty-eight years old, and just four years before his death.‡ Several of these later discourses involve two texts that Kierkegaard had already commented on previously, namely, 1 Peter 4:8, "Love hides a multitude of sins" and Luke 7:37–50, the story of the sinful woman who came uninvited to a dinner held at the house of Simon the Pharisee for Jesus and who fell at Jesus's feet, washing them with precious ointment and wiping them with her hair.

---

* Discourses 1–4 and 11–12 in the present collection come from the *Eighteen Upbuilding Discourses*.

† Discourses 5–7 in this collection are from *Upbuilding Discourses in Various Spirits*; Discourses 8–9 are from *Christian Discourses*. The three-part discourse *The Lily of the Field and the Bird under Heaven* was published as a freestanding booklet in 1849, under that title; it is presented here as Discourse 10, "Silence, Obedience, and Joy."

‡ Discourse 13 in this volume was published independently under the title *An Upbuilding Discourse* in 1850; Discourse 14 is from the collection *The High Priest, the Tax Collector, and the Sinful Woman* (1849). The final two discourses (15–16) were published together in 1851 with the title *Two Upbuilding Discourses*.

This collection, then, is far from being an exhaustive presentation of Kierkegaard's religious writings, and there are undoubtedly themes and topics that are not sufficiently represented. Nevertheless, I believe that the three sections into which I have grouped this selection—"The Gift," "Creation," and "Love"—do identify three key points in the overall architectonics of Kierkegaard's discourse literature and, more broadly, of his religious vision.

Of course, this will come as a surprise to those who see Kierkegaard exclusively in terms of anxiety, guilt, and despair. For it suggests that what is central to his religious outlook is not the anxious or despairing individual preparing to make an absurd leap of faith but, instead, a simple basic trust in the goodness of the life we have been given and faith in the power of love to overcome whatever might threaten such trust or mar such goodness. Paraphrasing Gerard Manley Hopkins, we may speak of a "goodness deep down things," and if this collection can be said to have an "argument" it is that just such a goodness deep down things is the ground bass of what Kierkegaard means by "upbuilding." Once this foundation has been laid, "love" (whether the love of human beings for one another, their love for God, or God's love for them) cannot be dismissed as an illusory consolation that, for a brief while, brightens the encompassing darkness of a tragic universe—for love is simply the ultimate and freely enacted fulfillment of this same goodness. Kierkegaard probably did not read Dante, but I think he would almost certainly have agreed with the Florentine poet—and, in one of the discourses on the lilies and the birds, virtually says—that the love of which religion speaks is nothing otherworldly but simply the human realization of "the love that moves the sun and other stars." We encounter this love already in the simple fact of our existence, in the humble life of nature, and in the possibilities of acceptance and renewal experienced by those who had, for a while, forgotten it or turned away from it.

The first section, then, "The Gift," includes three discourses on what Kierkegaard sometimes described as his "favorite" text, "Every good and every perfect gift comes from above, from the Father of Lights, in whom is no change or shadow of turning." This comes from the Epistle of James (James 1:17), a work that Luther had famously described as an "epistle of straw" because he saw it as undermining Paul's doctrine of salvation by faith alone without any involvement of human works. Be that as it may, it serves Kierkegaard as summing up the meaning of faith in divine providence, and here as elsewhere it is typical of his existential approach that this is not to be interpreted in terms of cosmic or metaphysical arguments but in relation to human experience. What we affirm in affirming that every good and perfect gift comes from above, according to Kierkegaard, is that there is nothing in what we are, nothing in what we have, and nothing we could ever experience that cannot or could not count as a "good and perfect gift." The first step in the path of upbuilding, then, is simply to acknowledge this and to give thanks for it—or, to put it another way, unconditionally to accept and to affirm ourselves as what we are, as where we are, and as how we are. And, at this point, perhaps it doesn't matter too much whether we think of the "giver" as "God" or "life" or, simply, "existence."

Immediately, then, we can see that although Kierkegaard seeks to speak to his contemporaries in a gentler tone in these discourses than he does elsewhere, he is from the very beginning setting his face against some of modernity's most cherished assumptions. In particular, he is taking issue with the modern aspiration to autonomy, an assumption that, from Kant to Sartre, sees only what we are able to think and do for ourselves as humanly valuable. As Sartre would put it, "You are the sum of your actions"—but for Kierkegaard we are never able to think or to do anything if we have not first been given and accepted the gift of being. We only "are" on the basis of life being given us in the first place. Of course, we must *accept* the gift and, as these discourses show, Kierkegaard was well aware of the many strategies by which people seek to evade the responsibility involved in such acceptance and how prone they are to indulge more or less disreputable fantasies about how much better life would be if they were somewhere else or someone else. In this Kierkegaardian perspective, then, acceptance is the first and most difficult of all the tasks with which life confronts us.

But Kierkegaard doesn't just offend our modern spirit of autonomy. He also offends, perhaps more seriously, against our modern sense of how the horrendous sufferings that afflict some human beings make a mockery of Christianity's talk about a good and loving God. From the Great Lisbon Earthquake of 1755 through to the Holocaust and beyond, modernity has been stalked by events that render ideas of progress and harmony almost laughable. It was in this context that the twentieth century rediscovered those passages in the Book of Job in which the eponymous protagonist railed against the injustice of God with a scalding rhetoric that few modern atheists have been able to match. Kierkegaard, however, seems quite out of step with this modern experience when, in a further discourse on the gift titled " 'The Lord gave, the Lord took away, blessed be the name of the Lord,' " he focuses on those earlier passages in which Job bowed patiently beneath the weight of his sufferings and refused his wife's advice to curse God and die. Yet Kierkegaard was far from being unaware of how Job then went on angrily to accuse God of injustice; in fact, in his pseudonymous book *Repetition*, it was just this aspect of Job he had emphasized. In doing so, he was one of the first to remind modern Europe that the biblical Job was so far from being the "patient Job" of pious legend that he rather resembled Dostoyevsky's Ivan Karamazov, and his words anticipated Ivan's famous "rebellion." Kierkegaard, then, fully understood that Job's words of acceptance are meaningless if they are mere platitudes, and that for those tested by extreme suffering acceptance is an act of seemingly infinite difficulty. Nevertheless, he insists in this discourse (as in others) that it is acceptance, and not anger, defiance, or denial, that is the only possible basis for reintegration and stepping forward into the future. Even in the hour of terror, our first task is to identify the good and perfect gift that God is giving us or to believe that there is a good and perfect gift in it. And, again, perhaps the point can also be understood by those who cannot speak of God but only of "life" or "existence."

The discourses on the gift focus strongly on the human being who accepts or who is striving (and perhaps even struggling) to accept their life as a gift. But the possibility of such acceptance is not grounded solely in human psychology. Rather (in Kierkegaard's view), human psychology reflects a broader and, in some sense, deeper context, a context that the modern world calls "nature" and that theology calls "Creation." It is especially in the discourses on the lilies and the birds that Kierkegaard explores this larger context, and a selection of these discourses make up nearly half of the present volume.

In these discourses Kierkegaard explores what he sees as a uniquely human propensity for being dissatisfied with life and a uniquely human sense of alienation from our natural instincts, needs, and passions—in short, our wanting to be other than we are. Everywhere else we look in nature, each creature is what and as it is and fulfills the law of its being simply by being what and as it is. We, on the other hand, constantly experience our lives as something we want to escape or to change in some more or less radical way. Again, this can be connected with our distinctively modern aspiration toward autonomy. We don't want to be as nature intended us to be; instead, we want to choose the values and the projects in which we find fulfillment so as to be fulfilled only on our own terms.

But, we might object to Kierkegaard, surely many people's lives are such that it is only too understandable that they want to change them? Again, Kierkegaard knows this, and the typical scenario that these discourses address is not that of those who merely want to assert their autonomy for the sake of it but of those whose alienation from their original or natural self is a reaction to adversity or to their wishes and longings being blocked and obstructed by external circumstances. In these terms, the lilies and the birds provide a counterpoint to human beings afflicted by melancholy, anxiety, worry, and a host of larger or smaller, real or imagined troubles. In fact, when Kierkegaard takes us out to the countryside to be alone with the lilies and the birds, he also shows us or reminds us of many of the angst-ridden characters we encounter in the pseudonymous works—only now we get to see them from the other side. Whereas the pseudonyms sometimes seemed to gild melancholy, anxiety, and despair with a certain tragic heroism or even glamour, the lilies and the birds make us realize that these characters are desperately in need of healing and that healing is there for them, if only they are willing to accept it. The reintegration of the self, becoming who we are and as we are on the basis of a radical and all-embracing self-acceptance is a therapeutic possibility because it is rooted and grounded in our fundamental human constitution or, as some might call it, our "nature," our being God's creatures, gifted with the divine image and likeness—a view that Kierkegaard explicitly endorses. Just being human is in and of itself a ground for joy, it is a glory and a promise, and no matter how much we may want to be other than we are, we can achieve nothing if we forget the infinite debt we owe simply by virtue of existing. In the spirit of the great German theologian F. D. E. Schleiermacher, who defined religion as a "feeling of absolute dependence," Kierkegaard insists that human freedom is inseparable from our absolute dependence on God.

Often it is external states of affairs that block our drive to self-fulfillment and that make us anxious and depressed. But more profoundly—or, at least, more sharply—we often sense that we ourselves are the cause of all our troubles, either because of the way we have treated others or because of how we have misused, abused, or simply failed to use the gifts and opportunities we have been given. We are not only afflicted by a mismatch between ourselves and our world but by a kind of split within ourselves: we are not as we want to be, or what we want to be is not what we are—and we ourselves are responsible, we ourselves are guilty of frustrating or undermining our own possibilities for a good and fulfilling life.

In a sense, if Kierkegaard is correct, this is indeed how it is, because we are in fact free to choose to be like the lilies and the birds, free to accept all that we have and are—including our troubles—as a good and perfect gift. But Kierkegaard does not say this in order to aggravate any guilt we might already feel. On the contrary, he does so precisely so as to help us be free of it. The overriding theme of the third group of discourses, collected here under the title "Love," is therefore the call to let go of guilt and sin in the sure and certain knowledge that we are loved. And, Kierkegaard counsels, if we are in any doubt as to this, the simplest and best way to learn it is that we ourselves should begin to love and to see the world and our neighbor with the eye of love, since, as he repeatedly reminds us, love hides a multitude of sins.

Kierkegaard knew how deeply the sense of guilt could strike a person, and he knew that the real problem of guilt is essentially the problem of self-hatred, the belief that we ourselves are responsible for everything that has gone wrong in our lives. Face to face with guilt, we are face to face with the question of whether we can endure to go on living with ourselves as we are. The stakes couldn't be higher.

That Kierkegaard was fully aware of this—and to a degree that most of us, understandably enough, don't want to be—is revealed in what is perhaps one of the most poignant and even terrifying passages in his entire authorship. This is to be found in the last of the discourses to be presented here, the discourse on 1 Peter 4:8. In this text, Kierkegaard addresses himself directly to Christ, something that is rare, perhaps even unique in his entire authorship. He admits to the one he addresses as his "Lord and Savior" that there is "one person on earth I hate and despise, one person whom I would fly to the world's end to avoid"—and then heart-wrenchingly adds that this "one person" is "myself." Self-hatred has rarely found a stronger expression, but—and the *but* cannot be emphasized strongly enough—love nevertheless has the power to hide a multitude of sins and, not least, to help us love even ourselves.

This, then, is the context for Kierkegaard's fascination with the sinful woman described in Luke 7. From some of his earliest discourses to some of his last, she is a recurring presence in his writings about love, and the image of her silently weeping at the Savior's feet

Seventeenth-century engraving by François Ragot illustrating Luke 7, after Rubens's *Feast of Simon the Pharisee.*

is an image to which he repeatedly returns. But this, he insists, is not an image of despair. Rather, it is an image, arguably the image par excellence, of how love enables us to make an act of infinite self-acceptance on the far side of guilt and sin, annihilating them, as it were, and leaving only love.

Kierkegaard's thought on this point is entirely in the mainstream of historic Christianity, Catholic and Protestant, and it is essentially the same thought that is familiar to many in the words of George Herbert's poem "Love":

Love bade me welcome, yet my soul drew back,
Guilty of dust and sin.
But quick-eyed Love, observing me grow slack
From my first entrance in,
Drew nearer to me, sweetly questioning,
If I lack'd anything.

"A guest," I answer'd, 'worthy to be here":
Love said, "You shall be he."
"I the unkind, ungrateful? Ah my dear,
I cannot look on thee."
Love took my hand, and smiling did reply,
"Who made the eyes but I?"

"Truth, Lord, but I have marr'd them: let my shame
Go where it doth deserve."
"And know you not," says Love, "who bore the blame?"
"My dear, then I will serve."
"You must sit down," says Love, "and taste my meat":
So I did sit and eat.

Again, we must acknowledge that many readers will not be able to accept the Christian beliefs about Christ being the Son of God whose death serves as an atonement for sin that underwrite Kierkegaard's (and Herbert's) views. But remember, for Kierkegaard himself this was not what he elsewhere called a matter of "objective" beliefs, not a matter of agreeing to some theoretical or historical truth, but subjective, existential truth. In this perspective the surest way to be convinced of love's power to annihilate guilt is by choosing to love. It is not our beliefs about love that matter but whether we are prepared to take love's risk. "Experience will decide," as a well-known hymn puts it.

There is a great deal more to be found in these discourses than has been mentioned in this introductory overview. Indeed, it is precisely in their detailed accounts of the manifold ways in which we are constantly seeking, losing, and finding our way to love that their extraordinary power and interest lies. Kierkegaard has long been celebrated for his psychological acuity, and his discourses do not fall behind the pseudonymous works in this respect. But they are also notable for their astonishing literary and rhetorical inventiveness, as Kierkegaard spins imaginary scenarios out of what in the biblical text he is commenting on are mere hints. The most striking example of this is when he starts making up fairy stories about the lilies and the birds, but there are many more. In this connection, the discourses richly illustrate Kierkegaard's exceptional gifts as a reader of the Bible. Underwritten by a rigorous academic training as well as by a deep familiarity with the Bible through private devotion and public worship, Kierkegaard offers something like a virtuoso performance of the biblical text, making it speak in unexpected, startling, and revealing ways. Some more solemn-minded Christians might feel that Kierkegaard-the-Bible-reader is a little too much like Kierkegaard-the-poet. Nevertheless, the overarching

vision that informs the way he reads each particular text is funda-
mentally congruent with historic Christianity, even as it restates
Christian teaching in a way that can speak to those of all faiths and
none. It is the purpose of my three keywords—Gift, Creation, and
Love—to hint at the trajectory of this vision, not in the sense that
they provide an instantly memorizable summary of the whole but
as an invitation to enter into dialogue with the discourses and as
an assurance that what these texts have to offer is for our good: to
build us up in gratitude for the gift of being, in joy at being who we
are, and in love for love itself.

George Pattison
Oxford University
January 2010

A Note on the Translation

A few words should be offered about the translation. I have followed the text found in the most recent and definitive Danish edition of Kierkegaard's writings and have been enormously helped by the extensive explanatory notes that not only identify Kierkegaard's many subtle references but also elucidate his sometimes archaic terms and phrases.* Kierkegaard himself rarely gave references to the biblical texts he cites or alludes to in passing. Where he does, I have followed his practice of putting these in parentheses in the text. I have added other direct references to Scripture in footnotes but have not attempted to note all the occasions when Kierkegaard alludes to or reworks the biblical text in developing his own thought. Beyond that, I have not sought to burden the text with a scholarly apparatus that would only prove off-putting for the purpose for which the collection is offered, namely, for readers to experience for themselves something of the existential edification that Kierkegaard is aiming at.

I have not used a standard English-language translation of the Bible for Kierkegaard's Bible references. This is because he himself rarely

---

* Niels Jørgen Cappelørn et al., eds., *Søren Kierkegaards Skrifter* (Copenhagen: Gad, 1994–). A full reference will be given for each discourse.

quotes the Bible in a precise form, preferring more or less free variations on the strict letter of the text. Generally, however, I have borne
in mind the tradition of translation of the King James and the Revised
Standard Version, because their idioms often have much in common
with the standard Danish translation of Kierkegaard's day. However,
as that was a combination of an eighteenth-century version of the Old
Testament and an 1819 translation of the New, it would not have been
experienced as antiquated by Kierkegaard's first readers in the way that
we experience King James as antiquated, and I have therefore avoided
thees and *thous* and other archaic spellings or formulations. The discourses on the lilies and the birds are prefaced by the set reading for a
given Sunday in the Church's year, and in this case I have given the full
text in the Revised Standard Version, with modernized English.

I have sought to bring Kierkegaard's text as close as possible to
current English usage without substantially compromising the fact
that it is, after all, a sample of mid-nineteenth-century religious literature and, as such, makes many assumptions contemporary readers will not share. Clearly, Kierkegaard held many of the views of his
age about gender roles, for example, and the relationship between
parents and children. He treats it as self-evident that a woman's
place is in the home, and that naughty children should be smacked.
I have not even attempted to soften the passages where these views
are made explicit and assume that anyone reading this will deal
with them as they deal with these or similar issues in other writings that predate the 1960s. However, it is important to add that
Kierkegaard's position on gender issues may be more complex than
it at first seems, and we should not forget that, in the end, it is a
woman (albeit a self-abasing sinful woman) who provides him with
the exemplary instance of a life that truly expresses Christian love.

More generally, I have been somewhat free in adapting Kierkegaard's often exclusive language to contemporary gender-inclusive

usage. Kierkegaard frequently uses *he* when speaking of nonspeci-
fied persons in general, and I have mostly handled this in one of
two ways, according to context. Often I have made such expressions
as *one* or *a person* the subject of the sentence and then employed
plural pronouns elsewhere, which is inelegant and, some would say,
barbaric but a widely used and understood solution nonetheless. My
second approach has been to utilize a plural form, *we* or *they*, and
although I have made extensive use of such constructions, I have a
slight worry that Kierkegaard wants us to be picturing his examples
as individual cases. However, I suspect—and hope—that in the pro-
cess of reading, the plural "we" or "they" will subtly transmute in
the reader's mind into a representative individual who *qua representative* has, in any case, something of the "we" about "them"—it
could be you, it could be me, it could be any of us!

There are passages in which I have wondered whether Kierkegaard himself wouldn't have benefited from editorial assistance, and
whether he himself hadn't got lost in the extraordinarily long sen-
tences and double or multiple rhetorical negatives that belong to the
genre. Because this is a translation intended for the general reader
rather than scholarship I have had few qualms about shortening sen-
tences and paragraphs, but occasionally—as is inevitable—I have had
to make strong interpretative decisions about just where Kierkegaard
is taking us.

There is one set of terms that merits particular comment, namely
those relating to the Danish words *Bekymring* and *Sorg*, terms that are
also closely related to that most Kierkegaardian of words, *Angest*, although this latter rarely appears in the discourses. Not least in connection with Kierkegaard's exposition of the Sermon on the Mount, these
are free and sometimes interchangeable expressions of a state of mind
that may variously be called anxiety, trouble, worry, care, sorrow, or
grief (the King James version of the Sermon on the Mount simply tells

us to "take no thought for the morrow"). Importantly, these would feed into Kierkegaard's bequest to modern existential philosophy, but here I am assuming that they are not technical terms and I have taken a certain amount of liberty in varying my translation of them for the sake of readability and to ensure that the echo of the biblical text is not lost.

Undoubtedly the discourses require patience. They were not written for those conditioned to our sound-bite culture, although there are some good sound bites in them. Sometimes I have speculated that part of their role is precisely to train the reader in patience. But if the discourses sometimes flow more slowly than we might want them to, they also offer an extraordinary array of charms, surprises, shocks, and even, occasionally, laughs. And don't we mostly need to learn to go a little more slowly if we are not to overlook just how many good things have already been given us?

G. P.

Part I

THE GIFT:
"Every good and every perfect gift is from above"

1

Understanding the Gift[*]

"EVERY GOOD AND EVERY PERFECT GIFT IS FROM ABOVE AND COMES DOWN FROM THE FATHER OF LIGHTS, IN WHOM IS NO CHANGE OR SHADOW OF TURNING."[†]

These words are so beautiful, so eloquent, and so moving that it is certainly not their fault if the listener does not attend to them or they find no echo in our hearts. They are spoken by one of the Lord's apostles, and even if we don't sense their deeper meaning we may nevertheless be assured that they are not spoken loosely or idly and are not a fanciful expression for some airy thought. No, they are trustworthy and steadfast, tried and tested—like the life of the apostle who wrote them. They are not spoken accidentally but with special emphasis, nor are they spoken in passing but are introduced by an urgent warning: "Do not go astray, dearly beloved" (James 1:16). We can therefore be confident that they not only have the power to elevate us but also the strength to support us—for they are words that supported an

---

* From Niels Jørgen Cappelørn et al., eds., *Søren Kierkegaards Skrifter*, vol. 5 (Copenhagen: Gad, 1998), pp. 41–56.
† James 1:17.

apostle through a tempestuous life. Nor are they spoken without any connection to what else is being said. When the apostle says, "Do not go astray, dearly beloved," he is warning the listener against the fearful error of believing that God might tempt a person and against the deception of a heart that wants to tempt God. We may therefore be certain that this saying has the power to expose the deception and to restrain the erring thoughts.

SOME WAYS OF MISUNDERSTANDING THE SAYING

"EVERY GOOD AND EVERY PERFECT GIFT IS FROM ABOVE AND COMES DOWN FROM THE FATHER OF LIGHTS, IN WHOM IS NO CHANGE OR SHADOW OF TURNING."

These words have been repeated over and over again in the world, and yet many live as if they have never heard them and perhaps it would have disturbed them if they had. They go on their way without a care, a friendly fate has made it all so easy for them—their every wish is granted, everything they undertake succeeds. Without knowing how, they are in the midst of life's onward movement, a link in the chain that binds past and future, and without bothering to know how, they are carried forward by the present moment, as if on a wave. They are as relaxed as if it was a law of nature that allowed a human life to unfold in the world in the same way that a carpet of flowers spreads across the earth. They live through life's changes happily and contentedly, and they never, not even for a moment, want to tear themselves away from how things are. They are reasonable enough to give credit to whom credit is due—they are grateful for the good gifts they have received, they offer help to those who they think need it and in a manner that they think suits their needs. They are aware that there are good and perfect gifts, and they also know where they come from, for the earth brings forth its growth, and the heavens give the early and the latter rain, and family and friends mean well by them, and their wise and sensible plans succeed—which is, of course, entirely natural, since they are wise and sensible. They do not see any riddles in life and yet their life itself is a riddle, a dream, and the apostle's earnest warning "Do not go astray" does not give them pause. They have no time to attend to it, not even to the words—and why should they worry about the wave that has borne them here, or where it will take them next? Even if one or two of them, whose minds aspired to something higher, did attend to the apostle's words, it wasn't for long. They let their thoughts be occupied by the words for a moment and concluded, "Now we've understood them, bring us new thoughts that we haven't understood." Nor were they entirely wrong in saying this, for the apostle's words are not difficult—and yet their readiness to leave them behind once they had understood them showed that they hadn't understood them at all.

"EVERY GOOD AND EVERY PERFECT GIFT IS FROM ABOVE AND COMES DOWN FROM THE FATHER OF LIGHTS, IN WHOM IS NO CHANGE OR SHADOW OF TURNING."

These words are so consoling and soothing, but how many have there been who really understood how to suck the rich nourishment of comfort from them, or who really understood how to take them to heart? Take, for example, those careworn people whom life never allowed to grow old and die in childlike confidence, who were not nourished by the milk of good fortune but on whom life turned its back; or take the sorrowful ones, whose thoughts sought to penetrate behind life's changing circumstances to what abides—such people received the apostle's words and attended to them. Indeed, the more they let their souls sink down into them, forgetting everything else, the stronger and more confident they felt. Yet it soon became clear that such strength was a delusion. No matter how much confidence they gained, they did not gain the strength to interpenetrate the whole of life. At one moment their minds, full of sorrow and wild thoughts, turned to that rich comfort, but in the next they once again encountered the opposite. Finally it struck them that perhaps these words almost posed a danger to their peace of mind because they aroused a confidence that was constantly disappointed: they gave them wings that could perhaps lift them up to God but didn't help them on their way through life. They didn't deny the inexhaustible comfort that the words offered, but even though they praised them they almost became afraid of them. It is as if a person owned a beautiful ornament whose beauty was beyond dispute. Such a person might take it out from time to time and find pleasure in it but, after a while, come to regard it as not suitable for daily use—even though the festive occasion when it would come into its own never arrived. So the ornament gets put aside, and its owner mournfully reflects that despite having such an ornament life never provided the opportunity for it to be joyfully brought forth.

And so they sat there in their quiet sorrow. They were not hardened against the comfort that the words offered. They were humble enough to acknowledge that life is a dark saying, and they allowed their thoughts to be quick to listen if any word of explanation should be heard—and likewise became slow to speak and slow to get angry. They did not presume to discard the words and waited only for the right time to come when they might be understood. If it came, then they would be saved, they thought. And perhaps it might be like that, you say, dear listener! But is there only a spirit that witnesses in heaven and no spirit that witnesses on earth? Is it only heaven, only the spirit that flees the earth, that is able to know that God is good? Does life on earth know nothing of this? Is there no harmony between what happens in heaven and what happens on earth? Is there joy in heaven and only sorrow on earth—or only the report that there is joy in heaven? Does God in heaven bring forth his good gifts and keep them for us in heaven so that we may one day receive them there?

Perhaps you have thought of it like that when your heart went astray. You didn't require signs and wonders to be performed for your sake. You didn't childishly want your every wish to be fulfilled. All you wanted, early and late, was some testimony—for your troubled soul harbored one wish. If this wish could be fulfilled, then all would be well. Nothing would then stop you thanking and praising God. It would be a time for celebration, and with all your heart you would testify that every good and perfect gift comes down from above. But look at what happened: it was not to be. And so your soul became restless, tumbled about in the passion of your desire. Not that you became defiant or wild: you did not impatiently throw aside the reins of humility, and you did not forget that you are on earth and God is in heaven. With humble prayers and fiery yearning it was as if you sought to tempt God: "This one wish is so important to me, it is my joy, my peace, my future," you said. "Everything depends on it. It is so important to me and so easy for God, for He is almighty." But it was not granted. In vain you sought rest. In your fruitless frenzy you left nothing unexamined. You climbed the vertiginous peaks of premonition to see if you might glimpse some possibility of fulfillment. If you believed that you saw something, then immediately you were ready with your prayers to see if they might help turn what was merely apparent into a reality. But it was a mirage. You came down again, and you resigned yourself to the dull weariness of sorrow. You knew that time would pass: morning came, and evening, but the day you were waiting for never came. And yet you did all you could; you prayed early and late, more and more inwardly, more and more temptingly.

Ah! But still it didn't happen. And so you gave it up. Instead, you decided to adapt yourself to being patient, to waiting with quiet long-ing—if only you could be certain that eternity would bring you your wish, the one thing that was your eyes' desire and your heart's long-ing. Alas, even this certainty was denied you!

But when your busy thoughts had worked themselves to a stand-still in this way, when fruitless wishes had exhausted your soul, then you perhaps became quieter in yourself. Hidden and unnoticed, it perhaps happened that your mind became more gentle and took to heart the words that had been planted in you and that were able to give a blessing to your soul—namely, the saying that every good and perfect gift comes down from above. Then in all humility you did indeed acknowledge that God had certainly not deceived you, that He took your earthly wishes and ignoble desires and exchanged them for heavenly comfort and holy thoughts. He didn't mistreat you by denying you your wish, since he gave you faith in your heart. Your wish, even if it could have encompassed everything, could at the most have given you the whole world—but instead of this God gave you a faith whereby you gained God and overcame the world. Then you realized with humble joy that God was still the almighty Creator of heaven and earth who had not only created the world from nothing but who had done something yet more wonderful: creating the incor-ruptible life of a quiet spirit from your impatient and unstable heart. Then, shamefacedly, you had to admit that it was good, so good for you, that God did not allow himself to be tempted. Then you under-stood the apostle's warning and why it was connected to the error of wanting to tempt God. Then you gained insight into how wrong your behavior had been. You had been wanting God's ideas about what was good for you to be the same as yours and wanting the proof that He was Creator of heaven and earth to depend on whether or not he was able to fulfill your wish. But, of course, if He shared your ideas,

He would cease to be the almighty Father. In your childish impatience you had been wanting to weaken God's eternal Being. You had been so blind as to deceive yourself into thinking that you would have been helped by God knowing no better than you yourself knew what was good for you. You had no thought at all for the fearful possibility that what you had wished for was something no human being could endure if it came to pass.

Let us for a moment speak in a foolish and human way. If there was someone in whom you had complete confidence because you believed he meant the best by you, and if you had one idea as to what was best for you and he had another, what then? Of course, you would try to persuade him, maybe even beseeching him to swear that he would give you what you wanted. But if he persisted in refusing, you would stop asking and would say to yourself that if your prayers had moved him to do what he didn't think was right then something really dreadful would have happened: "I would have been so weak as to make him equally weak, and I would have lost both him and my confidence in him even if in the moment of intoxication I had called his weakness love," you would have had to admit.

But perhaps that is not how it was for you. Perhaps you were too old to nurture childish ideas about God, and too mature to think of Him in a human way. Perhaps you wanted to move Him by your defiance. You certainly understood that life was a dark saying, but you were ready to leave it at that. Why should you be bothered to look for an explanation—and so your heart was hardened. Outwardly you were at peace, perhaps even well-disposed toward the world, and the way you talked was good-natured enough—but deep within the secret workshop of your mind you said, "No"; that is, you didn't say it, but you heard a voice that said, "God tempts a person." Cold despair froze your spirit, and its death-dealing breath brooded over your heart. And if, from time to time, life once more touched something

within you, then wild voices raged back, voices that didn't belong to
you but that seemed to come from inside you.

Why was your lament so forceful, your cry so penetrating, your
prayer so aggressive? Was it not because you believed that your sufferings were so great and your cares so crushing that your complaint
was fully justified? Isn't that what made your voice so powerful as to
resound in heaven and summon God forth from his hidden depths
where, as it seemed to you, He sat tranquil and indifferent, without
regard to the world or the fates of those on it? But heaven remained
locked against such presumptuous words and, as it is written, God
is tempted by no one.* Your speeches were powerless, your thoughts
were powerless, just as your arm was powerless. Your prayer was not
heard in heaven—but when you humbled yourself under God's powerful hand and, crushed in spirit, sighed, "My God, my God, my sin
is great, so great that it cannot be forgiven," then heaven opened
again. In the words of a prophet, it was as if God looked down from
His window at you and said, "Yet a little while, yet a little while, and
I shall renew the face of the earth."† And look: your face was renewed,
and in your barren mind God's merciful grace loved forth the gentleness that receives the word. Then you humbly acknowledged before
God that God tempts no one but that everyone is tempted when they
are lured and led by their own desires, just as you had been tempted
by your proud and lofty and defiant thoughts. Then you were ap-
palled by how you had gone astray when you believed that the idea
that God tempts a person might have explained life. For when life
had become a dark saying, you listened to an explanation that, as you
now had to admit, was precisely what made everything inexplicable.
Humbled and ashamed, you then acknowledged that it was good that

* See James 1:13.
† See Psalm 104:30.

God did not let himself be tempted, that He was the almighty God, crushing every presumptuous thought that might lead a person—as you were led in your despair—to explain life's dark saying with an explanation that no human being is able to live by.

GIFTS ARE GOOD AND PERFECT BECAUSE THEY ARE GIVEN BY GOD

"EVERY GOOD AND EVERY PERFECT GIFT IS FROM ABOVE AND COMES DOWN FROM THE FATHER OF LIGHTS, IN WHOM IS NO CHANGE OR SHADOW OF TURNING."

These words are so comprehensible, so simple, yet how many people have really understood them, really understood that they are like a commemorative coin that is more glorious than any other worldly treasure and yet also a coin one can use in daily life?

"Every good and every perfect gift is from God." The apostle uses two terms here. When he says, "every good gift," he is referring to what the gift is in itself, that it is a sound and blessed fruit concealing no unsound or harmful additives. And when he says, "every perfect gift," he is referring to the more particular relationship in which, guided by God, the good gift is offered to individual human beings who are to receive it in such a way that what is good in itself doesn't damage them or cause them to be lost. Two further terms correspond to these two. The gift is "from above and comes down from the Father of lights." "It is from above," says the apostle, thereby directing the believer's thoughts toward heaven, where everything good belongs—the blessing that satisfies the mouth and the blessing that satisfies the heart; toward heaven, from whence good spirits are sent to save us; toward heaven, from whence good resolutions return as heavenly gifts. "From the Father of lights," says the apostle, meaning that God's eternal light shines through all things, and that He understands human thoughts from afar and knows all their ways down to the minutest detail. In other words, His eternal love runs on ahead and makes everything ready, making "the good gift" also a "perfect gift." For God in heaven is not like a human being who, if he has a good gift to give, must give it, in a sense, in the dark, uncertainly: he is happy to be able to give a good gift and happy in giving it, but he is also anxious about it because he never really knows whether it will benefit the recipient or not.

"Every good and every perfect gift," says the apostle. But what does *every* mean here? Does the apostle mean that heaven's spacious stronghold is like a great storehouse, and that all that it contains are good gifts? Does he mean that God takes things from this rich store and dispatches them according to time and circumstance, now and then, now to one person, now to another, more to one and fewer to another, and none at all to yet another—but, in each case, what He sends is good and perfect? Pay attention to the following words, however: "in whom is no change or shadow of turning." If the apostle had wanted to say what has just been suggested, then he would have followed on with something like "from the God of love, the God of mercy and comfort, the giver of good gifts"—or however else he might otherwise have put it, better and more to the point than we are able to say it. He would almost have admonished believers to be sure to be thankful according to the time and circumstance that led to their receiving the good gifts. But he doesn't say this. What he warns against is the error of believing that God tempts a person, and the error of thinking that God lets Himself be tempted. What he emphasizes is that God is constant and remains the same while everything changes. He admonishes us to love God in such a way that we may become as He is, that we might win God by our constancy and save our souls in patience. He says nothing in these words about what the particular gifts are but about God's eternal relation to the believer. When joy makes everything clear and bright as if to show life's true meaning, then he warns against such an explanation and admonishes us to bring it back to the Father of lights in whom there is no change or shadow of turning. When care spreads its shadow over life, when discouragement clouds our vision, when anxiety's clouds hide Him from our eyes, then the apostle's admonitory words ring out: that in God there is no shadow of turning. What the apostle warns against is confusing God's blessed life with the inquietude of temptation, as if His heart had grown cold or weak. What he emphasizes is that just as God's might had made everything good in the beginning, so, too, even now, constantly, in every moment, He, the Father of lights, makes everything good: He makes everything into a good and perfect gift for the one who has heart enough to be humble, heart enough to be confident.

A DOUBTER'S OBJECTIONS

But doubt is wily and cunning and never, as it is sometimes said to be, loud or defiant. It is unassuming and sly, not bold or assertive—and the more unassuming, the more dangerous. It does not deny that these words are beautiful nor that they are full of comfort. If it did, then the heart would rebel against it. What it says is merely that these words are difficult and almost like a riddle. Doubt wants to help the troubled soul to understand the apostolic saying that every good and every perfect gift is from above, and so it asks, "What does this mean? Surely that everything that comes from God is a good and perfect gift, and that everything that is a good and perfect gift is from God." This explanation is so simple and natural—and yet doubt has unassumingly crept into it. So it continues, "In order for these words to help someone to find peace in their life, then we must either be able to say what it is that comes from God or else what really and truthfully can be said to be a good and perfect gift. But how is this possible? Is every human life a continuous chain of miracles? Or is it possible for the human understanding to find a way through the incalculable sequence of secondary causes and effects, to pierce everything intermediate and so find God? Or is the human understanding capable of deciding for sure what is good and perfect in relation to human life? Is this not something it comes to grief on over and over again? Hasn't humanity, hasn't every single human being repeatedly endured the painful experience that this is a piece of foolishness that does not go unpunished, that it is having the audacity to attempt something that is denied to human beings?" With this, doubt is finished with its explanation of the words and, moreover, finished with the words. It has transformed the authoritative, apostolic saying into the kind of folk saying that goes from mouth to mouth without any force or meaning. It was unassuming enough not to require that the words should be deleted and left to be forgotten forever, but it tore them from the heart and left them on the lips.

Is this not how it was, my listeners? Perhaps we do not owe these words to one of the Lord's apostles? Perhaps we owe them to that multitude of spirits who dwell beneath the heavens? Was there a curse on them that made them homeless in the world and prevented them from finding a place in any human heart? Were they destined to make human beings perplexed? Are we unable to halt that anxious movement in which thinking exhausts itself without ever getting any further? Is it not perhaps true that God does, in fact, tempt a person, if only by proclaiming something that merely confuses us?

THE ANSWER TO DOUBT IS GRATITUDE AND REPENTANCE
The apostle Paul says, "All God's creatures are good when they are received with gratitude."* In the first instance he said this in order to

---

* 1 Timothy 4:4.

warn against an earthly kind of cunning that was seeking to bind believers to the service of external rituals. How did the apostle respond
to this? He raised the believers' minds above their earthly and finite
anxieties, above worldly cunning and doubt by means of the divine
observation that one should always thank God. For the gratitude that
the apostle is talking about cannot be the kind of gratitude that one
person ought to show to another, comparable to the error of those
false teachers who believed that offending against ritual laws was
to sin against God. But doesn't the same thing hold of every human
relation to God, that every gift is a good and perfect gift when it is
received with gratitude?

It's true, isn't it, my listener, that you have interpreted that apostolic saying in that way, and you were not troubled by what were good
and perfect gifts or what it was that came from God because, you
said, all gifts are good when they are received with gratitude from
God's hand and it is from God that every good and every perfect gift
comes. You didn't ask anxiously about what it was that came from
God, but joyously and openheartedly you said that it was whatever
you thanked God for. You didn't trouble your soul by pondering what
would count as a good and perfect gift. Confidently, you said that
you knew that it was what you thanked God for, and that was why
you thanked Him for it. You interpreted the apostolic word by letting your heart expand. You didn't demand that you should learn a
lot from life but only wanted to learn one thing: always to be giving
thanks to God and thereby to learn to understand one thing, namely,
that all things work together for good for those who love God.*

Is the apostolic saying "Every good and every perfect gift is from
above and comes down from the Father of lights" really a dark and
difficult saying, then? And if you maintain that you cannot under-

---

* Romans 8:28.

stand it, dare you also assert that you really *wanted* to understand it? When you entertained doubts as to what it was that came from God, or what was a good and what a perfect gift, did you really dare to try it? And when pleasure's easy game called you, did you thank God? And when you were strong, so much so that it was as if you didn't need any help, did you thank God? And when your allotted share was little, did you thank God? And when your wish was denied, did you thank God? And when you yourself had to deny yourself your wish, did you thank God? And when people acted unjustly toward you and did you wrong, did you thank God? We are not saying that human injustice thereby ceases to be unjust—what would be the point of saying such a sick and stupid thing. Whether it was unjust is something you yourself can decide on, but the question is whether you traced the injustice and injury back to God and, by means of being thankful for it, received it from His hand as a good and perfect gift. Did you do this? If so, then you have interpreted the apostolic saying in a worthy fashion that honors God and furthers your salvation. For it is a beautiful thing when someone prays—and many things are promised to those who pray without ceasing—but it is always more blessed to give thanks. If you do this, then you have interpreted the apostolic saying in a worthy fashion, more gloriously than if all the angels were to speak in tongues of flame.

But who has such courage, such a faith? Who loves God like this? Who is the happy and steadfast warrior who stands watchfully at his post throughout his life and never drifts asleep? And if you do, my listener, have you not concealed it from yourself? Have you not said to yourself, "I do indeed understand the apostolic saying, but I also understand that I am too cowardly or too proud or too dull really to understand it"? Have you admonished yourself? Have you considered that, harsh as it may sound, the one who is overcautious also has a deceitful heart and is no genuine lover? Have you considered that timidity, too, is judged, while the humble heart does not come to judgment? Have you considered that those who sorrow do not love God with all their heart, but that those who are happy in God have overcome the world? Have you at the very least kept an eye on yourself? Have you kept the apostolic word in a holy fashion? Have you kept it in a pure and well-ordered heart? Have you resisted the cunning corruption of an over-clever mind that urged you to sell it off and thereby rid yourself of some deeply felt pain—acknowledging instead, over and over again, that you have never loved as you have been loved; that you were faithless when God was faithful; that you were lukewarm when He was aflame; that He sent you good gifts, but you used them in such a way as to damage yourself; that when He asked something of you, you did not answer; that when He called to you, you would not listen; that when he spoke to you in a friendly fashion, you did not pay attention; that when He spoke seriously to you, you misunderstood; that he fulfilled your wish, but you had not wished in the right way and were quick to become angry? Have you ever really felt how sad a thing it is that in order to depict your relation to God you need so many words? Have you at the very least been honest to yourself and to God in your relation to Him? Have you refused to postpone the reckoning and been unwilling to continue in your shame on your own? Have you been quick to bear the pains of reckoning? Have you considered that He loved you first? Have you been quick to judge yourself in case He didn't continue to love you, while you yourself were slow to love Him in return? If you have done all this, then you will from time to time find the courage to give thanks, also when what happens is wonderful in your eyes; you will find the courage to understand that every good and every perfect gift is from above; you will find the courage to explain it all in terms of love; and you will find the faith that receives this courage—for this, too, is a good and perfect gift.

"EVERY GOOD AND EVERY PERFECT GIFT IS FROM ABOVE AND
COMES DOWN FROM THE FATHER OF LIGHTS, IN WHOM IS NO
CHANGE OR SHADOW OF TURNING."

These words are so healing, so curative, and yet how often has the
penitent soul understood them in such a way as to let itself be healed
by them; how often has it understood not only the seriousness of the
judgment it implies but also its merciful grace?

Or, my listener, perhaps you never had occasion to find these
words difficult? Were you always satisfied with yourself, so satisfied
that you perhaps thanked God that you were not like other people?
Did you perhaps get so clever as to understand the deep meaning in
the meaningless saying that it was good not to be like other people?

What was it, then, that made it hard for you to understand the
apostle's words? If a human life is itself a good and perfect gift, if one
simply relates oneself receptively and receives everything from God's
hand, then, yes indeed, how might one ever receive anything but
good and perfect gifts? But when you submitted yourself to human
beings' universal lot, then you admitted that you were neither good
nor perfect, that you did not relate yourself purely receptively, but
that everything you received underwent a transformation. Can, then,
like be known by anything other than like? Can the Good become
good in anything other than in what is good? Can healthy food
remain healthy in a sick soul? Human beings do not relate themselves
purely receptively but are also communicative, and you found it hard
to understand how what was unhealthy, which came from you, could
be anything but damaging to others. You did indeed understand that
it was only by giving thanks to God that everything became a good
and perfect gift for you, and you held fast to the idea that others also
had to receive everything in the same way. But was the love that gave
birth to your thankfulness pure? Did it not transform what had been

received? But can a human being do more than love? Do thought or language have any higher expression for loving than always giving thanks? Indeed not, but there is a lower and a more humble expression for it. For the one who gives thanks loves in proportion to his degree of perfection, but God can love a person truthfully only when He loves him in proportion to his imperfection. What kind of love is this? It is the love seen in repentance, and it is more beautiful than any other love, since, in repentance, you love God more faithfully and more inwardly than in any other love—because, in repentance, it is God who loves you! In repentance, you receive everything from God, even the thanks you give Him, in the same way that parents enjoy the fun of receiving a present from their child when they are really only receiving what they themselves have given. Isn't that how it is, my listener? You were always willing to thank God, but this was somehow so inadequate. Then you understood that God is the one who does everything in you and then allows you the childlike pleasure of thinking that your thanks are a gift you give Him. He gives you this joy because you were unafraid of the pains of repentance and of the deep care in which a person becomes as happy as a child in God. And you showed this when you were no longer afraid of realizing that this is love: not that we love God, but that God loves us.*

And you, my listener, you who understood the deep meaning of the apostolic saying in a more simple and a more humble fashion, but in the sense that you were not like other people—was it so easy for you to misunderstand the apostle's words? You did indeed understand that every good and every perfect gift comes from God— Ah! But you could not understand that this could be anything but damaging in your case. Dew and rain are indeed a good gift from above, but if the harmful weed could understand its situation and could talk, then

---

* 1 John 4:10.

perhaps it would say, "Oh, stop! Go back to heaven and let me die from drought! Don't refresh my roots so as to make me flourish and grow and become yet more harmful!" If that is how you understood it, then you understood neither yourself nor the apostolic saying. For if that is how it is, then it is not true that every perfect gift comes from God, then God is not greater than an anxious human heart, and how then might every good and every perfect gift come from Him?

Perhaps there was something in your life you wished undone. If this were possible, you would then be able to gladly receive every perfect gift from God's hand with thanksgiving. Merely the thought of it makes you so happy that it seems to tempt God to make what is done undone. But God is not tempted by anyone. Perhaps you tried to forget about it, so your thanks became weak, like a flickering candle. Ah! But if you did forget it, how would it then be possible to understand the apostolic saying? If it was possible to forget it, then it is not true that every good and every perfect gift comes from God. Then you would have excluded yourself from being blessed not on account of what you had done but because of the feeble and egotistical and willful way in which you had understood the saying. It would be the same as in the case of those whose wish was denied and who exclude themselves from being blessed by wanting to believe that the wish that was denied them also was a good and perfect gift—even if, in your case, it was much harder for you to dare to understand this.

Perhaps you understood the apostolic saying in another way, such that the punishment God visited on you was a good and perfect gift. The wrath within you seemed to want to come to the aid of the divine wrath, so that you would be entirely consumed by the punishment. Yet the punishment you suffered was quite different from the one you intended. For you are not the only one affected by it, even though you are the only guilty one. It spreads out around you, even though you were the only one who should have been its object. Even if in the quietness of your thoughts you acknowledged that divine providence knows how to target a person and knows how to make itself understood by that person, even when no one else understands, the apostolic saying grew dark in your eyes, and the punishment itself became a fresh source of temptation. What was part of the punishment and what belonged to your circumstances in general became ambiguous. If you were only a victim of circumstances, then your soul craved punishment, but if everything was punishment, you could not accept it. You were ready to renounce everything—every wish, every desire. You were ready to give up your idea that the very best you had done, into which you had put the utmost efforts of which you were capable in the conviction that it was good was nothing but foolishness and sin. You were ready to suffer every punishment, but the "extra" that was added to what you had imagined was more than you could endure, and you asked yourself whether that, too, was a good and perfect gift. Then it grew dark in your soul. Could you not understand the saying? So what did you do? Did you throw the saying aside? Oh, no! In all your need you held it fast. And when all the devils were standing by to rescue your soul from the madness of despair by explaining to you that God is not love—isn't that how it was?—then you clung fast to the saying, even if you didn't understand it, and you did so because you had placed an obscure hope in it, and letting it go would have been the worst that could have happened.

Is that what you did, my listener? If so, then you discovered that even if the external self is ruined, the inner self may be renewed, and you understood that every good and every perfect gift is from above when it is received with thanks. Then you understood that repentance is a way of giving thanks not merely for the punishment you endure but also for the whole complex of circumstances of which it is a part, and that the one who merely seeks suffering in repentance is giving thanks in a very imperfect way. As the Lord Himself says,

"This very day."* Therefore, the Lord's apostle says, "This very day are every good and every perfect gift from above and come from the Father of lights in whom is no change or shadow of turning." "This very day"—and that irrespective of the fact that He is today as He was yesterday.

"EVERY GOOD AND EVERY PERFECT GIFT IS FROM ABOVE AND COMES DOWN FROM THE FATHER OF LIGHTS, IN WHOM IS NO CHANGE OR SHADOW OF TURNING."

These words are so beautiful, so eloquent, so moving; they are so full of solace and rich in comfort, so simple and comprehensible, so healing and curative. Therefore, Oh God, we pray that you will turn the ears of those who have not yet attended to them or been willing to receive them, that your Word will give understanding to the hearts that have misunderstood the saying and so heal them, that you will bend the straying thoughts to the saving obedience that the saying offers, that you will give the repentant soul courage to dare to understand the saying, and that you will make those who have understood it ever more blessed by ever and again understanding it anew. Amen.

* Psalm 95:7; Luke 23:43; Hebrews 4:7.

2

Evil and the Gift*

KNOWLEDGE OF GOOD AND EVIL

It was only from the tree of the knowledge of good and evil that human beings were forbidden to eat, lest knowledge should enter the world and bring it grief: knowledge of the pains of loss and of the dubious pleasures of possession, of the fear of separation and of the difficulty of separation, of the restlessness of reflection and of the worry of reflection, of the need to choose and of the decisiveness of choice, of the law's judgment and of the law's condemnation, of the possibility of being lost and of anxiety about being lost, of the sufferings of death and of the expectation of death. If this prohibition had been observed and not been breached, then everything would have remained as it was, so very good, and the witness that God Himself bore to Creation would have resounded from humanity in a ceaseless and blessed repetition.

Everything would then have dwelled safely in peace, beauty's festal smile would have been untroubled, and heaven's blessing would have overshadowed all. It wouldn't even have been as if heaven was

---

* From Niels Jørgen Cappelørn et al., eds., *Søren Kierkegaards Skrifter*, vol. 5 (Copenhagen: Gad, 1998), pp. 129–142.

mirrored in earthly life, since that might have aroused a premonition in the depths of innocence, nor would there have been any echo to summon longing from its hiding place. No—heaven was on earth, and everything would have been in a state of fulfillment. Human beings would then have woken from the deep sleep in which Eve was created, only to sink back in peace and glory. God's image would have been imprinted on all things as a radiance of His glory, lulling everything into an enchanted state of perfection, moving all things, itself unmoved. The lamb would have lain down with the wolf and the dove built its nest beside the bird of prey, the poisonous weed would have been harmless, and everything would have been so very good. All things would then have revealed truth, for Adam had indeed named everything by its right name, as what in truth it was. Everything would have been trustworthy, for everything was what it seemed to be, and righteousness would have flourished from the ground.

But would there really have been no difference between good and evil? This difference was precisely the fruit of the tree of knowledge. But would no one ever have asked where all this came *from*? Nevertheless, had things stayed as they were, the Lord's voice would not have wandered in the Garden of Eden to ask after Adam, and Adam would not have hidden himself in the Garden or in himself, for everything would have been in the open, and the one thing hidden would have been the Lord, even though He was unnoticeably present in all. And Adam would not, in fact, have had time to ask where it all came from, since it was offered anew in each moment—a gift offered in such a way as not to arouse a question about the giver in the mind of the receiver.

Then human beings broke the peace by plucking the forbidden fruit of knowledge; they went astray, and knowledge led them even further astray, for the serpent deceived Eve (Genesis 3:13), and so knowledge came into the world through deception, as a deception. The fruit of knowledge that humankind enjoyed planted a tree of knowledge inside them, a tree that bore fine fruits that now seemed very desirable to them. For the fruit of knowledge always appears desirable and is good to look at, but when one has enjoyed it, it leads to trouble, forcing a man to work in the sweat of his brow and sowing thorns and thistles in his path. What happened once in the beginning of days is constantly repeated in each generation and each individual, yet the fruit of knowledge is desirable to look upon. If the Lord's warning was not able to save the first human beings from being deceived, how might any human voice do anything more than to make that fruit even more desirable in the eyes of the individual?

Eden's gate was locked. Everything was changed. Human beings became afraid of themselves, afraid of the world about them. Anxiously they asked about what was good, about where to find perfection, about goodness's and perfection's origin and whether they existed. Knowledge brought with it doubt, which wrapped itself anxiously about their hearts, and the serpent, which had seduced them by making it desirable, tightened its grip. So it suggested, how could they know about goodness and perfection if they didn't know where they came from, but how could they know the eternal source without knowing what goodness and perfection were? Doubt offered to explain it now one way, now another, luring them on in such a way that the explanation itself made everything even more uncertain. What happened once in the beginning of days is constantly repeated in each generation and each individual, and the effects of the fruit of knowledge won't allow themselves to be brought to a halt. Thanks to knowledge, doubt became internalized, and the knowledge that ought to have guided humanity tied it up in neediness and contradiction. Now knowledge appeared as something unattainable, something one could only sigh for. Now it was thought of as a blessing that the soul was constantly losing. Now it was a kind of knowledge that the heart was ashamed to acknowledge. Now it involved the recognition of something that shook humanity. Now it was consciousness of something concerning the self, now consciousness of something concerning the whole world. Now it pointed each toward what they were capable of, now it made them flop down in exhaustion. Now it overpowered them with its riches, now it starved them out with its emptiness.

Is doubt, then, the stronger? Is the one who is triumphantly to enter into the strong man's house a new doubt? Does he disarm him by using the same weapons against him as he himself uses? But wouldn't that mean making him stronger? And isn't it precisely the subterfuge of doubt that it makes people imagine that they themselves can overcome themselves, as if they are capable of performing a miracle unheard of in heaven and on earth and under the earth—namely, the miracle that someone who is fighting against himself can be stronger in this fight than he himself is? But how does the unclean spirit behave when it itself has driven itself out of a person: doesn't it come back with seven others, so that the last state of that person is worse than the first (Matthew 12:45)? And how does it go when someone who is struggling with himself admits that even if he were capable of overcoming all things, he nevertheless had no power to overcome himself by himself? If such a thing were to happen, wouldn't the victorious self be transformed into something much worse than the corrupt self that it conquered? And isn't this corrupt self so secure because it knows that there is no stronger self in a person that would not be even worse for him? No! This is why one first binds the strong man or hands him over to be bound and only then goes into his house to take his weapons from him (Matthew 12:29).

Everyone who has honestly been prepared to experience something like this will certainly acknowledge that this is how it is—that is, everyone who has preferred a humble but, nevertheless, uplifting truth to a glossy lie that would enable him to deceive himself and, above all, make him capable of attracting admirers and of satisfying the deceitful demands of those who want to be deceived. If, on the other hand, one prefers to have little but with a blessing, to have a truth that one might care about, to suffer instead of celebrating imaginary victories, then one will not be so inclined to praise knowledge, which, whatever else it gives, also brings trouble. This is not to deny that the pain it causes may not serve to educate a person if that person is otherwise honest enough to want to be educated rather than deceived, to seek the one in the midst of the many, or what is needful in preference to what is superfluous, just in the way that this is simply and plainly offered, precisely as it is needed.

So let us focus our thoughts and do what we can to understand and, as we reflect on them, allow the apostle's words to make us prisoners in freedom's cause, words that explain both the what and the whence: "Every good and every perfect gift is from above."

THE ANALOGY OF HUMAN GIFTS

"If you, who are evil, know how to give good gifts to your children, how much more will your heavenly Father give good gifts to those who pray?" (Matthew 7:11, Luke 11:13.) These words address themselves so sympathetically to those who are troubled and speak with such concern to those who are full of cares that they lift them up and strengthen them in the free-spiritedness that comes from complete conviction. For what words could speak more appropriately than these to a person who, unlike the doubter, is not indifferent to himself but only preoccupied with the big issues of life and existence and who is first and foremost concerned about what matters to him and his small share of life? For just as he is always to a certain degree rather childlike, so, too, are these words. They remind us of life's first, unforgettable impressions by reminding us of a father's love for his child, his care in giving it good gifts. For if it is certain that God takes pity on those who call on Him in the same way that a father takes pity on his children, and that God gives good gifts to those who pray to him for them in the same way that a father gives good gifts to his child, if all this is certain, then the comfort that is being offered is the surest of all.

That is how a person once understood the saying. It made him happy, and he rejoiced over what it reminded him of and over what it promised, and it gave a further sign of his father's care for him by explaining that his father's love was most perfect when it offered him a means of understanding God's love. But it did not strike him that, like every word of Holy Scripture, the saying could at various times be milk for babes and strong food for adults, even though the word remains the same. He did not suspect that the saying could be given another interpretation, whereby it became even more glorious, or that what was said figuratively could be made even more comforting when reality explained the figures of this earthly life to him. Nor did he see that the conclusion of the saying became even surer when it was inverted, as he would need it to be when everything in his life got turned upside down.

So he became older, and everything was changed, shaken by a fearful upheaval. God's judgment was different from what he had imagined: it was that even human beings, the most perfect of all creatures, were evil. But this was not spoken by way of a wrathful judgment in order to induce terror. Rather, it was said in a figure of speech, seeking to express a heavenly truth that could be found in the world's most beautiful relationship. It did not say, "You who are evil," as if that was what was being talked about; rather, it was said as an acknowledged truth that merely needed to be mentioned. But the fact that it was thus presupposed disturbed the impression of the figurative saying. And perhaps it also disturbed him because he was convinced that life had taught him the truth that even the love of an honest person who wishes the best for the other sometimes serves only to do harm. He knew that he himself, even when he felt only sheer kindness and was willing to make every sacrifice by doing all he could for another, was only able to cause them pain. "So" he said to himself then, "there's not much comfort in these words if God's love doesn't know how to give good gifts better than a human father does." Thus, he came to think about the saying in the same way that he thought of fatherly love—as a beautiful, sacred, melancholy memory, a lofty mood that brought to life an idea of what is best in human life but also recalled human weakness; that brought to life a blessed longing but also revoked it, subordinating it to the melancholy of sorrow. Then he thought that he'd grown out of what the saying had to teach him and didn't grasp the care with which it was seeking to educate him; he didn't see that the saying hadn't changed, since it had always expressed its doubts as to a human father's ability to give good gifts while all the more forcefully bearing witness to God's heart and God's will.

Then he once more immersed himself in the saying. But he didn't let it raise him to its own level so as to forget the figurative element in light of what it was really saying. Instead, what should have been a word of comfort and empowerment became a seed of doubt. For if human beings, who are the most perfect of all creatures, are evil, then all earthly life must surely lie in wickedness. Or if it is only through human beings that whatever earthly life has to offer becomes evil, then it is merely indifferent and neither good nor evil; that is to say, it is mere appearance without being anything essential in itself—and so, once again, it is evil.

What is the Good? What is perfection? The figurative saying we are considering says that even though a father is evil he nevertheless knows how to give his child the good gift he is asking for. He doesn't give him a stone when he asks for bread or a serpent when he asks for a fish. And then comes the application: if you, who are evil, know how to give good gifts, how much more will your Father in heaven give them? But are bread and fish intrinsically good gifts, or is their being good dependent on what is needed (though, then again, isn't being needy in that way an imperfection in human life)? And even when people do need them, might it not be better for them to be refused them? In a higher sense, might they not need to become like the prodigal son who asked for bread and got pig swill—which made him look to himself and realize how far he had gone astray? So human beings can know how to give good gifts, but they cannot know whether what they are giving is a good gift, and, conversely, the wicked can know how to give an evil gift, but they cannot know whether what they are giving will work evil. The one who knew how to sow good, pure seed in his field did indeed know how to sow, but as he was doing so he couldn't know what might happen while he slept and whether what he saw when he woke up would be something terrible. Indeed, even if he didn't sleep he didn't know whether he might see something even more terrible. We can know what seems beneficial, whether on the basis of opinions that reflect our own experiences and reflections or of others' testimony, and we can know how to give it. The only way in which we can say that we know this, however, is at a level that is entirely indifferent to the question that really concerns us, namely, whether what we are giving is really beneficial.

Someone who had never been troubled by such thoughts wouldn't deserve the name of "father," for a father is distinguishable from others by such concerns: he is distinguished even from a person's best friend by being concerned in a much higher degree. So it seems that there is neither goodness nor perfection in the world. For the Good exists only in such a way as to be a dubious possession, and a dubious possession is not a good—and a good that cannot exist is no good at all. Or, it only exists in such a way that it presupposes something else that is not itself good.

In this way, doubt became the stronger. What the person we are considering had worked out and experienced for himself, what he had become convinced of through sympathetic concern or on the basis of his own sorrows—namely, that earthly life was vanity, and that even the good gifts that human beings can give express only the impotence of the will, an impotence that leads to exhaustion and restlessness—this is what he now found confirmed in the words of Holy Scripture. For it was now quite clear and apparent to him that this was what the saying meant, and that the words, far from furthering what was most beautiful in life and affirming it, rather passed a silent judgment on it and let it fade from sight. He thought this explanation would help him, even if he had to admit that it helped neither him nor anybody else. For how would it help you if you shut your eyes so as not to be troubled anymore by the dazzling lust of the eye? How would it help you if you shut your ears to the world's vain talk and refused it admittance? How would it help you if your heart became cold and all things became strange and indifferent to you? How would it help you if you knew that human beings do not give good gifts? How would it help you if you knew what would hurt most of all—that even when you loved you were unable to give good gifts? Oh! How would all this help you if your eyes were unable to look up and see a heavenly glory *above*, or your ears opened to receive the inexpressible words that echo *from above*, or if your heart was not stirred and enriched, your hand not ready to reach out and take every good and every perfect gift that comes *from above*, your left hand not knowing what your right is doing?

So how do you understand it? Doesn't the saying remain the same? Has it ever said anything different from what you think you found in

it, although you also forgot what it added? Did the saying ever conceal the fact that human beings are not able to give good gifts, for,
if they could, who would need God's? Or would the saying—would
life—have been more perfect and more comforting if all it meant was
that God gives good gifts in the same way that a father does? But
didn't it rather say just what you yourself discovered but didn't want
to understand in the right way, and didn't it say it as in passing, so as
to awaken the pain that would make you more receptive to what it
said next? If the whole world is evil, does that mean that God is not
good? Would it have been better for you if He had been good merely
in the same way that the world is? Isn't the one thing needful, the one
thing that is blessed in time and in eternity, in need and in joy, this:
that God alone is good and that none is good but God alone? Isn't the
only thing that saves us, the only thing that really guides us, whether
we find ourselves all smiles on the path of happiness or on sorrow's
narrow way, that "God's Spirit is good and leads you on a level path"
(Psalm 143:10)?

GOD'S WAY OF GIVING

So let's read on: "How much more will your heavenly Father give
good gifts." It doesn't say, "Your heavenly Father knows how to give
good gifts," but it says He "will give good gifts." For His knowledge is
not separate from His giving. His knowledge doesn't take leave of the
gift in the moment in which it is given and in the moment in which it
is received. Thus far, there is a certain aptness in the figurative saying
that a father's love is like or is a reflection of God's love, even if a
father's love is never such as God's, never so strong, so inward, and
therefore never able to achieve what God's love achieves, since the
power of God's love is almighty.

When the saying is understood like this, the figurative element
that made it comprehensible to the infant but also problematic for

the older person vanishes. Now the saying says what the apostle says, that every good and every perfect gift comes down from above. What earthly life does not possess and what no human being possesses is something that God alone possesses. It is not a perfection on God's part that only He possesses it, but it is a perfection of the Good that a human being can only participate in it by doing so through God. For what is the Good? It is what comes from above. What is perfection? It is what comes from above. Where does it come from? From above. What is the Good? It is God. Who is it who gives it? It is God. Why is the Good a gift, and why is this no figure of speech but the one reality, the sole truth? Because it is from God. For if human beings could give themselves or give each other anything at all, then this would not be the Good, nor would it be a gift but would only appear to be so. For God is the only one who can give in such a way that He also gives the condition for receiving the gift. He is the only one who, when He gives, has given already. God gives the power both to will something and to perfect it: He begins and completes the good work in a person.

My listener, will you deny that this is something that doubt is unable to reverse, precisely because it is beyond doubt and remains in God? And if you don't want to remain in it, isn't it because you don't want to remain in God, in whom you live and move and have your being? And why don't you want to do this? Even if doubt cannot understand this it doesn't make it untrue. On the contrary, it would become doubtful if doubt were able to understand it. Even though this truth neither can nor will get involved with doubt doesn't make it untrue. On the contrary, if it lets itself get involved with doubt it would be no truer than doubt itself. It is true because it breaks with doubt and disarms it. If it didn't do this, it wouldn't have any power over doubt but would itself be in doubt's service. Its quarrel with doubt would then be merely apparent, since it would be in league with doubt and its victory over doubt a deceit—since it would be doubt that really triumphed. Human thoughts know many of the world's ways, they mine their way into mountains, where all is gloom and dark as the shadow of death; they know the paths that lead where even birds cannot go; and they discern every animal's parts (Job 28:1–11). But they do not know the way to God, to where the Good lies hidden, for there is no way there since every good and every perfect gift comes *down* from above.

Perhaps you will say, Who would deny that every good and every perfect gift comes down from above? But not denying it is still a long way from wanting to understand it, and wanting to understand it is still a long way from wanting to believe it—and from believing it. But whoever is not for me is against me.* Does the fruit of knowledge still look so desirable? Instead of judging spiritually, could you wish for some sign of goodness and perfection, some proof that they really came from above? But what would such a sign be like? Should it be more perfect than what is perfect, better than what is good, because it gave itself the air of being able to prove that perfection was perfect? Should there be a sign, a miracle? Isn't the miraculous doubt's age-old enemy so that they cannot be in the same place? Should there be some experience? But doubt is precisely the restlessness that destabilizes a life based on experience and does so in such a way that it can never find peace or enter into its rest, never get through with being on the lookout—and, even if there were an experience, would never let it grant peace. Should flesh and blood grow stronger? Are flesh and blood not doubt's confidants, whom it constantly consults?

REMEDIES AGAINST DOUBT

But if no proof can be provided, does that mean doubt cannot be

---

* Matthew 12:30.

brought to a halt? By no means. If a proof could be provided in the way that doubt wants, then doubt couldn't be stopped any more than a sickness can be stopped by administering whatever medicine the sick person wants. If, on the other hand, you want to be convinced, then, in what he goes on to say, the apostle shows you a more perfect way, a way on which you will die to doubt while what is perfect comes to you. For the word of faith does not fight against doubt with its own weapons, and only when the strong man has been bound are his weapons taken from him.

First, the apostle draws aside the veil of darkness, puts away the shadows of turning, breaks through the alterations of what is changeable, and turns the believer's gaze to heaven so that, seeing it, he might seek what is above (Colossians 3:1–2). For what is high above all doubt must reveal itself in all its eternal glory—namely, what is from above, the Father of lights, whose clarity is unchanged by any shadow, whom no alteration changes, no envy darkens, no cloud removes from the believer's eye. If this does not stand fast, if you look for knowledge about this from your false friend Mr. Doubtful, then everything will ever and again become shadowy to you, confuse you with changes, bring the gloom of night mists upon you, and take everything you have from you, as if you had never had it. Therefore, the apostle says, "Every good and every perfect gift is from above and comes down from the Father of lights, in whom is no change or shadow of turning."

Next, he turns to the individual to explain the condition that makes it possible for him to receive the good and perfect gift. God himself has provided this condition, otherwise the Good would not be a gift; moreover, this condition is itself a perfection, otherwise the Good would not be a perfect gift. Having earthly needs is not perfection but rather an imperfection, and, therefore, if a human being were to be given something that was capable of completely satisfying these needs, then the gift would still be an imperfect gift, because the need itself was imperfect. But needing the good and perfect gift from God is a perfection, and therefore the gift, which is good and perfect in itself, is also a perfect gift, because the need is perfect. However, before this need awakens in a person there first must be a thorough shake-up. All the busy considerations that doubt set in motion were a preliminary attempt at bringing this about, but no matter how long they kept on, they could never be finished with—and yet they need to be finished with and brought to an end, that is, broken off, before the individual can become what the apostle calls the firstfruits of Creation.*

That this indicates a new order of things is easy to see, since when human beings were first created they were so far from being the first-fruits of Creation that they were created last. So there is a new begin-ning, which cannot be attained by doubt's constant efforts, efforts that can establish the kind of beginning that begins with doubt. So whereas human beings came last in the old order in such a way that doubt set itself the task of working its way back through everything that humanity presupposed, human beings are now the first, and there is nothing between them and God. They are now in possession of the condition that they cannot give themselves, which is a gift from God—and that is why the apostle says that God gave us birth in fulfillment of His purpose by means of the word of truth: He did it by Himself, unless it is to be supposed that He had some kind of agree-ment with human beings that would oblige Him to consult them about it. But those who are born by means of the word of truth are born into the word of truth. The condition is a gift from God and a perfection that makes it possible to receive the good and perfect gift.

The apostle says, "In fulfillment of his purpose He gave us birth

---

* James 1:18.

by the word of truth so that we would become a kind of firstfruits of His Creation." Do you want to make this, too, something to doubt? If you do, then doubt, as it always does, will only give you something by taking something else away. It will not allow the condition to be a gift, and so it takes away perfection and the possibility of receiving the perfect gift from you. For isn't it an imperfection when your need of God is not total and you therefore don't need His good and perfect gifts?

But because the condition is itself a perfection, it also matters that it is kept in perfect condition and is not shared out or divided up in such a way that it only yields a half-measure or becomes corrupted. While the eye of faith is unshakeable in its persistence in looking longingly toward heavenly things and is undisturbed in its vision of the open heaven, the apostle is nevertheless willing to allow or even to incite the individual to doubt, but so as to use doubt in the right way. That means not doubting what stands fast and will forever stand fast in eternal light but doubting only what is intrinsically transitory and will vanish away more and more, that is, doubting itself, its own power and capabilities—doubting them until they become unserviceable for anything and are laid aside. For false doubt doubts everything except itself, while saving doubt doubts only itself, with the help of faith.

HOW TO RECEIVE GOD'S GOOD GIFTS

The apostle therefore adds the following admonition in order to help strengthen and preserve the individual as the firstfruits of Creation: "Therefore let everyone be quick to listen."* But what do you suppose we should be quick to listen to? Do you suppose it is to doubt's long speeches or to human opinions or to what one's own heart has con-

---

* James 1:19.

ceived? Ah! But no matter what they achieve in the world or what they become, those who are quick to listen to such things scarcely become what the apostle next exhorts everyone to be: slow to speak. For being in haste to hear about what's going on soon engenders hasty talk. But those who are quick to listen to the divine word that is spoken today as it was in former times—when human beings fall silent, when Pharisees and Scribes have gone their way or been brought to silence, when the crowd has broken up and gone away—those are also slow to speak, since what they have heard is so indescribably satisfying and even more nourishes the desire to listen. And so they become even slower to speak—for what might they have to say? In the end, all there is to say is what David said: "Make haste, Lord, to speak!" And, to oneself, "Make haste, oh, make haste to listen!"

And when we have thus become quick to listen, then we should also be quick to listen to the admonition "Let everyone be slow to anger, for the wrath of man does not work the righteousness of God."* To begin with, anger produces what is certainly not righteous in relation to God, because it makes people slow to listen when they are being admonished. For even if someone was not so quick to grow angry, even if, humanly speaking, their anger didn't achieve very much because it had been subdued, it could nevertheless remain inside them and achieve what is not righteous in relation to God. This is because anger produces precisely that which, with the help of faith, we are to die to. Therefore, when anger gets power over people, even if their anger helps them triumph over the whole world, they lose themselves and harm their souls by it. But those who are quick to listen and who don't get worked up about answering back or speaking overhastily are also slow to get angry. They don't let the sun go down on their wrath and fear a yet more

---

* James 1:19–20.

anxiety-ridden darkness in which they would no longer be able to see the Father of lights, hidden by the shadows of an anger that thus changed the One who is unchangeable.

"Therefore rid yourself of all sordidness and rank growth of wickedness."* Human beings do indeed bear what is perfect in fragile vessels, which makes it hard for them to bear it—but it cannot at all be borne by those who seek an ill-gotten profit, who are aflame with lust or in fellowship with uncleanness. For there is a curse on whatever wickedness produces, which, in an inverse manner, makes it like the blessing that is given to what blessedness produces: excess.

"And with meekness receive the word."† For those who are quick to hear in such a way as to thereby become slow to speak do not take themselves by surprise in their haste, nor do they take God's kingdom violently. Instead, they learn what is heavenly, for "meekness discovers things that are hidden" (Sirach).‡ They know that no one can take what is not given to them, and that they cannot have anything unless they take it as something that is given to them—and the Good is a gift that meekness is willing to wait for. But meekness also has the assurance that God gives every good and every perfect gift and in this conviction is "watchful with thanksgiving" (Colossians 4:2).

Then they receive "what is implanted," and which was therefore there even before they received it. It is something that, when it is received, "has the power to save your souls."§ This is the good and perfect gift they receive, the gift that satisfies the need that is itself a perfection. That is why the figurative saying that we thought about at the beginning of this talk says, "If you, who

---

* James 1:21.

† James 1:21.

‡ Ecclesiasticus 3:19.

§ James 1:21.

are evil, know how to give good gifts to your children, how much more will your heavenly Father give good gifts to those who pray?" For it is a perfection on the part of human beings to need the Holy Spirit, and their earthly needs are so far from illuminating what this means by the analogy they provide that they are more likely to darken it. The need is itself a good and a perfect gift from God, and praying for it is, with God's help, a good and perfect gift, and communicating it is a good and perfect gift from above, coming down from the Father of lights, in whom is no change or shadow of turning.

3

Giving and Receiving*

Epistle: James 1:17–22.

DIVINE EQUALITY AND HUMAN DIFFERENCES

The same apostle from whom the text before us is taken goes on
in the very next section to warn against the worldly covetousness
that sought to worm its way into his congregation. It did so in order
to confirm the differences and divisions that only serve vanity and
that unravel the bonds of perfection that had bound the members
together in equality before God. In this way, it sought to get them
toiling in subjection to the law that holds sway and always has held
sway in the world—"flattering people for their own advantage" (Jude
16). The idea so often emphasized in Holy Scripture to encourage the
lowly and to humble the mighty—the idea that God has no regard
to persons—is what the apostle now wants to bring to life for the
individual, and in such a way that it can be applied in life. And so it
is in truth. For if we always used this idea to keep ourselves sober and
alert, then we would never go wrong in our view of life or of people

---

* From Niels Jørgen Cappelørn et al., eds., *Søren Kierkegaards Skrifter*, vol. 5 (Copenhagen: Gad, 1998), pp. 143–158.

or "put our faith in a person's regard."* Then our thoughts would be directed to God, and our eyes would not be distracted by seeing worldly differences instead of our equality before God. If a man with a gold ring and gorgeous raiment came in when the congregation was assembled, we would not fix our eyes on the gold ring or the gorgeous raiment or let the sensuous eye delight in such splendor. For such a sensuous attitude makes us slaves to human beings, since it doesn't know how to raise us above the worry caused by the fact that we ourselves lack such things. And if our thoughts were directed to God when a poor person in filthy clothes came in, our eyes would not direct him to the despised place at our feet.

And even if we did sometimes forget the equality, and life's confused divisions caused us to lose our way whenever we entered the holy place, our minds would be kept safe by the thought of our common equality before God. And we would then become more and more able to preserve this equality amid the din of worldly life and use it to pierce the confusion. For in the world there is a knowledge of differences that busies itself without rest in order to make life both more attractive and more bitter. This knowledge can be seen in the goals that allure us, in the rewards of victory, and in the heavy burdens we shoulder, and it accompanies our losses. In such ways, knowledge of differences in the externalities of life leads us vainly to puff ourselves up in pride or else to sigh over them, to become worried and afraid. But in the holy place, the voice of the ruler is heard just as little as in the grave. Here, there is no difference between man and woman, any more than there will be in the Resurrection. Nothing is heard of worldly wisdom's arrogant demands, and the world's glitter and glory are not to be seen, since they are seen as what is not seen. Here, the teacher is a servant, and the greatest is the least, and the one who is most powerful in the world is

---

* James 2:1.

the one who most needs praying for. For everything external has been laid aside here as something imperfect, and our essential equality is true, saving, and equally saving for all.

But even when the one who has the world is like the one who does not, and when the one who does not have the world is like the one who does not desire it, or "when the lowly person rejoices in his exaltation and the rich in their lowliness" (James 1:9–10), or when the woman who was caught in flagrant sin here finds forgiveness and the man who looks at a woman with nothing but lust is condemned, even then equality is not present in truth nor has enslavement to the world been done away with, nor has its law vanished like a shadow and been forgotten like a childhood lesson. For everything is not yet made perfect under equality's "divine law, to love the neighbor as oneself," and to do so in such a way that nobody is so lofty as not to be your neighbor in absolutely the same sense as nobody is so lowly or wretched as not to be your neighbor, and that their equality is demonstrated beyond dispute by the fact that in each case you love the neighbor as yourself! Woe to those who are so proud as not to be able to forget what makes them different, but woe, too, to those who are so lowly as not to forget what makes them different.

Equality, figuratively speaking, stands on guard at the entrance to the holy place and keeps watch in case anyone tries to enter without having put off what belongs to the world—power and wretchedness—so that intercessions can truly and with the same intention be made both for the rulers and the mighty ones and for the sick and sorrowful, for those who bear the scepter and those who are hard-pressed and must be content to have God as their rod and staff. In just the same way, every upbuilding view of life only finds repose or only becomes upbuilding when it avails itself of the thought of the divine equality that raises the soul to what is perfect and makes the eye of sense blind to the differences. This divine equality burns ever more strongly in the midst of the differences without, humanly speaking, consuming them.

In the holy places and in every upbuilding view of life we see the thought that helps us fight the good fight with flesh and blood, with principalities and powers, to free ourselves so as to become equal before God. And it is the same whether this is more a war of conquest against those differences that want to burden us with worldly fortune or a war of defense against the differences that, by means of anxiety, will cause us to lose our way in the world. Equality is only a divine law, the strife is only truthful, and victory is only legitimate when we are, each of us, fighting for ourselves, with ourselves, and in ourselves—but not if we preemptively presume to make the whole world equal in an external sense, which would mean that all the rest would then owe a debt of gratitude to those who had brought about this "external equality" and no longer be their equals. Those who make haste in such an uncomprehending and worldly way may well really believe that one or another external set of circumstances is the true state of equality to which what is higher has to be reduced and to which what is lower has to be raised. But all it produces is confusion and self-contradiction, as if true equality could be expressed as such in anything external or could triumph or be preserved in anything external. This would be like arguing that a monochrome-painted surface is the true likeness that could represent the life, truth, peace, and harmony of all things, whereas, in fact, it tends to destroy everything in a spiritually consumptive uniformity.

Yet the differences are so many and so changing that what one person experiences as insignificant becomes something monstrous for another. For this reason, it is difficult to talk about them or to find a characteristic or decisive expression for any one of them. Yet thinking about the apostolic saying "Every good and every perfect gift is from above" suggests a way of stating more particularly what these differences consist in. This is something everyone will have an idea of, whether as something they have lived through and laid aside or as something that is still relevant to them and that seems to describe a more general polarity. It is the difference between *giving* and *receiving*, a difference that embraces a great manifold of human situations even if it also contains within itself a mass of more particularly defined forms. To be able to give and to have to receive is a way of dividing humanity into two great classes, and as soon as this difference is uttered in all its brevity, everyone is able to expand on it and to connect it with many happy or burdensome memories and with many joyful hopes or painful expectations as to what is to come.

GIVING AND RECEIVING

How many reflections these simple words have given rise to! The old person who has grown old in the wearisome service of this difference has much to tell! Even the young person, who, coming across this inscription on life's door for the first time, will discover much if, before experiencing what the difference really is, he allows himself to speculate about whether it is more fortunate to give and how fortunate that might be, or whether it is more burdensome to receive and how burdensome that might be. Which is more to be desired? How would he choose if the decision was up to him? Was what has been said true—that the most glorious life is one in which one has nothing to do with the world, so as to be able to say, "I came naked into the world, I owned nothing, I was a stranger in it, and, naked again, I left it"?* Is it such a heavy and burdensome thing to have earthly treasures? Is having to share with others such hard work, and does it carry such responsibilities?

---

* Job 1:21.

But such reflections that superficially play around with the conditions and presuppositions of life as if it were a game designed to stimulate the imagination merely serve to bring freedom's power of action to a halt and to dull the spirit in fantastic cravings and agonies. Even in the case of a deeper contradiction, Paul pithily indicates that there is no time for protracted reflections: "If you are a slave when you are called, do not worry about it, if you can gain your freedom, choose to do so."* Even if no one else speaks as powerfully in as few words as an apostle does, we shall refrain from extending our reflections and seek to summon the soul back from its state of distraction to the equality that becomes apparent when, with the help of the apostolic saying, we pierce through the differences. So let us then seek to take the saying and, as it were, to wander out into the differences, while constantly letting the saying remind us that every good and every perfect gift is from above, for if this stands fast, then difference has been abrogated. For a difference between two imperfect things, which are what remain for human beings to give, cannot be anything but transitory. Thus, the apostolic saying rings out like a divine chorus, fulfilling every difference by bringing it into a state of equality before God.

The apostolic saying demands that those who give humble themselves and their gift under the word. If they are not minded to give, then this saying has no meaning for them. If they brood like dragons over their earthly treasures, or if they are ready with the hypocritical explanation that what they have and could help others with has already been given away, because "it is a gift," or if they hoard their spiritual gifts in a miserly and jealous way—how, then, can they be helped by a saying that teaches them to give in the right way? They don't think they need any such instruction. They cannot be

---

* 1 Corinthians 7:21.

helped by this saying, even though it has been able to help the most wretched.

But if you are willing to give, then the saying keeps an eye on you in order to see whether your good will means that you are a cheerful giver who is well pleasing to God. If, on the other hand, your willingness is not an expression of joy, pour out your rich gifts and give away the wealth that tires and wearies your soul, for its price is a curse. If it is possible, change your earthly form, so that you are the only one who has to beg— Ah! But every good and every perfect gift comes down from above, and providence needs your treasures and your goods so little that it always has twelve legions of angels at hand to help it serve each individual! And even if it did need what you owned, it could take what it had given. But you had learned a different wisdom, namely, that there are no good gifts, neither there above nor here below, and so you could just as well keep all you had or give it all away, since you could neither attain nor produce the divine equality. Or perhaps what you owned was not yours by right, and your hand was sullied—what would your gift then be if not a mockery of God? How would you know that the good gift is from above if you did not understand what it meant to give each their own?

If you are willing to give, then the saying keeps an eye on you in case you are inclined to take it back. For the equality before God that it wants to bring about is not the equality that is involved when equals look out for one another, or when the rich entertain the rich so that they may be invited back, or when the powerful support the powerful. You were willing to help the person in need who had nothing to give in return, and yet you demanded something of them: their respect, their admiration, their submission—their soul. But how much is the little that you own, even if you are the richest of all, even if your name were to be remembered instead of that man whose name has for centuries been synonymous with "the richest" and after whom the richest are named? How high was the mountain from which nothing could be seen but what you owned? Have you forgotten that it was one who could climb the highest mountain, the summit of which reached into the clouds, who, pointing to all the kingdoms of the earth, could say to the one who hungered, "I will give you all this if you bow down and worship me"?* Have you forgotten that this was the Tempter? And do you really want to do good to others in such a way as to do them wrong? Do you want to be their benefactor in such a way as to become their souls' enemy? How much does a person need to live on, since life does not consist of food and drink? You who want to frighten the needy into submission, are you not afraid that, with a single word, they will take the shine off your glory and make your silver and gold into false coinage that no one wants? Would you thus betray your neighbor with a kiss and kill the soul while you saved the body? Ah! But every good and every perfect gift is nevertheless from above, and no one has promised that earthly treasures are to be called "good" and "perfect," nor have they any intrinsic right to be so. If, then, you are able to give, then never forget—neither for your own sake nor for that of the other—that what you give is from above. Otherwise, although you want to be a benefactor to others—and are able to be that—you might oppress them and oppress them in such a way that they refuse what you offer and teach you that you are not suited to each other, since they are not as lowly as you are proud, and even if you have the power to let their bodies suffer you are not able to corrupt their souls.

Don't use your goods for profit; don't be like those who knew how to let their gift be even more productive for them after they had given it away; and don't do what is still more terrible, for which neither you nor the whole world can compensate: don't damage the soul of the

---

* Matthew 4:8–9.

one to whom you give. Give your gift, keep an eye on it, and even if it is not your fault, if you notice that the needy person is tempted by it, then offer an admonitory word, point him to God, or simply refrain from giving. In all the charitable grandiloquence that your wealth allows you to indulge in, don't forget that it is better and more blessed and infinitely more important to save a soul. Once this idea has come alive in you, then humble yourself in fear and trembling under the apostolic word, so that you will see your gift as being poor enough and you yourself as even *lowlier than the gift*.

Or is it that you are certainly willing to give, but you need to think about it for a long time first in order that the people will know how much thought you have put into the gift? Ah, but there are many ways of thinking about things that may indeed make a person cleverer and show how clever they are but without making them better or being more well-pleasing to God. It is well enough known that all the careful thought that your left hand discovers is not for the good if your right hand takes counsel from it—and even if you were to discover something new, it would be a dubious honor. And why is it generally the case that the reflections that such a charitable deed inspires are also very protracted if not because there is no profit in it and one must be content with thinking about it? If, on the contrary, you consider that every good gift is from above, then, even as it reaches out to give, your right hand will quickly hide itself, and your left hand will never find anything out. Then you shall rejoice in secret in a manner that befits a genuine benefactor, rejoice like the one who received the gift, and both of you rejoice that the gift came from above. For it was an invisible hand that gave it—your hand—and an invisible hand that (you are convinced) will make it into a good gift: God's hand.

Or you are willing to give and you put the gift to one side in readiness for the needy person but let him wait for it. My friend!

"Hope deferred makes the heart sick, but a desire fulfilled is a tree of life" (Proverbs 13:12). Would the other be able to understand your behavior otherwise than that you were wanting to make yourself the one he was waiting for? No matter how marvelous the explanation you wanted to give him, wouldn't making him understand it this way damage him in a matter that concerned his essential happiness? And how would it benefit you? Would it make you any more perfect? God in heaven still knows best what is the highest a human being can seek after and bring to perfection. Scripture says that no more can be asked of someone than to be a faithful steward, but a steward is lower than the house and the property he manages. You, however, wanted to be the master and so wanted to be perfect. By making the needy wait, you wanted them to understand that you had other things to attend to, that they had to give you time, that they were insignificant and had to wait. Ah! God in heaven does not let a sparrow wait for Him. So don't let the needy have to keep asking you or it will become apparent that you are not giving for God's sake but perhaps merely to free yourself from having to hear their requests. Wasn't it unjust on the part of the judge that he only did what righteousness demanded in order to be quit of the widow's prayers? Was he not unjust even when he acted justly? Was it not an injustice against the widow that she had to thank him merely because he did his duty, as if this was some great act of charity? But the longer you let the needy go on asking, the more they will be subject to their earthly needs, until they are no longer able to raise themselves above them, not even with the help of your gift. And what you have to give is no good and perfect gift, or, if it is, it is not thanks to you, since you are only a steward and therefore *lowlier than the gift.*

Or perhaps you were willing to give, but your gift was so lowly that you didn't dare to give it. Ah! But every good and every perfect gift is nevertheless from above, and therefore your lowly gift can be the good gift, just as much as the greatest. And those who give in the right way close their eyes so as not to see the gift, or how little it is, until what God makes of it is revealed. Then you will once more acknowledge that you are *lowlier than the gift*, which, when they give a good gift or do what they can for the gift to become good, those who give always are.

NONMATERIAL GIFTS

But it is not only with external, earthly goods that one person can help another. Guidance and counsel, comfort, advice, and empathy are also goods, and here the giver would seem to play a more important role. Perhaps you had to pay a high price for your experience; perhaps you acquired the advice you have to give in the day of need; and if life's adversities wrung it from you with great difficulties, then you will not squander it or make a jest of it but know how to value what you acquired so bitterly. Ah! But the one you bought it from was life and since, when you bought it, it was (you say) good for you, will you now act toward another as life did to you, so that he, too, would one day say, "I bought it dearly and must pay for it bitterly"? If you have advice to offer, is it a gift if you cannot separate it from yourself and yourself from it? Would your advice be at all diminished if the one to whom you gave it saw that, although you were now less in need of it than formerly, you still felt its force, as if it chiefly affected you and you needed it more than anyone else in such a way that it became as fresh and living when you repeated it as it had been on the day when you acquired it? Thus, you yourself would be *lowlier than your advice.*

If, then, you have advice to give, don't raise your head in a judgmental way, don't peer inquisitorially at the one who needs it, but bow your head and lower your eyes under your own advice, so that it might be heard from above—for you as much as for the other. Every good and every perfect gift is nevertheless from above, and even if you could offer the best advice that could be given, you don't know whether it will provoke others to contrariness or keep them humble, whether it will be for their salvation or their ruin.

Or is the sympathy that you have and are willing to bestow on those who need it conditional on their being weaker than you, having less strength in the hour of need, or not being so intrepid in the face of difficulties? Is it only then that your sympathy hastens to strengthen the weary and raise up the fallen? Ah! But every good and every perfect gift is nevertheless from above, and those who offer their gift must first see to it that they have nothing against their brother in case their sympathy is offered opportunistically and brings no reward because they are themselves benefited by it. What the other needs is not you yourself but your sympathy, so be *lowlier than your sympathy* in order that it might be from above—something higher than you can offer, a sympathetic rather than an injurious act, not something that came from your heart but something that is in your heart as having come from above.

Or perhaps you are intellectually gifted as few others are, and your thoughts are able to penetrate all truths. You know how to use this power to lure other people in, so they are happy to bind themselves to you with indissoluble bonds—but you are unable to put yourself out of the picture in such a way that they become able to see the truth without your help and remain in it without you. Is that how you are? If so, we don't presume to instruct you any more than we presume to instruct the lowly, but we speak only of what happens and what could happen. Ah! But every good and every perfect gift is nevertheless from above, and even the most certain truth established by a human being may appear doubtful to others unless they can acquire it in absolutely the same way as the first person did. What would people gain if they put their confidence in you in this way, and what would you gain if you were satisfied in the way that you want to be? For it is not only with food and drink that people seek to nourish their souls but also with worldly honor and human admiration. And what is worldly honor, with its painted face, and where is the sanctuary in which it sanctifies itself so that it might be truly worth seeking? And what is human admiration, which is squandered on the ungodly and the dissolute as often as it is offered to the righteous? Indeed, even if it was given to the right person, how uncomprehending and mistaken such admiration often is. It is as if instead of taking care for itself it cares only about admiring others, which burdens the one who is admired with a new concern (that is, whether he is more concerned about them than hungry for their admiration).

If, then, you have some truth to offer, then try not to make such a strong impression, annihilate yourself, sacrifice yourself even as you offer your gift, so that people do not get you instead of the gift and their lives are not wasted in the deceit of thinking that they have the truth when they don't. You know best how this might be done, for you are the powerful thinker, and if you can do it, then you are indeed the giver but still *lowlier than the gift*, and every good and every perfect gift is nevertheless from above, even if it also comes from you.

Or perhaps you were so simple that you therefore remained silent, and it was far from you to think that anything you said could give guidance to or help another person. Ah! But a simple word from a simple person has worked wonders in the world. It has imprinted itself on the memories of the wise to remind them when, in all their wisdom, they forgot about it. It has halted the mighty and disarmed the violent. Clever people have been shaken by it and doubters saved. And if that is not how it is, your gift would nevertheless be a good gift and you yourself *lowlier than the gift*.

HOW TO RECEIVE

The apostolic saying turns to you, whose humble lot it has been to receive, and, like every sacred word, it is a gospel for the poor, a heavenly summons calling out to them. It inspires them with courage to fight for victory in their terrible strife, a strife in which it is as if one fights with one's friend or in which it is so hard to tell friend from foe. It gives them courage to raise their hearts in thanksgiving to God whenever they are in danger of being imprisoned on earth by becoming another's debtor.

Do you think we are praising ingratitude? Is the apostolic saying unable to bring about equality before God, or does it teach an inequitable equality when it says that "every good and perfect gift is from above," and therefore everyone—those who give and those who receive—has to be essentially grateful to God? For only the good rightly merits gratitude, and the good comes only from God. Oh, no! The saying certainly doesn't intend to do away with gratitude. For it is shameful of those who give to know that they are giving and not even to try to make themselves in every sense invisible (even though they may know how to make themselves invisible in a higher sense, even when they are visible in a physical sense), but it is also shameful of those who receive not to know or not to make every effort to find out from whom they receive the gift. But when one tries to find what the other tries to conceal, both will be united in finding God, and, when He is found, the shame is taken away from both of them, both from the one who was found when he should have been hidden and from the one who should have found out but didn't.

Those who are the recipients of a good deed but do not seek out their benefactor in order to give thanks will never find God. For it is in such seeking that they find God, whether they do or don't find their human benefactor, whether they find him to be one who does as he should and helps them to find God, or whether, despite his wrong attitude, his desire for gratitude also helps them to find God. For those who forget about earthly gratitude in order, in some fantastic way, to give thanks only to God had better watch out. For if you are not willing to give thanks to the benefactor whom you see, how can you truly thank God whom you do not see? Even if a Pharisee were to propound what is true but go on to apply it in the wrong way, the truth nevertheless remains. One must honor God for what one owes a sinful human being, so that no one can raise himself above another in such a way as to make it impossible for the other to thank God because he has gotten in the way. And no one should dare to be so base, so cowardly, so easygoing, so soft, so lost in earthly things as to be satisfied with thanking others only because they gave him what he wanted.

Therefore let it not be denied that openly to deny your benefactors while you secretly accept their gifts is like being ashamed of your parents: it offends both God and humanity; it is an abomination that amounts to a real and serious mistreatment of those who have given to you. We praise the man born blind for using the sight he was given first of all to seek out his benefactor.* We praise him because the world's judgment was unable to make him do what Peter did: forget his benefactor. We praise him because he would rather be despised at the side of his benefactor than be honored for perhaps serving as a weapon in the hands of the mighty. But if he didn't want to do more than this, if his benefactor had been a sinful man like one of us, and if the good deed had bound them together in indissoluble friendship instead of uniting them in common thanks to God to whom glory was due—would this outcome not have ruined what had been so beautifully begun? And if Christ accepted the blind man's adoration, was it not rather for his faith than on account of the good deed,

* John 9:1–38.

and, in any case, wasn't His relation to him of a kind such that no
sinful human being could be tempted to demand anything similar?
The good deed itself concealed Christ as much as was possible, for
when He had made it possible for the man to have his sight back, He
sent him away saying, "Go, wash yourself in the Pool of Siloam." It
was there that he got his sight, but the Lord no longer stood by him.
Thus, the one who was the benefactor knew how to make Himself
invisible—even though the good deed was the gift of sight.

We have already seen many of the different ways in which one
person can become indebted to another, since we have been talking
about those who were fortunate in being able to do good. If, then,
you are willing to give thanks, the saying keeps watch on you in case
your soul is damaged by having to receive and thanking only your
human benefactor. Perhaps you were low down on the social scale,
your place was at the rich man's door, and your life bore witness to
the experience that one can also live from crumbs, and that these are
sometimes thrown to human beings as if they were dogs. You took
the gift that was thrown to you. Having to be in such need was heavy,
but you couldn't do anything else. It only helped you momentarily,
and then you again felt just as heavy, and you felt how heavy it is to
have to receive. Before you had raised your bowed head again, your
benefactor had vanished, although not quite because he wanted to be
unknown and had hurried off to conceal himself, but because he had
other things to attend to. You sent your thanks after him, but they
couldn't reach him, although not quite because he ashamedly felt
himself to be lower than the gift, but because he wasn't listening and
was indifferent to the whole affair—it was absolutely unimportant to
him. Even if your thanks had reached him he would probably have
said, "It's scarcely worth thanking me for"—and this would have been
his honest opinion, as would his thought that your thanks were also
worth nothing. Ah! But every good and every perfect gift is neverthe-

less from above. The mighty must be satisfied with the fact that the lowly serve them, but the mighty also serve the lowly, and when you raised yourself to God in thanksgiving you used that mighty man as a means to help yourself.

But perhaps your circumstances were more favorable. You had a frugal livelihood and lived contentedly and peacefully in your humble dwelling at the foot of the rich man's palace. But you owed it to him, you owed everything to him, and you yourself felt that the only service you could do for him was just a paltry recompense—but that made you all the more ready to thank him. Sometimes you saw him at your door, but his glance made it clear how insignificant your thanks were and that he did not know how to accept payment in such coinage, although he knew how to get paid in other ways. Then you might have wished yourself a bird of the heavens that had only God to thank for its livelihood, or a lily of the field that had only God to thank for its glorious raiment, only God to thank—whom it is a joy beyond all measure to thank again and again. Ah! But every good and every perfect gift is nevertheless from above. If your benefactor pays no attention to your thanks, raise yourself to God from whom his gift came, but don't leave off thanking him; do what you can for him (which is not so little) and let him have used his unrighteous mammon to have bought himself a friend in you who will be able to receive him in the eternal mansions.

Or perhaps you had no such care. Perhaps you had no need to thank anyone for the earthly gold or goods you had been given. But you had been tossed about in life's confusion, and you had not been able to rescue yourself from the difficulties in which you had been placed and which overwhelmed your mind and weakened your will. You went to someone who could give you advice and help, someone who had a clear view of what lay beyond the darkness in which you were enclosed. Now you were happy and at peace, your life ran on quietly and calmly, but both in your heart and with your lips you acknowledged that you owed this to him. But he would not accept your thanks. When you spoke to him about it, it was not hard for you to discover that your life and its complications had indeed occupied his thoughts, but he had not been occupied about you and that was why he couldn't accept your thanks. Indeed, the one to whom you owed it all was perhaps even your enemy, and that was why he wouldn't accept your thanks! Ah! But every good and every perfect gift is nevertheless from above. If human beings cease to be human, if they want only to be like a power of nature, then indeed you cannot thank them any more than the seafarer can thank the wind when it fills his sails and he makes good use of it, or the archer can thank the string when it drives the arrow so that it hits the target. So don't let yourself be snared in worldly worries but raise yourself in gratitude to God; however, don't for that reason omit to thank your benefactors. Your thanks are still owed to them. You have them on trust, like the property of someone who has died or has traveled abroad, and you have to have them well looked after and ready for him to take back if he should ever want them.

Or perhaps you owed to another what you could never forget any more than he could—your knowledge, your education, your sureness of thought, your eloquence. He regarded you as his debtor and would allow no jubilee on which to give it all back to you as your own. He was indeed willing to accept your thanks but not in such a way as to free you from the debt. Ah! But no one can give what they have not been given: the highest that one person can give to another is life, but a father will teach a child to thank God even for this—God, who gave it and who will also be the one to take it. Every good and every perfect gift is from above, and the disciple is indeed not higher than the master. But if the master loves him, then he wishes him to be as he himself is.

EQUALITY IN GIVING AND RECEIVING

"It is more blessed to give than to receive."* This saying expresses the differences that are to be found in earthly life, but it does not reflect or borrow from what human passions tell us—that it is better, happier, more glorious, or more desirable to be able to give than to have to receive. Instead, the saying depicts the difference as it is found in a loving heart. Those who say that it is better or happier or more glorious or more desirable do not say how they will use the power given them; even less do they testify to what they know about how to use it in the right way. But those who know that it is more blessed to give than to receive have understood life's differences and have learned how to be reconciled with them by giving cheerfully and finding their blessedness in giving. Yet a difference still remains if the one who receives is not able to know a similar blessedness. Shouldn't this be possible? Shouldn't those who were tried in a harder struggle not have a similar reward? And isn't it in fact true that it is a greater thing to receive than to give if, that is, both are done in the right way? So let us now consider the apostolic saying in order to see whether it reveals something about this kind of equality.

The one who gives acknowledges that he is *lowlier than the gift*, for this was the confession that the apostolic saying was glad to receive, whether it was freely given or forced out of a person. The one who receives acknowledges that he is lowlier than the gift, for this was the acknowledgment that the saying made a condition for his being raised up, and this acknowledgment is indeed often heard in all its humility in the world. But when the one who gives is lowlier than the gift, and the one who receives is lowlier than the gift, then equality has been brought about—namely, equality in lowliness, equality in lowliness over against the gift, because the gift is from above and

---

* Acts 20:35.

therefore does not really belong to either of them or else equally belongs to them both—in other words, it belongs to God.

The imperfection did not, therefore, consist in the fact that someone was needy and could only receive the gift but in the fact that
the rich person possessed it. But this imperfection is done away with
when the rich person gives the gift away. Now equality has been established, not by the needy person coming into possession of the gift
but by the gift no longer being the property of the rich person, because he has given it away. But it has not become the property of the
needy person, since he has received it as a gift. When the rich person
thanks God for the gift and for having had the opportunity to give it
away in a beautiful manner, he gives thanks both for the gift and for
the poor person who receives it, and when the poor person thanks the
giver for the gift and God for the giver, then he also thanks God for
the gift. Thus, equality is established in gratitude to God, equality in
thanksgiving in relation to the gift. There is nothing difficult in this,
and it is easy to grasp. Insofar as a difficulty might tempt a person on
this point it is because earthly goods, about which we unfortunately
tend to think first when thinking of the difference between giving
and receiving, are in themselves so imperfect and therefore have imperfection's power to bring about a difference. But the more perfect a
gift is, the clearer and more indisputably equality, too, reveals itself,
and does so straightaway. This is indeed the "good and perfect gift"
which the apostle says comes from above, but the only good and perfect gift a human being can give is love—and in every age all have
agreed that love dwells in heaven and comes down from above. If any
are unwilling to accept love as a gift, then let them take care as to
what it is they are receiving, but if they accept it as a gift, then giver
and receiver are indistinguishable in the gift—both have been made
essential to and are entirely equal to each other in relation to the
gift. Only the earthly mind in all its imperfection will then be able

to find any ambiguity in what has one and the same meaning. And the more we wean ourselves from understanding the imperfect as a means of grasping the perfect, the more we will make our own that understanding of life that gives comfort while it is still day and that remains when the night is come, when we lie forgotten in our graves and we ourselves have forgotten what moth and rust have consumed and human cleverness discovered. For there is one thought that can fill the longest passage of time—it is a thought that cares to know nothing of the differences that bring only trouble but thinks solely of the equality that is from above: equality in love, which alone abides. This is the equality that does not allow anyone to be another's debtor in any other sense than, as Paul says, being in the debt of mutual love.

4

"The Lord gave, the Lord took away, blessed be the name of the Lord"*

JOB AS A TEACHER OF HUMANITY

Those who are called "teachers of humanity" are not only those who, thanks to an especially fortunate opportunity or to tireless effort and unflagging persistence, discovered or fathomed one or another truth and bequeathed what they had achieved as a contribution to knowledge that subsequent generations can strive to understand and, by understanding, make their own. For, perhaps in an even stricter sense, those were teachers of humanity who had no teaching to hand on to others but who left behind only the pattern of their own lives as a signpost that each and every human being could follow, whose names give comfort to the many, whose deeds encourage the afflicted. Job is such a teacher of and guide to humanity, and the meaning of his life is by no means in what he said but in what he did. He did indeed leave behind an epigrammatic saying that, thanks to its brevity and its beauty, has become proverbial, passed on from generation to generation, and no one has ever been so presumptuous as to add

---

* From Niels Jørgen Cappelørn et al., eds., *Søren Kierkegaards Skrifter*, vol. 5 (Copenhagen: Gad, 1998), pp. 115–128. The reference is to Job 1:21.

anything to it or subtract anything from it. But the saying itself does not provide guidance, and Job's significance does not consist in the fact that he said it but that he followed it up by what he did.

The saying itself is indeed beautiful and worth pondering—but if someone else had said it, or if Job had been someone else, or if he had said it in another context, then the saying itself would have meant something different. It would have been meaningful, to the extent that it is anyway, but not meaningful because of how he acted when he said it, for in its context to say it was to act. If Job had spent his whole life refining this saying, if he had regarded it as the sum total of what a human being ought to learn from life, if all the time he had merely *taught* it but had himself never tried it, never acted as he did in saying it, then Job would have been a different person, and the meaning of his life would have been different. Then Job's name would have been forgotten or, at least, it would have been a matter of indifference whether one knew it or not, since the main thing would have been the content of the saying and the depth of thought that lay in it.

If the next generation had received the saying, then this would have been what was handed on to the following generation, and so on—but as it is, it is Job himself who has become the human race's companion. When a generation has completed its service, accomplished what it had to do, and fought the good fight—then Job has accompanied it. When a new generation, both en masse and each individual within it, stands in its assigned place ready to begin its journey—then Job is there again, taking his place, at humanity's frontier post. If the human race knows only happy days in fortunate times, then Job follows faithfully along; and if some individuals nevertheless come to think frightening thoughts, growing anxious at the idea of how much horror and neediness life might conceal or how no one knows when they might come to the hour of despair—then their troubled minds seek out Job, they rest with him and are quietened by

him. For Job follows faithfully along and gives comfort. But the comfort he gives is not given by implying that what he had suffered was
suffering of a unique kind such as no one has ever suffered since, but
he speaks as one who is able to testify that what seems frightening is
really only a little thing, that the horror has been lived through, that
the battle with despair has been fought—to God's honor, for his own
salvation, for the joy and benefit of others.

In happy days and fortunate times, Job goes side by side with the
human race and confirms it in its joy, taking on its anxious forebod-
ing that some sudden horror might fall upon a person with the power
to destroy his soul and take it as its assured booty. Only the frivolous
could wish that Job was not alongside—Job, whose venerable name reminds him of what he is trying to forget, namely, that frightful things
can happen in life and that there is much to be anxious about. Only
the egotistical could wish that Job was not there—Job, the memory of
whose sufferings and the rigorous earnestness that they inspire disturb
his feeble joy and scare him out of a self-assurance that springs from
the intoxication of hard-heartedness and of being lost.

In stormy times, when the foundations of existence are shaken,
when each moment shudders in anxious expectation as to what is
coming next, when every explanation grows dumb at the sight of
the wild tumult, and when what is innermost in a person groans in
despair and in "bitterness of soul" screams out to heaven—then, too,
Job still walks alongside the human race and vouches for the truth
that there is a victory to be won, vouches for the truth that even if the
individual loses his fight there is nevertheless a God. And just as this
God made every temptation human, even if a human being could not
withstand temptation, so, too, will He make its outcome such as we
can bear—in fact, He will make it glorious beyond all human imagining. Only the defiant could wish that Job were not there in order
that they might free their soul from the last vestige of love that still

remained in the despairing cry of lament. For they want to complain about life—to curse it—in such a way as to eliminate every note of faith and confidence and humility from what they say. In their defiance they want to be able to stifle their cries so as not to let it seem that there was anyone whom they were intended to provoke. Only the hypersensitive could wish that Job was not there, so that they might have an excuse for letting go of every thought and renouncing every effort in favor of a repellent weakness, annihilating themselves in the most wretched and miserable kind of self-forgetfulness.

LEARNING TO UNDERSTAND JOB'S SAYING

The saying that calls Job to mind as soon as it is spoken, and that springs to life and comes to mind at the very mention of Job's name, is an entirely simple saying that does not conceal any secret wisdom such as only a deep thinker could discern. When a child learns this saying and it is entrusted to her as a dowry that she will not be able to make her own until such time as she needs it, she nevertheless understands the saying and understands it in essentially the same sense as the wisest of the wise. Yet the child doesn't understand it or, more accurately, doesn't understand Job. For what she doesn't grasp is all the neediness and wretchedness in which Job was tried. A child can have only a shadowy premonition of this, and yet good for the child who understood the saying and got the impression that what she didn't understand in it was the most frightful thing of all; what such a child acquires—before sorrow and adversity make her sly—is the conviction and, in a childishly lively way, the realization that there really is something truly frightful. When a young person turns his mind to this saying, he, too, understands it and understands it as saying essentially the same as what the child and the wisest of the wise also understand. Yet perhaps he does not understand it or, more accurately, doesn't understand Job.

Perhaps he doesn't understand where all that neediness and wretchedness in which Job was tried could come from. And yet good for the young person who understood the saying and humbly bowed himself under what he didn't understand until the time came when affliction made him self-willed and he discovered what seemed like something no one before him had known. When those who are older ponder this saying, they understand it and understand it in essentially the same way as the child and the wisest of the wise. They also understand the neediness and the grief in which Job was tried, and yet perhaps they do not understand Job, for perhaps they cannot understand how Job was able to say it. Yet good for the man or woman who understood the saying and admiringly held fast to what they didn't understand before grief and need made them also mistrustful of Job. When those who have been tried, who fought the good fight by remembering the saying, say it, then they understand the saying and understand by it essentially the same thing as the child and the wisest of the wise. They understand Job's wretchedness, and they understand how Job could have said it. Such a person understands the saying and, even if he or she never speaks about it, interprets it more gloriously than those who spend a whole lifetime explaining it.

Only those who have been afflicted, only those who have tried the saying by being themselves tried, can interpret it in the right way. These are the only kind of disciples and interpreters whom Job wants, the only ones who can learn from him what he has to teach—namely, what is most beautiful and most blessed and in relation to which every other art or wisdom is so inessential. That is why we call Job a teacher of humanity in the truly proper sense. He is not the teacher of some individual, because he presents himself as a pattern for all, he summons all to heed his glorious example, and in his beautiful saying he calls out to all. There are sometimes those

simpler souls, less gifted than others or less favored by time and circumstance, who, not necessarily envious but anxious and dejected,
want the ability or the opportunity to grasp and to ponder deeply
what the wise and the educated of various ages have researched.
Such types also sometimes feel in their souls a desire to be able to
teach others and not always to be merely the recipients of others'
teaching. But Job does not tempt people in that way. For how can
human wisdom be of assistance here? Can it make any clearer what
the simplest person and even the child easily understood and understood just as well as the wisest of the wise? And how might the
arts of eloquence or the power of the word be of assistance here?
Is such a power able to make the speaker or anyone else do what
the simplest person is as capable of doing as the wisest—trying it?
Isn't it more likely that human wisdom actually makes everything
more difficult? Don't the arts of eloquence, which, splendid as they
are, never manage to say at a stroke all the many things that at any
one time dwell in a human heart, rather serve to dim the power of
action and let it drift off into vacuous reflections?

The individual who is able to be clear about this and therefore
seeks to avoid speaking in such a way as to intrude himself in a
disturbing way into the relationship between the one who is struggling and the beautiful prototype of Job (who is equally near to all
human beings), not offering to increase wisdom in such a way as
also to increase sorrow—such a one is careful not to let himself be
trapped by the splendid but fruitless speeches of human rhetoric.
Yet it doesn't at all follow from this that carefully pondering and
developing a thought is without meaning. For those who ponder
the saying but didn't know it before, it will always be beneficial to
learn about it. For those who knew the saying but had never had
occasion to use it, it will always be beneficial to learn to understand
something they will perhaps have occasion to use at some point.

For those who have tried and tested the saying but betrayed it by thinking that it was the saying that had betrayed them, it will be beneficial to think about it once more before they again flee from it, thrown off balance by conflict or by the press of battle. Perhaps pondering it further might then become meaningful to them, and perhaps such reflection might become vital and present in their soul precisely because they need it in order to penetrate their restless heart's confused thoughts. Perhaps what they understood partially by pondering the saying will come together in the moment of decision, as if reborn, and what that reflection sows in perishability will rise again in the day of need as the imperishable life of action.

Therefore, we shall attempt to understand what Job said in his beautiful saying "The Lord gave, the Lord took away, blessed be the name of the Lord."

THE STORY OF JOB

In a land in the East there lived a man whose name was Job. He enjoyed the blessing of the land, having numerous flocks and fruitful meadows, and "his words lifted up those who had fallen and he strengthened the weak knees."* His tent was as delightful a dwelling as the very lap of heaven, and he lived in this tent with his seven sons and three daughters, and "the confidence of the Lord" dwelled with him in this tent. Job was an old man whose joy in life was the joy of his children, over whom he kept watch so as to prevent any misfortune from affecting them. One day, he sat by his fire, while his children had gathered at their eldest brother's house for a festive occasion. After Job had offered a burnt sacrifice for each of them, he let his heart rejoice in his children's joy. As he sat there in the quiet assurance of joy, a messenger arrived and, before he had finished speaking, another, and while this

---

* Job 4:4.

one was still speaking, a third messenger came, but the fourth came from his sons and daughters, announcing that the house had collapsed and buried them all. "Then Job stood up, tore his cloak, shaved his head, threw himself onto the ground, and prayed."* He did not use many words in his sorrow, or, rather, he didn't say a single word. Only his body bore witness that his heart was broken.

Could you wish it any other way? Would you rather be like the one who takes pride in not grieving in the day of mourning, but who, to his shame, is equally incapable of being joyful in the day of joy? Isn't the sight of such impassibility unpleasant and unenlivening? Isn't it some-how disturbing—whereas it is so deeply moving to see the venerable old man who had recently sat with his fatherly countenance radiant with his joy in God now cast down on the ground with torn cloak and shaved hair? Now that he has given himself up to grief with genuine human feeling but without despairing he is quick to judge between himself and God, and his judgment is as follows: "Naked came I from my mother's womb, and naked shall I return."† With this, the issue was settled, and every demand that he might have made on the Lord, asking for what he wouldn't give or desiring to keep something back that was not to be granted, was brought to silence in his soul. There-upon follows the confession from the man who had been cast down to earth not only by sorrow but by the spirit of adoration: "The Lord gave, the Lord took away, blessed be the name of the Lord."

THE LORD GAVE

"The Lord gave, the Lord took away." The first thing that gives pause for reflection is that Job said, "The Lord gave." Isn't this saying rather inappropriate? Doesn't it contain something that is not actually pres-

---

* Job 1:20.
† Job 1:21.

ent in the immediate circumstances? If someone lost everything in a single moment, everything that was dear to him and what was dearest of all—then the loss would perhaps overwhelm him in such a way that, although he couldn't comfort himself by saying it, he would nevertheless know in his innermost self, before God, that he had lost everything. Rather than letting the loss remain in his soul with its crushing weight, wouldn't he do better to put it at a distance by following the natural movement of his heart and saying, "The Lord took away"? And this, too, would indeed be praiseworthy and merit imitation, namely, to fall silently and humbly at the feet of the Lord in such a way. Those who behaved like that would also have saved their souls in the time of trial, even if they lost all their joy in life.

But Job! In the moment when the Lord took everything away, the first thing he said was "The Lord gave." The saying is brief, but in its brevity it fully depicts what it intends: that Job's soul is not broken down by grief's dumb oppressiveness, but that his heart expands in thankfulness. The loss of everything first of all made him grateful to the Lord for having given him all the blessings that He had now taken away. In his case, it was not as in Joseph's prophecy, which told of seven lean years in which the surplus that had been enjoyed in the seven fruitful years would be entirely forgotten. His gratitude now was indeed of a different kind from how it had been in that now already long-vanished time when he thankfully received every good and every perfect gift from God's hand. And yet his gratitude was honest, as was the idea of the Lord's goodness that was now vital in his soul. Now he remembered everything that the Lord had given, and some particular things with perhaps even greater gratitude than when he had received them. They had not become less beautiful to him because they had been taken away, nor had they become more beautiful, but they were just as beautiful as they had been before—although, because the Lord had given them, there remained what could have seemed even more beautiful to him than the gift, namely, God's own goodness. He remembered his wealthy circumstances, and his eye rested one more time on the fruitful meadows and followed after the numerous flocks. He remembered what a joy it had been to have had seven sons and three daughters, now, when there was no further sacrifice to be offered on their behalf except the sacrifice of thanksgiving for having had them. He remembered those who perhaps also still remembered him with gratitude, the many he had instructed, "whose weary hands he had strengthened and whose trembling knees he had raised."* He remembered his days of glory, when he was powerful and respected among the populace, "when the young men hid out of respect for him and the old men stood up and remained standing."† He remembered with gratitude that his feet had not strayed from the path of righteousness, that he had rescued the poor who complained to him and the fatherless who had no helper, and even in this moment the "blessing of those who are abandoned" was upon him as before.

"The Lord gave." It is a brief saying, but for Job it said so much. For Job's memory was not so short and his gratitude not so forgetful. Thankfulness, and its quiet sorrow, rested in his soul. He took a mild and friendly farewell from it all, and in this farewell it all vanished like a beautiful memory. Indeed, it seemed as if it was not the Lord who took it but Job who had given it back to Him. Having said, "The Lord gave," Job was now well prepared in his mind to thank God also in the next thing he said: "The Lord took away."

THE LORD TOOK AWAY

Perhaps there have been others who remembered on the day of mourning that they had seen happy days, but the memory only made

---

* Job 4:3–4.
† Job 29:8.

them more impatient. "If he had not known joy, then pain would never have overcome him—for what is pain except an idea that someone who knows nothing else cannot have, but joy is precisely what forms and develops a person in such a way that they can experience pain." Their joy thus became their ruin. It was not so much lost as missed and thereby became more tempting than ever. Their eyes once more desired what had been their eyes' delight, and their ingratitude punished them even more by making them imagine it as more lovely than it had ever been. They now thirsted for what their soul had delighted in, and ingratitude punished them by depicting it as more pleasurable than it had ever been. They wanted to achieve again what they had once achieved, and ingratitude punished them with mirages that had never truly existed. Then their soul was condemned to live with a hunger and craving that could never be satisfied for what they now missed.

Or perhaps a consuming passion awoke in them, because they had not enjoyed the happy times in the right way and had not sucked all the sweetness out of their voluptuous superfluity. If they could only be granted just a favorable moment, if they might get their splendor back for just a short time, so that they could satisfy themselves with joy and thereby be able to face the pain with indifference! Then they yielded to a feverish restlessness. They would not face the question as to whether the pleasure they desired was worthy of a human being, or whether they might not have done better to have thanked God that their souls had not been so wild in the happy times as they had now become. They would not let themselves be alarmed by the thought that their desires might provide an occasion for them to be lost. They would not be concerned about the fact that the undying worm of desire in their soul was more wretched than all their wretchedness.

Perhaps there were those who, in the moment of loss, remembered what they had possessed, but who presumed to limit the loss by finding an explanation for it. Even if it was lost, their defiant wills would nevertheless be able to preserve it in such a way that it would seem as if it wasn't really lost at all. Rather than trying to bear their loss, they chose to waste their energies in powerless defiance, losing themselves by holding on to what was lost in a crazy kind of way. Or else, in the very moment of loss, they fled like cowards from all humble efforts to come to terms with their loss. Then the abyss of forgetfulness opened up—not so much for what had been lost but for those who sought to forget. Far from evading their loss by forgetting it, they cast themselves away. Or others might have secretively sought to defraud the good that had once been bestowed upon them by pretending that it had never really been beautiful, never really brought them joy. They thought that they would find strength in such wretched self-deception whose power was the power of falsehood. Others again became utterly thoughtless, assuring themselves that life wasn't as hard as they had imagined, and that what had been described as frightful was not so hard to bear. But that is only possible if one begins by not finding anything frightful in what really is frightful!

Who would ever get to the end of talking about what has often happened and will often happen again in the world? One would soon become exhausted by it, long before one had exhausted the passion of finding ever new variations on the explanations and understandings that people come up with to deceive themselves with, and that always let them down. Let us therefore rather turn back to Job. In the day of mourning, when everything was lost, he first of all thanked God who had given it all. He deceived neither God nor himself, and while everything was shaken and cast down, he remained as he had been from the beginning, "honest and upright toward God."* He ac-

---

* Job 1:1.

knowledged that the Lord had shown mercy in blessing him, and he thanked Him for it—therefore it did not now remain as an aching memory. He acknowledged that the Lord had richly blessed his undertakings beyond all measure, and he thanked Him for it—therefore the memory of it did not linger on as a consuming restlessness. He did not hide from himself the fact that everything had been taken from him, and therefore the Lord who had taken it remained in his upright soul. He did not flee from the thought that it was lost, and therefore his soul became quiet, until the Lord would come to him again and make all things clear. And when He did, He would find Job's soul like the good soil that had been cultivated by patience.

"The Lord took away." In saying this, Job said nothing other than the truth. He didn't use some indirect expression for what might be said directly. The saying is brief and depicts the loss of everything. It is natural for us to use his words, since the saying has become a holy proverb. But is it just as natural for us to connect it with what Job meant by it? Wasn't it rather the Sabaeans who had fallen upon his peaceful herds and cut down his servants? Wasn't it rather the lightning that had consumed the sheep and their shepherds—isn't that what the messenger said, even if he spoke of the lightning as "God's lightning"? Wasn't it rather a storm from the far side of the desert that overturned the house and buried his children? Did the messenger mention any other perpetrator or anyone who had sent the storm? Yet Job said, "The Lord took away"—and in the same moment he received the news he understood that it was the Lord who had taken everything. Who explained this to Job? Or was it a sign of how he feared God that he thus attributed everything to the Lord? But who instructed him in how to do this—and are we more devout, we who sometimes think about it for a long time before speaking like that?

Perhaps there have been those who lost everything. Then they sat down to ponder how it had happened. Their joy vanished like a dream, and sorrow came over them like a dream, but they could never discover how they had been thrown from the glory of the first to the wretchedness of the latter. It was not the Lord who had taken it, it was an accident. Or else they persuaded themselves that it was human deceit, or subterfuge, or open violence, that had robbed them of it all, as it was the Sabaeans who had cut down Job's herds and their minders. Then their souls rose against their fellow human beings. They did not want to do an injustice to God by reproaching Him. They understood how it all had happened. Their immediate explanation was that it was these men who had done it, and their more considered explanation was that humankind is evil and people's hearts corrupt. They understood that other human beings are the ones who most directly harm them, and perhaps they would have understood it in a similar way if it had been a matter of being benefited in some way. But the idea that the Lord who dwells far off in heaven might be nearer to them than the human beings who are closest to them, whether they act well or badly, is an idea very far from their thoughts.

Maybe they did understand how it had happened and knew how to describe it with the eloquence born of terror. For who does not understand that when the sea rages wildly and rises up toward the heavens, human beings and their feeble dwellings are tossed about like a toy? Who does not understand that when the storm breaks out and rages, human undertakings are like childish things; or that when the earth quakes with elemental anxiety and the mountains sigh, human beings and their glorious undertakings are as nothing in the abyss? Such explanations were enough for them and, above all, served to make their souls indifferent to it all. For it is true that what is built on sand does not need a storm to overthrow it. But is it also true that there is no place else on which a human being can build and dwell and find salvation? Or else they understood that it was their own fault, because they had not been clever enough. If only they had planned properly it wouldn't have happened! And this reasoning explained everything once it had made clear that they had let themselves be corrupted in such a way that it was impossible for them to learn anything from life and, above all, from God.

But who would ever get to the end of talking about what has happened and what will certainly happen over and over again in life? Wouldn't it be better to come to an end of all this talking rather than to carry on like the sensuous person who deceives himself with superficial and vain and deceptive explanations? Let us therefore turn away from that from which there is nothing to learn, and with which we were already sufficiently acquainted to be able to know how little this world's wisdom is worth, and turn back to him from whom we can learn what is true—to Job and his devout saying "The Lord took away." Job attributed everything to God. He did not drown his soul or wear out his spirit with pondering it all and explaining it all. That would only have issued in and given nourishment to doubt in the one who dwells within, even if unnoticed. In the same moment that everything was taken away from him, he knew that it was the Lord who had taken it. Therefore, in his loss, he preserved his confidence in the Lord. He saw the Lord and therefore he didn't see despair. Or is it only those who see that God gives who see God's hand and not also those who see that He takes away? Or is it only those who see God's countenance turned toward them who see God and not also those who see Him turn His back, just as Moses only ever saw the Lord's backside? But those who see God have overcome the world, and therefore Job, with his devout saying, had overcome the world. In his devout saying, he was stronger and mightier than the whole world, which, while it was not now seeking to lead him into temptation, was trying to overpower him with its might and bring him to his knees before its limitless force. But how weak, how almost childish, are the storm's wild billows when they have tried to shake a person by taking everything from him and he answers them, "It is not you who are doing it but the Lord who is taking away." How powerless is the arm of the man of violence, how wretched is the cunning of the crafty, how almost pitiable human might becomes when it tries to plunge a weak person into despairing submission by taking everything from him and he faithfully says, "It is not you. You are unable to do anything. It is the Lord who takes away."

BLESSED BE THE NAME OF THE LORD

"Blessed be the Name of the Lord." In this way Job not only overcame the world, but he did what Paul wished on behalf of his struggling congregation: he stood, having overcome all (Ephesians 6:13). Ah! Perhaps there have been those in the world who overcame everything but then fell in the moment of victory. Blessed be the name of the Lord! Has the Lord then remained the same? Is He to be praised in the same way as before? But has He in fact changed? Isn't He in truth the same, as Job, too, is? Blessed be the name of the Lord! So the Lord did not take everything, for He did not take the word of blessing from him. Nor did He take Job's peace of heart, his openhearted faith from which that word proceeded. But Job remained confident in the Lord as before, perhaps even more inwardly than before, since there was now nothing at all that could by any means distract his thoughts from it. The Lord took everything away, and Job, as it were, gathered all his grief together and "cast it on the Lord"*—and then He took even that from him, leaving only the word of blessing behind and therewith an imperishable joy of heart. For Job's house was a house of mourning if ever there was one, but where "Blessed be the name of the Lord" is spoken, joy also dwells. Job indeed stands before us with grief imprinted in his face and in his whole form, but whoever speaks

---

* 1 Peter 5:7.

this saying nevertheless still bears testimony to joy, as Job did. And this is also true when his testimony is not given to the happy but to the sorrowful, and it speaks yet more understandingly to the many who have ears to hear. For the ears of the sorrowful are formed in a singular manner, and just as the ears of lovers hear many voices but really only ever hear one, that is, the voice of the one they love, so, too, do the ears of those who mourn hear many voices that merely pass them by and do not find a way into their hearts. For just as faith and hope without love are a sounding gong and clanging cymbal, so, too, is all the joy that is proclaimed in the world a sounding gong and clanging cymbal if sorrow is not heard along with it. It tickles the ears but repels the soul. But such a voice of comfort, this voice that shakes with pain and yet proclaims joy—the mourners' ears hear that, they keep what it says in their hearts, they are strengthened and guided by it to find for themselves the joy to be found in the depths of grief.

My listeners! It's true, isn't it, that you have understood Job's blessing? At the very least, it has seemed very beautiful to you as you quietly pondered it in your minds. So beautiful, perhaps, that in thinking about it you forgot what you didn't want me to have to remind you of—namely, what is sometimes heard in the day of need instead of praise and blessing. So let it be forgotten. You, as little as I, will want the memory of it to come back to life by being remembered.

APPLYING THE SAYING

We have spoken about Job and sought to understand him in his devout saying without speaking in such a way as to want to intrude on anyone. But does it follow that it should therefore be without meaning or application and not concern anyone? If you yourself, my listener, were to be tried as Job was and stood firm as he did in the time of trial, then what has been said would apply quite precisely to you, if we have spoken correctly about Job. And if you have not yet been tried in life, it still applies to you. Perhaps you think that this saying can be used only in some exceptional circumstances, such as those in which Job found himself. Do you then perhaps expect that if such things happened to you, the terror of the situation would itself give you this strength and produce this humble courage in you? But didn't Job have a wife—and what do we read about her? Perhaps you think that horrors cannot themselves exert such power over a person as being bound to the daily slavery of much lesser adversities. If so, then see to it that you are not the slave of any adversity any more than you are a slave to anybody and learn from Job to be, above all, honest to yourself and not to deceive yourself with imaginary powers with which you experience an imaginary victory in an imaginary conflict. Perhaps you will say that it would be one thing if the Lord had taken everything away from you, but in fact you were never given any-thing—and perhaps you think that while this may not be as terrifying as Job's sufferings, it saps you all the more relentlessly and is therefore more difficult to struggle against. We will not argue with you, for even if it is your struggle it is useless to argue about it, and doing so only makes it more difficult. But if you are in agreement with us that you can learn from Job, and if you are honest with yourself and love your fellow human beings, then you cannot wish to let go of Job in order to try yourself in hitherto unknown needs while keeping the rest of us agog until such time as you are able to testify that victory is also possible in difficulties such as these. So you can learn from Job how to say, "Blessed be the name of the Lord." This serves you well, even if what went before suits you less.

Or do you imagine that such things could never happen to you? Who taught you this wisdom, or on what do you build your convic-tion? Are you wise and understanding, and is this your comfort? Job was teacher to many. Are you young, and is your youth your security? Job had also been young. Are you old and drawing close to the grave?

Job, too, was an old man when grief came to him. Are you powerful, and is this your free pass? Job was well regarded among the people. Are riches your surety? Job owned the blessing of the land. Is it your friends who will protect you? Job was loved by all. Do you seek comfort in God? Job was God's confidant.

Have you really considered such thoughts, or do you rather flee them in case they force from you an admission that you might be inclined to call a depressive attitude? And yet no hiding place has been found anywhere in the whole wide world where grief cannot find you, and yet there has never lived anyone who was able to say more than you are able to say, namely, that you do not know when sorrow will visit your house. So take your situation seriously, fix your eye on Job. Even if the sight of him can make you afraid, this is not what he wants to do unless this is what you yourself want. When you look back over your life and imagine that it has come to an end, you could not want to say of yourself that you were fortunate and were not like other people, that you never suffered anything in life and let each day look after itself or, more accurately, bring you fresh joys. Even if it were true, you would not want to say that of yourself, because it would be shameful. Why? Because even if all around you was at peace, peace such as no one else had enjoyed, you would still want to say, "Indeed, I have not been tried, but my mind has often thought seriously about Job and how no one knows the time or the hour when the messengers will come bearing ever more terrible tidings."

Part II

CREATION:
What We Learn from the Lilies and the Birds

5

Be Satisfied with Being Human*

Father in heaven, you give only good and perfect gifts, and so it must be beneficial to follow the guidance and teaching of those whom you give to human beings as teachers and as guides for the anxious. So give the anxious the true benefit of learning from those divinely appointed school-teachers, the lilies and the birds.

The Gospel is written in the sixth chapter of the Gospel according to St. Matthew, beginning at the twenty-fourth verse.

No one can serve two masters; for either he will hate the one and love the other, or he will be devoted to the one and despise the other. You cannot serve God and mammon. Therefore, I tell you, do not be anxious about your life, what you shall eat, or what you shall drink, nor about your body, what you shall put on. Is not life more than food, and the body more than clothing? Consider the birds of the air: they neither sow

---

* From Niels Jørgen Cappelørn et al., eds., *Søren Kierkegaards Skrifter*, vol. 10 (Copenhagen: Gad, 2004), pp. 258–280.

nor reap nor gather into barns, and yet your heavenly Father feeds them. Are you not of more value than they? And which of you by being anxious can add one cubit to his span of life? And why are you anxious about clothing? Consider the lilies of the field, how they grow; they neither toil nor spin; yet I tell you, even Solomon in all his glory was not arrayed like one of these. But if God so clothes the grass of the field, which today is and tomorrow is cast into the oven, will he not much more clothe you, Oh you of little faith? Therefore do not be anxious, saying, "What shall we eat?" or "What shall we drink?" or "What shall we wear?" For the Gentiles seek all these things; and your heavenly Father knows that you need them all. But seek first his kingdom and his righteousness, and all these things shall be added unto you. Therefore do not be anxious about tomorrow, for tomorrow will be anxious for itself. Let the day's own trouble be sufficient for the day.

Who has not known this holy gospel from their earliest childhood and often had joy of its glad tidings? And yet it is not unqualifiedly joyful. For it is essential to it being a gospel, that is, good news, that it is directed to the anxious. Indeed, every line in the gospel alludes to anxiety in such a way as to show that it is not addressing the healthy or the strong or the happy but the anxious. And it shows this in such a way that the glad tidings are delivered in a manner that echoes what God himself is said to do, that is, to take up the anxious and care for them—in the right way. Ah! But this is indeed needful. For everyone who sorrows—and especially when their grief has penetrated more deeply or for longer into their soul—is perhaps also tempted to impatience and does not to want to hear what others have to say about comfort and hope. Perhaps those who sorrow are wrong in that regard; perhaps they are too impatient when it seems to them that no human being can speak to the point about what grieves them. For, they think, the happy do not understand them, and when those who are strong offer comfort they seem precisely to place themselves far above them by doing so, while what other anxiety sufferers have to offer only depresses them further. So if that's how it is, then it's best to look for other teachers who do not address us in such a way as to show they don't understand, whose exhortations don't contain some secret reproach, who do not look at us judgingly, and whose comfort does not serve more to stir us up than to calm us down.

It is to such teachers that the gospel for the anxious directs the sorrowful: to the lilies of the field and the birds of the air. In relation to these teachers, so cheap that they ask for neither money nor deference, no misunderstanding is possible, because they keep silent—out of consideration for the anxious. For it is from speaking that all misunderstanding arises, which can be more precisely explained by noting that all speaking, especially speaking in company, implies an element of comparison. So when the happy person says, "Cheer up," to someone who is suffering from anxiety, this also implies, "Be happy as I am"; and when the strong person says, "Be strong," then he is understood as meaning "in the same way as I am." But silence honors anxiety and the anxious person, as Job's friends did when, out of respect, they sat silently with the sufferer and thus showed their respect. And yet they looked at him—but already the fact that one person looks at another implies a comparison. The silent friends did not compare Job with themselves: that only happened when they broke with the respect in which they silently held him and broke silence in order to fall upon the sufferer with their speeches. Nevertheless, merely the fact of their presence gave Job occasion to compare himself with himself. And so no human being can be present, even silently, without that presence arousing some possibility of significant comparison. At the most a child can do it, for a child is a bit like the lilies of the field and the birds of the air, and how often a sufferer has experienced and been moved by noticing that when a child is there it is as if no one is there. And as for the lily of the field—no matter how richly it is attired, it does not compare its prosperity with anybody else's poverty. Even if it is without a care in all its glory, it neither compares itself with Solomon nor with the most wretched. And even if the bird soars lightly in the sky, he doesn't compare his easy flight with the heavy trudge of those weighed down with anxiety, and if the bird is richer than those who have filled their stores—even though he never stores what he gathers—he doesn't compare his rich independence with the plight of those who suffer need and who gather in vain. No. For if you seek comfort where the lily flowers in loveliness—in the field—and where the bird is free and at home—in the air—there you will find uninterrupted silence: no one is present, yet everything constantly speaks to you.

But this is only true if those who sorrow really pay attention to the lilies and the birds and forget about themselves in thinking about them and their life. Thus, by forgetting about themselves in considering these creatures, they learn something about themselves without noticing it. Without noticing it: for there is unbroken silence and no one is there; there is no one to find out anything about their anxiety except God Himself—and the lilies.

In this discourse, then, let us consider how, by observing the lilies of the field and the birds of the air in the right way, the anxious person might learn

TO BE SATISFIED WITH BEING HUMAN.

"Consider the lilies of the field." Consider them, that is, observe them closely, make them the object not of a quick glance as you pass by but of observation. That is why an expression is used that is customarily employed by the clergy on the most serious and solemn oc-

casions, when they say, "In this quiet time, let us consider this or that." And the summons or the invitation that is issued here is indeed solemn. There are perhaps many who live in the big cities and never see the lilies and many who live in the country and indifferently pass them by every day. Ah! But how many are there who rightly consider them in the manner proposed by the gospel!

"The lilies of the field." We are not talking about some rare plants that are carefully cultivated in a garden and that are objects of study by specialists. No, just go out to the field where there is no one who cares about the abandoned lilies, and where it is so clear that they have been left to themselves. Ah! If such an exhortation does not seem inviting to the anxious, then they, too, are like the abandoned lily—abandoned, unrecognized, overlooked, without human care— until, by rightly considering the lily, they understand that they have not been left alone. So then, the anxious one goes out to the field and stops to look at the lily—not in the same way as a child or a childish adult might do, running around to find the prettiest or, in order to satisfy their curiosity, to find the rarest. No. Quietly, solemnly, he considers them as they stand there, a numerous, brocaded multitude, each as good as the other.

"How they grow." Strictly speaking, we cannot see how the lilies grow, for, as the proverb says, one cannot see the grass grow, but we can see how they grow, or, precisely because this is incomprehensible, we can see that there must be one who knows them as intimately as the gardener knows the rare plants he cultivates, one who daily looks after them, morning and evening, as the gardener looks after the rare plants, one who gives them growth. Presumably this is the same one who gives growth to the gardener's rare plants, although the role of the gardener can easily cause a misunderstanding in this regard. The lilies that have been left to themselves, however, the common lilies, the lilies of the field, give those who consider them no occasion for

misunderstanding. For where there is a gardener to be seen, where no effort or cost is spared in order to bring on the rich man's rare plants, it might seem to be easier to understand that they grow well. Out in the field, however, where no one, no one, no one cares about the lilies, how is it that they grow? And yet they do.

But that must mean that the poor lilies themselves have to work all the harder. No, *"they toil not"*—it is only rare plants that need a lot of work in order to grow. There, where the carpet is richer than in a royal chamber, no one works. As you observe the scene and are delighted and refreshed by it, you do not need to worry yourself about how the poor little lilies have to work and slave to make the carpet look so lovely. It is only in relation to the products of human artifice that while the eye is dazzled by the quality of the work it is also filled with tears at the thought of the sufferings of the poor lace maker.

The lilies *"neither toil nor spin."* In fact, they do nothing except adorn themselves or, more precisely, be adorned. As in the preceding verses of the gospel, where the birds are being discussed, and it is said that "they neither sow nor reap nor gather into barns," as if indicating a man's work in securing a livelihood for himself and his family, so what is said about the lilies (who neither toil nor spin) seems to allude to women's work. The woman stays at home and does not go out in order to seek the necessities of life; she stays at home, sowing and spinning and seeking to keep everything as neat as possible. Her daily tasks and all her busy work are first and foremost about keeping a neat and well-ordered household. So too, the lily—it stays at home, it doesn't leave the spot, but it doesn't work, it doesn't spin, it merely adorns itself or, more precisely, is adorned. If the lily was to be anxious about anything, it wouldn't be for its livelihood, such as the bird might seem to be anxious about as he flies so far and wide to gather his food. No, the lily's care would be of a more feminine kind, namely, as to whether it was lovely and well adorned. But it has no anxiety or care.

MCDOUGALL, ST

It is adorned—that is certain. Looking at it, you can't take your eyes off it: bend down to just one lily, any one at all, *"yet I tell you, even Solomon in all his glory was not arrayed like one of these."* Look at it carefully and close up, and, if your mind was troubled (ah, as a human mind can be troubled!) and if your heart was pounding loudly (ah, as a human heart can pound!), you will be struck silent just by considering this lily. The more closely you look, the more you will marvel at its loveliness and the ingenuity with which it has been formed. For it is only in relation to the products of human artifice that when you look more closely you discover lack and imperfection, and if you augment your natural vision with a magnifying glass, then even the finest piece of weaving will be seen to have rough threads. Ah! It is as if the very invention that human beings are so proud of has caused them to be humbled, for when they learned how to make an artificial lens the magnifying glass they produced revealed that even the finest works of human hands were crude and imperfect. But the discovery that humbled human beings gave glory to God, since no magnifying glass has ever revealed that the lily was less lovely or less ingenious. On the contrary, it has shown it to be even lovelier and even more ingenious. Indeed, it honored God as every discovery must do, for it is only in relation to a human artist that those who know him well and are close to him in his everyday life discover that he is not so great. But in the case of the artist who weaves the carpet that is spread over the field and who produces the loveliness of the lily, the more closely He is known the more wonderful He is seen to be, and the closer we get to Him the greater the distance our adoration reveals.

So then, the anxious one who took his sorrows out to the lilies now stands among them in the field, wondering at the loveliness of the lilies he is looking at. He has fixed his eyes on the first one he came across, without distinguishing one from another, since it hadn't occurred to him that there could be a single lily or a single blade of grass in the field of which it couldn't be said that even Solomon in all his glory was not arrayed like one of them. If the lily could talk, wouldn't it then say to the anxious, "Why are you so full of wonder at me? Isn't it just as wonderful to be human? Isn't even all of Solomon's glory as nothing in comparison with what every human being is just by being human? And if Solomon really wished to be the most glorious of all and knew what that meant, would he not have to relinquish all his glory and be just a human being? Shouldn't what is true of poor little me not hold also for being human, since human beings are the marvel of all Creation?" However, the lily cannot talk, but precisely because it cannot talk, precisely because there is unbroken silence out there and there is no one present, if the anxious one talks and talks with the lily, he will actually be talking to himself. For little by little he will discover that he is talking about himself, and that what he is saying about the lily he is saying about himself. It is not the lily that says it, for it cannot talk. Nor is there any *other* human being who says it to him, because if there was *another* human being, then there would be all the disturbing thoughts that originate from comparing oneself with another. But among the lilies the anxious person is merely a human being and—content with being human. For it is in exactly the same sense that the lily is a lily—in exactly that same sense and despite all the anxieties that only a human being can have—that we are human. And it is in exactly the same sense that without working or spinning the lily is more beautiful than Solomon's glory that, without working or spinning or doing anything to deserve it, a human being is more glorious than Solomon's glory. The gospel does not say that the lily is more glorious than Solomon but that it is better adorned than Solomon in all his glory. Ah! But in constant association with human beings, in the multitude of differences between them and all the different ways they interact with one another, in busily or anxiously finding out how to compare them, one forgets what it is to be a human being: the differences between one human being and another cause one to forget it. But in the field, with the lilies, where the sky is arched high above—as if over a ruler, freely—it is like breathing properly, where the great thoughts of the clouds dispel all pettiness. The anxious one is the *only* human being there and learns from the lilies what cannot perhaps be learned from any *other* human being.

"Consider the lilies of the field." How brief this saying about the lilies is, how solemn and how equable. There isn't a trace, not the slightest hint, of any sense that there might be a difference between one lily and another. It speaks about them all and about each one and speaks about them all in equal terms: "the lilies." Perhaps you think that it would be rather peculiar and asking too much for human language to start exploring the respective differences between the lilies and all the possible anxieties that these differences might occasion. Perhaps you think that "such differences and such anxieties are not worth attending to." Let us understand each other. Do you mean that it isn't worth the lily's while to pay attention to such anxieties— that is, that the lilies should be sensible enough not to pay attention to such things; or do you mean that it is beneath a human being's dignity to bother about what worries the lilies might possibly have, because a human being is a human being and not a lily? In other words, are such anxieties irrational in themselves and therefore not worth bothering about, whether it is simple lilies or rational human beings we are talking about? Or is the same anxiety essentially different when a lily has it from when a human being has it and in such a way that it is bad for the lily to worry about such things but not for human beings? If, however, the lilies really did have such anxieties, and the speaker thought that anxieties of that same kind acquired great significance in the case of human beings, then it would by no means be a mark of wisdom or compassion but of human self-love to be able to speak so shortly and so dismissively of the poor lilies, to be so lofty about the lilies' "petty troubles," so lofty as to call them "petty troubles" and not worth bothering about. Now, if it were the case that there were differences between one lily and another that, in their little world, corresponded to human differences, and if these differences preoccupied the lilies and worried them, just as they do human beings, then, if it were so, what would it mean to say that such differences and such anxieties were not worth bothering with?

Let us think about the matter more carefully. Since it was precisely to avoid all comparisons with other people, and it was because of his reluctance to have any other human being talk with him about his trouble that the anxious one went out to be with the lilies in the field, we have wanted our discourse to respect this anxiety and not speak about any other human being or any anxious human being, but instead we have preferred to talk about *the anxious lily*.

Once upon a time there was a lily that stood in an out-of-the-way place by a little running stream. It was well known to some nettles and a pair of other small flowers in the neighborhood. As in the gospel's truthful description, the lily was more beautifully clad than Solomon in all his glory and, furthermore, happy and carefree all day long. Time passed happily by without anyone noticing, just like the running water murmuring as it flowed. But then it came to pass that one day a little bird paid a visit to the lily. The next day, he came again and then stayed away for a few days before he came once more. This seemed very peculiar and quite inexplicable to the lily. It was inexplicable that the bird didn't stay in one place, like the small flowers, and it was peculiar that the bird could be so unpredictable. But as often happens, so, too, it happened to the lily that it fell more and more in love with the bird, precisely because he was so unpredictable.

Now, this little bird was a bad bird. Instead of putting himself in the lily's place, instead of taking pleasure in its loveliness and sharing its joy in its innocent happiness, he wanted to make himself important by feeling his own freedom—and making the lily feel tied down. And that's not all. The little bird was also a gossip and chattered away fast and loose, telling both what was true and what was not about other places, where there were great masses of lilies that were splendid in quite other ways, and where there was joy and cheerfulness, scents, splendid colors, and birdsong that were beyond description. That was how the bird talked, and every one of his tales ended with the remark—so humiliating for the lily—that, in comparison with such glory, the lily didn't look anything special at all; indeed, it was so insignificant that it was open to question whether it really had the right to be called a lily.

So the lily started to worry, and the more it listened to the bird the more worried and anxious it became. It no longer slept peacefully at night, and it was no longer joyful when it awoke in the morning. It felt as if it was imprisoned and tied down, and it found the babbling of the water getting boring and the days seeming long. It started to be preoccupied with itself and to be anxious about itself and its circumstances in life—the day was long enough for that! "It might be a fine thing," it said to itself, "to listen to the babbling brook now and then, for the sake of a change, but to have to hear the same thing all the time, day in and day out, is much too boring." "Maybe it's pleasant enough," it said to itself, "to be in an out-of-the-way place all alone now and then, but to be like this—spending one's whole life being forgotten, being without company or with only stinging nettles for company—what sort of company is that for a lily? It's not to be endured!" "And then," the lily said to itself, "to look as lowly as I do, to be as insignificant as the little bird says I am: Oh! Why wasn't I born somewhere else, in other circumstances? Why wasn't I born a crown imperial?" (For the little bird had told it that of all the lilies the crown imperial was regarded as the most beautiful and was the object of all the other lilies' envy.) Unfortunately, the lily began to notice that it was starting to worry and thought to reason with itself about the situation. But instead of finding reasons not to worry, it rather found reasons that proved it was right to be anxious. "For," it said, "I'm not wanting anything unreasonable, I'm not asking for the impossible or to become what I'm not, like becoming a bird. No, all I want is to be a splendid lily or maybe even the most splendid!"

All this time, the little bird flew back and forth, and every time he came and every time he went away made the lily more restless. Finally it confided itself entirely to the bird. One evening, they agreed that the next morning they would change things in such a way as to put an end to all the worry and anxiety. Early the next morning, the little bird came and with his beak pecked away the soil from the lily's roots so that it was set free. When he had done this, the bird took the lily under his wing and flew off. The agreement was that the bird would fly with the lily to the place where the splendid lilies blossomed. Once they were there, the bird would once more be of service by planting it there, so that the change of place and the new environment might help the lily to become a splendid lily along with all the others—or perhaps even a crown imperial, envied by all the others.

Alas, as they were going, the lily withered up. Had the anxious lily been content with being a lily it would never have become anxious, and if it had not become anxious it would have remained standing where it stood—where it stood in all its loveliness. If it had remained standing there, then it would have been the very lily about which the priest spoke on Sunday when he repeated the words of the gospel: "Consider the lilies of the field, how they grow; they neither toil nor spin; yet I tell you, even Solomon in all his glory was not arrayed like one of these." If it were not so, the gospel would make no sense at all. On the contrary, it would be troubling and even frightening if some-one who had to interpret the passage of Holy Scripture concerning the lilies were to use the occasion to explain—as the little bird did—that those were regions where crown imperials grew wild, so that it was easier to understand that the loveliness of the lily surpassed that of Solomon and better to understand the gospel as referring to them than to the insignificant lily.

This, however, is what happened to the lily who anxiously wanted to become a more splendid lily or even a crown imperial. The wicked little bird represents the restless thoughts aroused by comparing oneself with others, thoughts that roam far and wide, inconstant and unpredictable, gathering all the unwholesome knowledge there is to be had about the differences. And just as the bird didn't think to put himself in the lily's place, no more do we when we make acts of comparison, whether by putting ourselves in another's place or putting another in our place. The little bird is the poet, the seducer, or what is poetic and seductive in a person. The poetic is like the bird's discourses, true and untrue, poetry and truth. For it is indeed true that there are differences, and that there is much to say about them, but it is poetic license to say impassionedly that the differences are what is highest, whether one says it in despair or triumph, for this is eternally untrue. By comparing himself to others, the anxious one can finally go so far as to forget that he is a human being and can even think that he is somehow different from the rest of humanity, just as the little bird thought that the lily was so insignificant that it was open to question whether it really was a lily. And it is always assumed that a reasonable response to such anxieties is to say that one isn't asking for anything unreasonable, such as to become a bird, etc., but only to become this one particular thing one isn't—even though it is something that other anxious people regard as utterly unimportant. After such comparisons have aroused the passion of anxiety and, moving to and fro like the bird, have torn the anxious person from the soil in which he is rooted (that is, from wanting to be what he is), then it seems for a moment as if comparison is going to be able to fetch the anxious and take him to where he wants to go. And it does indeed come to fetch them, but only in the sense that death fetches a person: it lets the anxious perish by swinging backward and forward in discontent.

When you imagine how the lily became anxious about not being a crown imperial and so perished on the journey, it is not without a smile, but if you consider how a person can become just as causelessly anxious, then you can't help crying. Just as causelessly? But no—how could I let that stand, how dare I in all seriousness accuse those whom God has appointed as teachers, the lilies of the field? No, the lily does not become anxious in this way, and that is precisely why we should learn from it. And so, those who are like the lily in being satisfied with being what they are, that is, with being human, do not become sick with temporal anxieties; and if they do not become anxious about temporal things, they remain in the place appointed them; and if they remain there, then it is true that to be a human being is more glorious than Solomon's glory.

What, then, do those who suffer from anxiety learn from the lily? They learn to be content with being human and not to become anxious about the differences between one human being and another. They learn to speak just as briefly, just as solemnly, and just as upliftingly about what it is to be a human being as the gospels speak briefly about the lilies. And this is indeed customary precisely on solemn occasions. Imagine Solomon: when he is clad in his royal purple and is enthroned majestically in all his glory, then one is indeed to speak solemnly, and those who address him must say, "Your Majesty." But when, in the most solemn moments of all, one has to speak the serious language of eternity, it is a matter of simply, "Man!" And we say exactly the same to the lowliest when, like Lazarus, they have been laid low and made almost unrecognizable by poverty and wretchedness: we say, "Man!" And in the decisive moments of a person's life, when a choice between two different paths is to be made, we say to them, "Man!" And in death's decisive moment, when all differences have been done away with, we say, "Man!" But that doesn't mean that we are talking in a belittling way. On the contrary, we are saying what is highest, because just being a human being is not lower than being characterized by any of the differences between human beings but is elevated far above them. For the glory that is essentially alike among all human beings is not the sorrowful likeness they share in death, as little as this is the essential likeness among all lilies, for what they are truly alike in is their loveliness.

All *worldly* anxiety has its basis in human beings being unwilling to be content with being human and, under the influence of comparison, becoming anxiously desirous of being different in some way. However, one cannot immediately and without further ado say that *earthly* and *temporal* anxiety are invented by comparison, for the fact that in moments of real need human beings need food and clothing is not something we discover by comparing ourselves with others. For the one who lived alone among the lilies of the field would also discover this. Being worried about what to eat or, as it is more commonly called in a pitiable plural, having worries about what to eat, is not directly invented by comparison. It is something else, even if there are innumerable ways in which comparison ambiguously works away at deciding just what it means to be worried about what to eat and whether there shouldn't be— But no: the anxious don't want any other human being to talk to them about this, precisely because they want to avoid comparing themselves with others. And so, let us say it another way and see whether one might not be able to learn much about such care from the birds.

We shall now consider those whose worries about what to eat cause them to become anxious and how, by rightly considering the birds of the air, we might learn to be content with being human.

"Consider the birds of the air." Consider them, that is to say, pay careful attention to them. That is what the fisherman does when he comes in the morning and looks at the nets that have been set all night. It is how the doctor looks at the invalid. It is how the child looks when its elders are doing something it has never seen before. That is how—and not with divided attention or distracted thoughts but with focused attention and reflection—one is to carefully consider the birds. If anyone says, "We've seen birds so often that there's nothing particular to say about them," it just shows that they haven't understood what the gospel is inviting us to consider with regard to the birds of the air.

"The birds of the air"—or, as it says elsewhere, "the birds under heaven."* One does indeed also see birds down on the ground or on the earth, but if one is really to benefit from seeing them, one must see them under heaven or else constantly remember that they belong to the heavens. If anyone was misled by constantly seeing a bird on the ground into forgetting that it was a bird of the air, then he would have prevented himself from understanding the gospel about the birds of the air. *"They neither sow nor reap nor gather into barns."* How indeed could they do so there, where the birds belong, under heaven; there, where they live without looking into the future in a temporal sense, innocent of time, in the moment. The earthly person who looks to the future learns from time how to use time, and when their store is full of what has been gathered in the *past* so that they are well provided for in the *present*, then they go on to sow again for a future harvest, so that they can again fill their store in *time to come*. And, so, there are three words that are used to signify the labors of the provident person. It is not said as briefly as in the case of the lilies—they neither toil nor spin—but the three

---

* Psalm 8:8; Jeremiah 4:25.

words signify the categories of time that are the basis of providence. *"And yet your heavenly Father feeds them."* The heavenly Father—yes, that is clear, it has to be Him when you consider the birds "under heaven." For where it is a case of the farmer coming out morning, noon, and night to call the birds together and feed them, then it is easy to make a mistake and to believe that it is the farmer who feeds the birds. But there, where there are no farmers, in the field; there, where there are no barns, "under heaven," there, where the carefree birds swoop lightly over woods and lakes without sowing, reaping, or gathering into barns and without any worries about what to eat: there it must indeed be the heavenly Father who feeds them. "He feeds them"—or should we not perhaps say, rather foolishly, what many a foolish farmer might have said, "The birds steal" (by which he means that it is really the farmer who feeds them, because they steal from him)? Ah! If a person's thoughts had sunk so low in miserable wretchedness as to be capable of thinking such a thing in all seriousness, how might they then learn to be uplifted by the birds of the air, how would it help such a one to consider the birds of the air? And yet it certainly would help, were they willing simply to look at them, that is to say, to pay careful attention to them and learn once more to forget that miserable way of reasoning that made them so inhumanly petty. No, it is the heavenly Father who feeds the birds, and He does so despite the fact that they do not sow nor reap nor gather into barns, which is to say that the heavenly Father also feeds those who do sow and reap and gather into barns, so that those who provide for themselves shall learn from the birds of the air that there is also a heavenly Father who feeds them. But those who own nothing, nothing at all on earth, those who thus also live "under heaven," those who sorrowfully realize that they are very close to the happy company of the birds of the air—such also learn that the heavenly Father feeds them.

"Consider the birds of the air: your heavenly Father feeds them." How briefly, how solemnly, how equitably this is said. It includes all the birds; not one single one is forgotten in a discourse that explains how the heavenly Father does not forget a single one, He who opens his merciful hand and satisfies all that live with His blessing. There is not the slightest hint about any difference in what the gospel says about the birds, such as that one is richly provided for while the other scarcely at all, the one perhaps getting a supply that lasts a little longer while the other gets only what it needs in the moment, or that sometimes there are those who have to wait and wait in vain and maybe even go hungry. No, the gospel speaks only of the birds and their being fed by the heavenly Father.

But perhaps some people might say that from time to time there are birds that get too little and also birds that die of hunger, but that's nothing for us to get worried about. How could a person bear to talk like that about the birds! Isn't anxiety about getting the wherewithal to live the same, whether in the case of a bird or a human being? Should a human being loftily disregard this anxiety, because it was only the bird who knew of it, while human beings were free from it? Or was it unreasonable of the bird to be anxious about such insignificant things, although it was not unreasonable of reasonable human beings to be anxious about the same insignificant things?

Suppose the bird was not without a certain knowledge of the differences with regard to a livelihood, a knowledge that is unfortunately so prevalent among human beings. Suppose these differences occupied and worried the bird in the same way that they worry human beings! Assuming this to be so, the discourse can then avoid what the anxious one is so reluctant to have—namely, *another* human being talking to him about his anxiety—and the discourse can remain out in the field among the birds and talk about *the bird's anxiety*.

Once upon a time there was a wood pigeon that had his nest

in the murky wood, where awe mingles with fear among the tall, lonesome trunks. But nearby, where smoke rose from the farmer's cottage, there lived some of his distant relatives, some tame doves. He often met up with a couple of these when he sat on a branch stretching out over the farmer's yard, while the two tame doves sat on the ridge of the roof, but not so far away that they were unable to exchange thoughts in a conversational kind of way. One day, they were talking about time and its occasions and about their livelihood. The wood pigeon said, "Until now, I've had my livelihood, letting each day have its troubles, and that's how I get through life." The tame dove listened closely, although he couldn't help noticing a certain pleasurable movement run through his whole body, and preening himself he answered, "No, it's quite different for us. Among us, that is, at the wealthy farmer's place where we live, one's future is assured. When it's harvesttime, I or my spouse, one of us, sits up on the roof and watches. The farmer brings in one load of grain after the other, and when he's brought so many that I've lost count, then I know that there are provisions enough for a long time—I know that from experience." When he had thus spoken, he turned to his spouse, not without a certain self-satisfaction, as if to say, "Isn't that right, little wifey, we two are well provided for."

When the wood pigeon went home, he thought more about all this, and it immediately struck him that it must be very agreeable to *know* in that way that one's livelihood was assured for a long time, whereas it was worrisome constantly to live in a state of uncertainty such that one never dared to say that one *knew* one would be looked after. And so he said to himself it would be best for him to see if he couldn't succeed in gathering a larger supply and storing it in one or another very safe place.

The next morning, he woke up earlier than usual and was so busy gathering his supplies that he scarcely had time to eat or to eat enough. But it was as if there was some fate that wouldn't allow him to gather a good supply. For each time he had got together a little morsel and hidden it in one or other of the places he supposed were safe—when he then came to take a look at them, they were gone. For the time being, there was no real change with regard to his livelihood. Each day he found his food as before, and inasmuch as he took rather less for himself, this was because he wanted to save it up, and because he didn't allow himself time to eat. Otherwise he would have had as good a livelihood as before. Ah! But a great change had nevertheless taken place. He was far from suffering from real need, but he had started to *imagine* what he might need in the future and his peace was shattered—he had acquired *worry about what to eat.*

From now on, the wood pigeon became anxious. His feathers lost their iridescent colors, his flight lost its lightness, his days passed in a fruitless attempt to gather a good supply, and his dreams were the powerless plans of fantasy. He was no longer happy; indeed, he was almost envious of the wealthy doves. He found enough food each day and became tired, and yet it was as if he was not tired because his worries about what to eat made him hungry for more time. He had snared himself in a trap in which no bird catcher could have snared him, because only those who are free can catch themselves—in imagination. "It is indeed true," he said to himself, "it is indeed true that when I have as much as I can eat each day, then I have a livelihood. I couldn't eat the great supply I want to gather up all at once, and in a certain sense one couldn't do more with it than to tire oneself out with eating. But it would nevertheless be a great pleasure to be free from this uncertainty that makes one so dependent." "It may well be," he said to himself, "that the tame doves have paid dearly for their livelihood. It may well be that at bottom they have many anxieties that, until now, I've been free from. But I can't get this idea of security for the future out of my head. Oh! Why was I born a poor wood pigeon and not one of the rich doves?" Thus, he indeed noticed how he was becoming troubled, and he began to reason with himself—although he did not reason in such a way as to strike the anxiety from his thoughts and restore his peace of mind but rather in such a way as to persuade himself that his worries were entirely proper. "I don't want anything unreasonable," he said, "or anything impossible. I don't want to become like the rich peasant but simply like one of the rich doves."

Finally he thought up a plan. One day, he flew down and sat on the ridge of the farmer's roof between the tame doves. When he had spotted the place where these flew into, he also flew in, for that must be where the supply store was. But when the farmer came in the evening to lock up the dovecote, he immediately discovered the strange pigeon. The wood pigeon was immediately placed in a little cage on his own until the next day, when he was killed—and thus relieved of his worries about what to eat. Ah! The anxious wood pigeon had not only caught himself in anxiety but also caught himself in the dovecote—fatally!

If the wood pigeon had been content with being what he was, a bird of the air, then he would have had his livelihood; then the heavenly Father would have fed him; then, on condition of being uncertain, he would have remained where he belonged, there, where the straight, lonesome tree trunks have a melancholy but good understanding with the cooing wood pigeons. Then he would have been the one about whom the priest spoke on Sunday when he repeated the words of the gospel: "Consider the birds of the air: they neither sow nor reap nor gather into barns, and yet your heavenly Father feeds them."

This wood pigeon represents a human being. But no—let us not forget that this is only a discourse that, out of respect for the anxious, has allowed the wood pigeon to have his turn. It is rather like when a poor boy is used in bringing up a royal child by having to take the punishment owing the young prince—in the same way the discourse has let everything fall on the wood pigeon. And he was happy to play that role, for he knows well that he is one of those divinely appointed teachers from whom we are to learn, and that a teacher sometimes teaches by displaying the error he is warning us against. The wood pigeon himself is carefree, for he is indeed the one of whom the gospel speaks. So the wood pigeon represents a human being. If, like him, that human being is content to be human, then he understands what he learns from the bird of the air: that the heavenly Father feeds him. But if the heavenly Father feeds him, then he does not have to worry about what to eat, and he does not so much live like the tame doves at the rich farmer's but lives with the one who is richer than all. And he truly lives with Him, since heaven and earth are God's house and God's possession and thus a human being indeed dwells with Him.

This is what it comes down to: to be content with being human, to be content with being the lowly one, the creature that is as incapable of keeping itself alive as it is of creating itself. If, on the other hand, a human being forgets God and takes upon himself the task of feeding himself, then he will worry about what to eat. It is certainly praiseworthy and well pleasing to God that human beings sow and reap and gather into barns, and that they work to get their food. But if they forget God and think that it is their work that provides them with what they eat, then they will worry about what to eat. If the richest man who had ever lived were to forget God and think that he provided his own food, he would start to worry about food. But let us not talk foolishly or pettily by saying that the rich are free from having to worry about what to eat and the poor are not. No, only those are free from such worry who are content with being human and who understand that it is the heavenly Father who feeds them— and the poor person is as capable of this as any of the rich.

Worrying about food is therefore the snare in which no outward force, nothing *real*, can catch a person, but in which we—both rich and poor—can entrap ourselves when we are not content with being human. And if we are not content with that, what more is there that we could ask for? The "more" is simply wanting to be one's own provider for one's whole life, or perhaps just for the next day. And when we want to be that, then we—*cunningly*—get taken by the snare, rich as well as poor. It is as if we want to entrench ourselves on some smaller or larger spot that is not to be the object of God's providence or of the heavenly Father's care in providing. Perhaps we do not notice before it is too late that we live behind our defenses as if in a prison. We do what the farmer did to the pigeon: we turn the lock and believe that we are now safe—but in fact we have become prisoners, or, to put it another way, we are utterly excluded from being cared for by providence and given up to being worried about what to eat. For only those are caught and excluded who have locked themselves up, with many or few possessions, in the belief that they can provide for themselves; and only those are free and without a care as to what they are to eat who, with many or few possessions and even in poverty, understand that their heavenly Father feeds them. And, spiritually speaking, those who by their presumptuous reasoning have cunningly locked themselves in and thereby imprisoned themselves have, like the wood pigeon, condemned themselves to death. In this way, we can already see that worrying about food is a result of making comparisons and, especially, of the frightful way in which those who are not content with being human want to compare themselves with God and to give themselves a kind of security that no human being should dare to have, a security that therefore ends up with worrying about what to eat.

But there are also other ways in which it can be shown that worrying about what to eat is a result of making comparisons, insofar as worrying about what to eat has nothing to do with the real needs we experience this very day but with imagined future needs. Again, the comparison is a result of someone not being content with being human. The poor bird of the air compared himself with the rich birds, and in making this comparison he discovered anxiety about what to eat. He had long known what it was like to be hungry and to look for food, but he had never before worried about what to eat. Now he learned to distinguish between the rich and the poor, who, far from being separated by a yawning gulf, are in constant association and continually arguing over how the boundary between them is to be defined. Furthermore, the distinctions between them and their relations to one another are altered according to what is at issue, and this third element in the comparison can be hugely varied. Worrying about what to eat is therefore a matter of not being content with being human but being marked by or having one or another distinguishing feature: being rich, affluent, comfortably off, fairly secure, and so on. Such a one does not look to the birds of the air and, so, away from the differences that characterize human life, but he compares himself to others and to the differences that distinguish them from one another, and his worry about what to eat is a relationship of comparison.

And even if the anxious don't fix their attention in this way on some degree of difference or other and confuse anxiety about what to eat with worldly worries (for worrying about whether one has just as much as this person or that is not being anxious about what to eat)—even if this isn't the case, and if their anxiety about what to eat is not an expression of an actual but only of an imagined need, there is still an act of comparison at the root of it. Why was it that the bird didn't worry about what to eat? It was because he didn't compare one day with the next and, as the gospel instructs us to do, he let each day have troubles enough of its own. But even

if the anxious don't compare their circumstances with those of any
other human being and, in this sense, "keep themselves unsullied
by the world"* (ah! but comparison is perhaps one of the most ruin-
ous types of contagion), if they nevertheless anxiously compare one
day with another and they are richly provided for today, they say,
"But what about tomorrow?" or when they have only just enough
for the day, they say, "It'll be even worse tomorrow"—then they are
engaged in making comparisons.

Ah! If such anxious people were to read this, they would soon
get impatient with the speaker. From respect for the subject of the
discourse I would gladly act like the pagan wise man who covered
his face, and, in the same way, I would willingly hide my face out of
respect for what it is to be anxious and not be looking at anyone in
particular but speak only of the birds of the air. For it was thanks
to this kind of comparison that the wood pigeon discovered what
it was to worry about what to eat, letting anxiety's careworn self-
preoccupation go on for day after day. He acknowledged that he had
enough to live on, but the element of uncertainty distressed him, and
it seemed to him that he had become so dependent—on God. He was
vexed that he could never speak with assurance about tomorrow—although let us not forget that, in a godly sense, he could dare to speak
with confidence if he said, "The heavenly Father will certainly feed
me tomorrow"; and let us also not forget that he could have spoken
with the greatest confidence about tomorrow if he had with true inwardness limited himself simply to giving thanks for what he had
today! Isn't it so? If a girl in love was visited by her beloved and she
asked whether he was also going to come the next day, wouldn't that
show an element of anxiety in her love? But if, without mentioning
the next day, she threw her arms around his neck and said, "Thank

---

* James 1:27.

you for coming today," then she could be quite at ease about the next day. Or, if there were two girls and one said to her beloved, "Are you also going to come tomorrow?" while the other said, "Thank you for coming today"—who would you assume was most convinced that the beloved really would come again the next day?

We often encounter the pointless and perhaps vain conflict that occurs when the poor say to the rich, "You can do what you like, because you are free from having to worry about what to eat." May God grant that the poor really understand how much better the gospel's intentions concerning them are, how much more equitable and loving. For, in truth, the gospel does not let itself be fooled by the sense deception of visible differences, nor does it let itself be fooled into taking one person's part against any other—neither with the rich against the poor nor with the poor against the rich. Not being worried about what to eat is in truth well pleasing in God's eyes. But does this mean that the advantage is given to the rich and the poor are excluded? No, it does not. If the poor really choose to be content with being human and learn from the birds of the air how not to worry about what to eat, then they will in all simplicity be elevated above all the apparent differences, and sometimes they might even have occasion to say, "Ah, those miserable rich people! How they really suffer from worrying about what to eat!" For who, really, is truly able to say that he is without any worries about what to eat? If the rich say it and point to their wealth, does what they say make any sense at all? Doesn't the contradiction in what they say cry out to the heavens above in the moment they say it, since the fact that they are keeping such worry at bay by means of their wealth requires them to keep a close watch on it and increase it—because of worrying about what to eat? Now, if the rich were to give all their goods away and to cast aside all their money—and their worries about what to eat—and then say they didn't worry about what to eat, only then would what they had to say make any sense. And so, too, in the case of the poor, when those who have nothing and, to that extent, nothing to give away cast their worries about what to eat onto God and then say, "I have no worries about what to eat." Is it not the case that riches have to be got rid of if it is to be at all possible to speak meaningfully on this point? If someone who owned a costly collection of amazing medicines, some of which he used every day, were to point to them and say, "I am not sick"—wouldn't that be a contradiction that cried out to the heavens above?

We often find people quarreling with one another in a niggling dispute that hinges on the comparison between dependence and independence and how fortunate it is to be independent and how burdensome to be dependent. And yet, and yet—human language and human thought have never discovered a more beautiful image of independence than heaven's poor bird; and yet, and yet—nothing would be more peculiar than to say that it would be burdensome to be as light as a bird. To be dependent on one's wealth is not only to be dependent, it is to suffer a burdensome thralldom. To be dependent on God, utterly dependent, is to be independent. The anxious wood pigeon was foolishly afraid of becoming entirely dependent on God and so lost his independence and ceased to be an image of independence, ceased to be heaven's poor bird that depends entirely on God. Dependence on God is the only independence, for God is without weight—only earthly things and especially earthly treasures have weight—and therefore those who are entirely dependent on Him are light. That is how it is in the case of the poor, when, content with being human, they look to the birds of the heavens and look to them "under heaven," to which those who pray always look up. Those who pray? No, they are independent—but they give thanks.

To be content with being human. This was the subject of the discourse: how the anxious might learn from the lilies of the field and the birds of the air, and how comparing ourselves with someone else produces only worldly anxieties and generates worries about what to eat. It is of course a human being who has been talking but, with the support of the lilies and the birds, he has spoken of the lilies and the birds. The fact that he has been speaking does not involve any comparison with anyone else, as if he was superior to anyone else by virtue of being the speaker. No. Here, too, is equality before the divinely appointed teachers, the lilies of the field and the birds of the air.

6

The Glory of Being Human*

If it is true that anxiety and care—especially when they have been working their way into the soul over a long time, penetrating deeply into it—are more firmly lodged the longer they have deeply penetrated the soul, then it will assuredly be worthwhile to think about how to distract the anxious, although not in the way in which the world often enough and foolishly enough vainly recommends: rushing about madly or anesthetizing oneself by being noisy as a means of distraction. For when people are anxious and feel themselves abandoned and yet (in a self-contradiction typical of states of grief) don't want any sympathy (because sympathy would make them feel constricted or pressured and hurt them almost as much as what was troubling them in the first place), the best thing to do is to take them somewhere where there is nothing to remind them of their trouble, not even sympathy. That is, take them somewhere where it is as if sympathy is both present and absent, somewhere that is intimate and touching, as sympathy can be, but also with sympathy's soothing distance, since there is no one to offer sympathy.

---

* From Niels Jørgen Cappelørn et al., eds., *Søren Kierkegaards Skrifter*, vol. 10 (Copenhagen: Gad, 2004), pp. 281–296.

It is in this way that the gospel that has just been read* leads the anxious out into the fields, to a place where they will find themselves woven as a part into the great common life, and so win them for the great fellowship of existence. But if anxiety has a firm grip on someone, then it will be necessary for them to do something to look away from it and stop thinking about it, and it is to this end that the gospel recommends two distinct movements. For when the anxious "consider the lilies" that are at their feet, they look *down*—and looking down at the lilies they no longer see their anxiety. And when, following the gospel's advice, they look at the birds under heaven, they look up—and looking up at the birds they no longer see their anxiety. Of course, it may well be that the troubled also now and then look up and send a worried sigh up to God that they follow with a troubled gaze. But when they look up at the birds under heaven, they look away from their anxiety.

How might one better describe what it is like when anxiety has a firm grip on a person than to say that it is as when the eyes are *staring*? For when the eyes are staring they look straight ahead without deviating to right or left, only ever looking in one direction and yet seeing nothing, since, as science has shown, all they can see is their own act of seeing. The doctor's advice to such a person is to move their eyes, and, in the same way, the gospel says let your thoughts be distracted, look down at the lilies or look up at the birds, and stop staring at your anxieties. And when your tears stop as you look at the lilies, it is not as if it was the lilies that dried them for you, and when the wind dries up the tears of the person who looks up at the birds, it is not as if it was the birds that dried them. If someone you love sits with you and dries your tears, but whatever is worrying you won't let you stop crying, then your tears are not really being dried, are they?

---

* Matthew 6:24–34; see pp. 85–86.

But if someone is able to stop a troubled person crying, then they really do dry their tears.

This is what one might be so bold as to call a "divine distraction." It is not like worldly and vain distractions that incite a person to impatience and feed their anxiety, but the more one devoutly gives oneself up to it, the more it distracts, calms, and persuades. Human beings have been very clever in devising many things to please and distract their thoughts, and yet these kinds of inventions are subject to a law that renders all their efforts fruitless and self-contradictory. Art itself serves impatience, as it more and more impatiently teaches us how to distill many amusements into one brief moment. But the greater the sophistication of the artifice, the more it works against itself, since it shows how one is amused by the distractions it produces for less and less time the more artful it is. Fireworks, for example, nicely illustrate the feebleness and self-contradictoriness of feeble and worldly pleasures. They can indeed delight the eye and distract our thoughts by lighting up the night with their artful, fiery flashes—but even after an hour the watchers grow tired of them, and even if there is only the shortest of intervals between each new piece they find them wearisome. The task of the technician is therefore to be able to fire them off more and more rapidly, and the pinnacle of perfection would be to burn the whole lot in just a few minutes. But since the point of these amusements is to distract us from the passing of time, the self-contradiction is quite clear. The most perfect amusement that art can devise can only pass away a couple of minutes, thus making all the clearer how fearfully long time is. One pays to be brought to a state of impatient excitement as one waits for the start of the show, and in that very moment it is all over. And just as those entertaining flashes of fire flare up and in the same moment vanish into nothing, so, too, do the souls of those who know only that kind of amusement, and, in the minute they find amusement, they also despair over how long time is.

Ah! But how different it is with divine distractions! Have you ever looked up at the stars on a clear night, and have you ever found any surer vision? It doesn't cost anything, and so there is nothing for impatience to fret about. There is no poster saying, "Tonight, on the stroke of 10." On the contrary, the stars wait for you—even if, in another sense, they do not wait for you, since they have been burning away and lighting up the night like this for thousands of years without changing. And just as God makes Himself invisible, so that, alas, there are perhaps many who never paid heed to Him, so, too, do the stars above make themselves similarly insignificant, so that there are perhaps many who never really saw them. In comparison with the divine majesty, whatever is imposing in the visible or untrue world is but little, and the solemnity of the starry heavens is more than unassuming. Ah! But if you just stand quietly, perhaps having gone out without any special aim in view—there, where year in and year out they are to be seen, even if no one pays any attention to them—if you were quite by chance to stop and look up, you must have experienced how the stars win you over more and more each moment you are looking at them. More and more movingly they steal time from you, and for each moment you look more and more deeply at them, what ought to be forgotten sinks into forgetfulness. Oh, divine distraction, you don't call yourself amusing in the sense of those faithless and treacherous distractions that, emptily noisy and rampantly impatient, are in league with boredom and plunge those who indulge in them ever deeper into it, since you are in league with the eternal. That is why what you offer is difficult only at the beginning; once a start has been made, the distraction increases, as does the silence and, therein, your power to win us.

This is true of everything in nature. It seems insignificant, and yet it is so infinitely rich. Imagine yourself hurrying on your way on some important errand and along a path that runs by the edge of the wide sea and then think of how the sea affects you. Of course, no one is calling to you, no invitation is issued, no one is screaming out, and no cannons are roaring to advertise some human entertainment—but think of how it affects you: if you stand still for just a moment, won't the movement of the waves, even by their monotony, win you over? And so it is with the lilies of the field and the birds of the air. If you were busy going about "to your farm, your business, or your wife" and a bird flew by, perhaps you would stop and look after him for a long time. Or if it was while you were at work, plying your trade, as when the harvester diligently whets his scythe and swings it through the hay—if he were to catch sight of the lily at his feet, wouldn't it win him over, so that both the harvester and the lily remained standing?

As for the anxious, they are not warned but rather urged by the gospel to go out to the fields and just stand there quietly and look at the lilies and the birds in order that the divine distraction might cause the staring eyes to move and distract them from the thoughts by which they are anxiously held fast. Consider the lily; look how it stands there so delightfully at your feet. Do not despise it, for it is waiting for you to have joy of its loveliness. Look how it refreshes itself in the wind, giving itself over to being moved until, once more still, it delights in its happy existence. Look how gentle it is, always ready to jest and play, although it can triumph over the most powerful of storms by the way in which it yields and so endure. Look at the bird under heaven, see how he flies. Perhaps he has come on a long journey from far, far happier climes—but, then, he has brought something of them with him. And if he is perhaps flying back to them, back to those far distant parts—then let him take your anxieties with him. For he does so without even noticing the burden, so long as all you do is keep on looking at him. Look at how he now pauses, stopping and resting in infinite space, stopping and resting where it seems impossible. Look how he finds his path—and no matter how full of trouble and strife a human life might be, what path is so difficult, so incomprehensible as a "bird's mysterious path through the air"? And so, there is a path and a path to be found, there, where a path seems impossible.

But distractions are not only provided to pass the time, they are also meant to give the anxious something else to think about. Therefore, we shall now consider how, by considering the lilies and the birds and making use of the divine distraction they offer and their power to dispel the fog of care, the anxious may find something other than anxiety to think about. That is, we shall consider how, by being distracted into forgetting their anxiety, the anxious are led to think about

HOW GLORIOUS IT IS TO BE HUMAN.

"If God so clothes the grass of the field . . . will he not much more clothe you, Oh you of little faith?" God, then, clothes the grass, or the grass is clothed: the beautifully formed casing atop the stalk, the delicacy of the leaf, the lovely shadings of its various colors, all its wealth of frills and buckles and bows (if I may dare put it like that). All of this belongs to the lilies' attire, and it is God who clothes them thus. "Will he not much more clothe you, Oh you of little faith?"

"You of little faith." This is a gentle way of reproaching those who are being admonished here. It is how love talks to someone who is in the wrong when it doesn't have the heart to speak severely. It is not so much a matter of wagging the finger threateningly and saying reproachfully, "You of little faith," since it is said so gently that the reproach doesn't hurt, distress, or humiliate those being spoken to but rather raises and cheers them. Imagine that a child came to an adult and asked in distress for something that it, in fact, already possessed and had done so for a long time but without noticing it, so that it

thought it had to ask for it instead of being grateful for already having received it. Wouldn't the adult gently reproach it and say, "Yes, my dear, you will certainly get it tomorrow, Oh you of little faith," meaning that when you realize the truth you will recognize that you both have it and have had it for a long time, so that it is a kind of lack of appreciation on your part to ask for something you already have—even though it is forgivable and even becoming in a child?

But if this is what the saying means, then the gospel is not only saying that human beings are clothed like the grass of the field, but that they are far more gloriously arrayed. By adding the reproach ("You of little faith"), what it really says is, "Has not God all the more clothed you already?" It is not the new Sunday dress or the new dress one so greatly needs that is being talked about, but how unappreciative we are when we forget how gloriously human beings are clothed by God's own hand. But isn't there, then, a misrelationship in first saying that the lilies are more gloriously arrayed than Solomon and then concluding, "Will not God much more clothe you," since this would seem to suggest that it is about some items of clothing that a human being might need?

Let us consider the matter carefully. It is said that the lily is "clothed." But this is not to be understood in the sense that the lily first of all exists and is only in the second instance clothed. No. How it is clothed is what it is for it to be a lily. It is in this sense that it is asked whether a human being shouldn't be far more gloriously clothed. Or should anxiety be allowed to forget about this primary clothing because of its preoccupation with items of clothing? "Oh you of little faith, how unappreciative your imagined needs have made you, you anxious ones, if—even if you are greatly in need—you have so entirely forgotten how God has clothed you. Learn wisdom from the ant, but learn from the lily how glorious it is to be human, how gloriously you are clothed, Oh you of little faith!"

Worldly anxiety always tries to lead a person out into the petty restlessness of comparison and away from the sublime calm of simple thoughts. Being human is then absorbed into being clothed—and being well clothed. Worldly anxiety busies itself with clothes and all the different kinds of clothes—and isn't it, then, like the child that came all distressed and asked for what it had, the child whom the adult gently reproached, saying, "You will certainly get it tomorrow, Oh you of little faith!" Even if it is someone in need, the gospel first wants to remind him not to forget entirely how glorious it is to be clothed by God. In fact, it is very far from being the case that we are all in a more serious and stricter sense in need, but we are perhaps nevertheless all too inclined to worry about clothes and unappreciative enough to forget what should be thought about first—our original clothing. Looking at the lily, however, the anxious are reminded to compare their clothing with the lily's, even if poverty has dressed them in rags.

Shouldn't the invitation to learn from the lilies be welcome to everyone who can benefit from what it reminds us of? Ah! But in the everyday worldly life dominated by comparison, those great, uplifting, simple, elementary thoughts are more and more, perhaps even completely, forgotten. People compare themselves with one another, and each generation compares itself with the other, so that comparison piles up in a great mass over our heads. As artifice and industry increase, each generation contains more and more individuals who slavishly work their whole lives through deep down in the low, subterranean regions of comparison. Indeed, like miners who never see the light of day, these unfortunates are thus never able to see the light—those uplifting, simple, elementary thoughts about how glorious it is to be human. And meanwhile, up on comparison's high places, vanity smilingly plays his false game and deceives even the fortunate, so that they get no impression of those sublime, simple, elementary thoughts.

To be a ruler: how much people fight about that in the world, whether it is a matter of ruling over realms and nations, over thousands, or maybe just over one other human being—only to rule over oneself is something no one cares for. But out there among the lilies, everyone quietly and in solitude is suckled by the milk of those elementary thoughts as every human being was designated to be by God: a ruler—there, where no one wishes to rule!

To be marveled at: how much effort there is in the world to attain this envied goal, and how much effort the envious make to prevent it. But out there among the lilies, everyone is as God made them: Creation's wonderwork—there, where no one wishes to be marveled at!

The few who understand things better may smile while the shrill laughter of the crowd will mock the fool who could then talk about ruling or being marveled at. Yet what could the preacher have meant when he said that "God will set human beings apart to see whether they will regard themselves as animals do"?* Those who want to be calmed, comforted, edified, and uplifted by the unconditionality of those elementary thoughts without going apart, and who are willing to give themselves over to and vanish into and perish in the insignificant service of comparison—those really do regard themselves as if they were animals, whether they emerge from the comparison at the top or at the bottom of the pile. That is why God set human beings apart and made each human being this one individual being who is encompassed by the unconditionality of those elementary thoughts. For the individual animal is not set apart, is not unconditionally an individual. The individual animal is an individual only in a numerical sense and belongs to what the most renowned of pagan thinkers called the attribute of animality: the mass. In this way, those who despairingly turn away from those elementary thoughts in order to

* Ecclesiastes 3:18.

plunge into the mass element of comparison make themselves into mere numerical individuals, regarding themselves as if they were animals, whether they emerge from the comparison at the top or at the bottom of the pile.

However, among the lilies, the anxious have been set apart and are far removed from all such human—or, perhaps, more accurately, inhuman—comparison between one person and another. And not even the one who turned his back on the greatest city in the world has left behind such a variegated mass, such a confused, monstrous multitude as the one who turned his back on these inhuman comparisons in order to humanly compare his clothing with the lily's.

It is certain, then, that "clothing" signifies being human. A pagan thinker was already aware of this, since, although he did not know to lead everything back to God, he did think that it was the soul that, as he cleverly put it, is like the weaver who wove the body that is a human being's clothing. And with a beautiful wonder he praised the skillful piece of work that is a human body and its glory, which was such that no plant or animal could bear any comparison with it. He thought of this glory in terms of what distinguishes the human being, its upright carriage, and, thinking of this, his mind, too, was lifted up. He marveled at the cleverness of the human eye and still more at its capacity to look, for while animals have eyes, only human beings look. And that is why the mother tongue of that much-admired man calls human beings "the upright ones." In that language, this has a double meaning: first, that the human form is upright, like a straight tree trunk, and second, that this upright one looks up—so that whereas the straight tree trunk is always striving to grow higher, the upright one can look up in such a way as to raise his head higher than any mountain. In this way, the human being stands proud, a commanding figure—and that is why it also seemed to that much-admired man to be so glorious that human beings were the only creatures to have hands, for when the one who rules gives a command, he stretches out his hand. And thus, in many ways, that much-admired man continued to speak gloriously of human beings' glorious attire. Perhaps there have been many who have talked more knowledgeably, with more insight, or with greater scientific accuracy about it, but, wonderfully enough, no one has talked about it with greater wonder than that noble wise man. He did not begin by doubting everything but rather the opposite: as he became older, when he had seen and heard and experienced much, he really began to be filled with wonder, wonder at that simple elementary truth about which nobody else seemed to be bothered. Not even the learned men of science seemed to care about it, since it did not concern them as an object of wonder. Yet all that he said about wonder is nevertheless imperfect to the extent that he related the clothing to the soul. To speak in such a way as to forget that solemn elementary truth is utterly imperfect and even foolish: when one thoughtlessly and without further ado treats being human as if it were nothing, or when one takes humanity in vain and straightaway starts on all this foolishness about costumery, about trousers and tops, purple and ermine. But it is also imperfect to speak in such a way that, although one is indeed mindful of that elementary truth, one is not properly mindful of God. No: if we are to compare ourselves with the lilies, then we must say, "Everything that I am by being human is my clothing, and I owe none of it to myself—but it is glorious."

How are we then to talk about this glory? One could talk for a long time before being finished with it, but this is not the place for that. Let us therefore rather talk briefly and bring everything to a single statement that Scripture itself uses authoritatively: *God made human beings in His own image,* and, again for the sake of brevity, let us understand this as meaning just one thing.

God made human beings in His own image. Shouldn't it be glorious to be thus attired? If the gospel praises the lilies by saying that they exceed Solomon in all his glory, should it not be infinitely more glorious to be like God? The lily is not like God. No, it is not. It has a mark whereby it reminds us of God, and it bears witness to God, since there is nothing in what has been created that does not bear witness to God—but the lily is not like Him.

When a person looks at his image in the mirror of the sea, he sees his image for himself, but it is not the sea that is the image, and when he moves on, the image vanishes. The sea is not the image and cannot even retain the image. What lies behind this but the fact that, just as a body's bodily presence makes it impossible for it to be omnipresent, the visible form, precisely by virtue of its visibility, is powerless to reproduce itself in another in such a way that this other might retain its image when it is absent. But God is Spirit, which means He is invisible, and the image of what is invisible will itself be invisible. Invisibility is an attribute of Spirit, and the image of God is therefore an invisible glory. If God were visible, then there would be no one capable of being like Him or being His image. For the image of anything visible *cannot be another existing entity*, and of all visible things there is nothing, not even a leaf, that is like another or is its image. If this were the case, then the image would have itself to be the object. But since God is invisible, no one can be like him in a visible way, and that is why the lily is not like God, since its glory is visible. That is also why that pagan spoke imperfectly about what it is to be human: even when he spoke most perfectly about the glory of the human body, he said nothing about how the invisible God had made every human being in His image.

To be Spirit—that is human beings' invisible glory. So when the anxious stand out there in the fields surrounded by all those witnesses, when every flower says to them, "Remember God," a human can answer, "That I shall, little one, for I shall worship Him, which you, poor things, cannot do." The one who stands upright is thus a worshipper. The upright carriage was a mark of distinction, but to be able to cast oneself down in worship is still more glorious, and nature is like a great company of servants that reminds humankind, its ruler, to worship God. This is what is expected of us: not that we should come and assume dominion, which is also glorious and for which we are suited, but that we should worship the Creator and praise Him. This nature cannot do, since it can at most remind human beings to do it. It is glorious to be clothed like the lily and more glorious still to be elevated into the role of ruler—but most glorious of all is to be nothing and to worship.

Worshipping is not having dominion, and yet it is precisely in worshipping that a human being is like God, and to be able to worship in truth is the superiority of the invisible glory over all Creation. The pagan was not aware of God and therefore sought the likeness in having dominion. But that is not where the likeness lies—on the contrary, that is to claim it in vain. It is only to be found in truth in the context of the infinite difference, and that is why being able to worship is both being like God and being superior to all Creation. Human beings and God are not alike in a direct way but inversely. Only when God has become the eternal and omnipresent object of worship in an infinite sense and the human being has become and forever remains a worshipper, only then are they like each other. If human beings want to be like God by exercising dominion, then they have forgotten God, and God has departed from them, leaving human beings to play at being God in His absence. That is what paganism was like—living a human life in the absence of God. That is why paganism was like nature, and the heaviest charge one can bring against it is that it was incapable of worshipping. Even though that noble, simple wise man was able to fall silent in wonder, he was incapable of worshipping. But being able to worship is no visible glory. It cannot be seen, and yet nature's visible glory sighs and implores its master, reminding each one of us never to forget—to worship. Oh! How glorious it is to be human!

Thus, the anxious get something very different from anxiety to think about when they are distracted by the lilies: they get to think rightly about how glorious it is to be human. If they then forget about it again in the worldly to and fro of comparison and the clash of differences between one human being and another, it is not the lilies' fault. On the contrary, it is because they, too, have forgotten the lilies and forgotten that there was something they should have learned from them and something that, in a finite sense, they ought to remember to do for them. If there is a single phrase by which to sum up worldly anxiety, it is not that it is anxiety about what to wear but anxiety about how one is seen. That is why being built up by means of the invisible glory lifts one as high as is possible above worldly anxiety, and why the lilies also serve by showing how to worship.

That, then, is the instruction offered by the lilies. We shall now consider how the anxious might learn *how glorious it is to be human* from *the birds.*

"They neither sow nor reap nor gather into barns." That is, birds do not worry about what to eat. But is this, in fact, a perfection? Is being heedless of danger, not noticing it, not knowing it's there, a perfection? Is being sure-footed because one is blind or walking with a firm tread because one is sleepwalking a perfection? Not at all. It would be truer to say that it is a perfection to know the danger, to look it in the eye, and to be awake to it. Thus, it is a perfection *to be able* to worry about what to eat precisely in order to overcome such fear, and to let faith and confidence drive fear out so that one truthfully doesn't worry about what to eat, because one has acquired the carefree outlook of faith. For only being carefree in faith is, in a godly sense,

the kind of hovering of which the birds' easy flight is a beautiful but imperfect image. That is why we also speak about raising ourselves on the wings of faith, and such wing beats are in a godly sense the perfect reality of which the bird's wing beats give only a weak, figurative hint. For when a weary bird's wings grow tired and he slowly sinks to the ground, it is apparent that even the proudest flight of the boldest of birds is, in a worldly and temporal sense, mere weakness in comparison with faith's power to keep itself way up high or, in comparison with faith's easy ascent, merely a slow descent.

Let us consider this more closely. Why does the bird not worry about what to eat? It is because he lives only in the moment and, therefore, because there is nothing eternal in the bird. But is this a perfection? For where does the possibility of worrying about food come from if not from how eternity and time come into contact in a conscious mind, or, more precisely, in the fact that human beings have consciousness? By virtue of consciousness, human beings are far, far beyond the moment. No bird could fly so far into the distance, and yet it is precisely for that reason that human beings are alert to the danger of which the bird is unaware. Because human beings are conscious of eternity, they are also conscious of "tomorrow." Consciousness reveals a world that the most well-traveled bird doesn't know—the future, or what is to come—and it is when we take this consciousness of "what is to come" back into the present moment that we discover an anxiety that the bird does not know. For no matter how far away he flies and no matter how far he flies back, he has never yet flown into what is still to come and never yet returned from there.

Since human beings are consciousness, they are the place where time and the eternal constantly come into contact, or where the eternal breaks into time. It is because of the element of the eternal in consciousness that time can seem long, since we measure our moments by it, although time never struck the bird as being long. Human beings thus have a dangerous enemy that the bird does not know: time. Time is an enemy—indeed an enemy or a friend—that we cannot cease from pursuing or associating with, because our consciousness has a sense of eternity with which it measures time. There are many ways in which time and eternity painfully afflict each other in human consciousness, and one that causes us to moan more than most is worrying about what to eat.

This kind of worry seems to be so infinitely remote from the eternal. We can't talk about it in the way we talk about filling our time with some glorious deed, some great thought, or some lofty sentiment, as in those hours of which we say that we are living for eternity. Ah, no! All there is to talk about is the wretched work that is measured by the hour, about what really is living for temporal life: the wretched work that secures the conditions of existence. And yet being able to worry about what to eat is a perfection and is simply the expression, under the form of oppression, for human beings' lofty dignity. For as high as God raises up, so deeply can He also cast down—but this implies that being cast down and oppressed is also to be high and lifted up. And as God lifted human beings high above the bird by means of the eternal element in consciousness, so He pushed them back down below the bird, if one can put it like this, by virtue of their knowledge of care, of the earthly, lowly care of which the bird knows nothing. Oh, how superior it seems on the part of the bird not to worry about what to eat—and yet it is far more glorious to be able to do so!

Human beings can therefore indeed learn from the bird and also call the bird their teacher, albeit not in the highest sense. For, like the bird, the child, too, does not worry about what to eat—and who would not gladly learn from a child! And when either imagined or real needs make a person dispirited, out of sorts, or downcast, then he might well want to learn from a child and, with a quiet, grateful mind, call the child his teacher. But if the child wanted to speak and to talk like a teacher, the adult would gently say, "Ah, indeed, my dear child, but there is something you don't understand here." And if the child wouldn't keep quiet, then the adult would say that it was naughty and even be tempted to think about smacking the "teacher"—and perhaps even do so and do so rightly. Why? Because the adult is in all seriousness the child's teacher, and the child is only the adult's teacher in the beautiful sense of a jest that seriousness allows itself. And thus it is nevertheless a perfection to be able to worry about what to eat, and a human being is far superior to the bird, even if we also follow the hint provided by the gospels and learn from the bird and, with a quiet, grateful mind, call him our teacher.

The bird, in not worrying about what to eat, is, then, our exemplar. And yet, by being able to worry about what to eat, we are far more perfect than our exemplar. Therefore we dare never forget that the One who pointed us toward the birds of the air as to an elementary childhood lesson, He is the One who in all seriousness and in truth is the real exemplar, that it is He who is the true, essential exemplar of human perfection. For when it is said that birds have their nests and foxes their holes but the Son of Man has nowhere to lay His head, this is not to say that His situation is more helpless than that of the bird, and that He is conscious of it into the bargain. But there's the point: to be conscious of being without a nest, without a place to live, and yet to be carefree. Yes! This is an exemplar for a sublime creature, a divine exemplar of humanity. The bird doesn't have such an exemplar, nor does the child, but it is by means of this that being able to worry about what to eat is a perfection. Is it not so? Do we say that it is a perfection in a woman that, being the weaker sex, she should not go to war? Or that it is a perfection on the part of the prisoner that he cannot be released and so go out to risk his life? Or that it is a perfection in the sleeper who sleeps unaware of danger? Do we, then, say that it is a perfection to be excluded from daring to call this sublime One our exemplar? If not, then why do we speak differently, even with regard to worrying about what to eat—for do we say that woman is more fortunate than man because he has to go out and earn a living, or the prisoner fortunate because the state feeds him, or the sleeper fortunate because he dreams of being rich? Or do we say that someone is most fortunate of all when perhaps his very riches have led to him being excluded from calling the God-man his exemplar?

But out there, in company with the bird, the anxious cannot talk like that. They look at the bird and entirely forget their imagined worries and, for a moment, even their real needs, and so they are built up. But if the bird were to start to speak to him in a teacherly way, the anxious might well reply, "My little friend, there is something you don't understand"—that is, the consciousness that it is a perfection to be able to worry about what to eat.

"They neither sow nor reap nor gather into barns"—that is to say, birds do not *work*.

But is it a perfection not to work at all? Is it a perfection to steal the daylight hours as sleep steals the nighttime? For the bird indeed wakes early to song, and yet, when he has slept, what he really awakens to is a dream, for even the most beautiful song is but a dream of unhappy love. Thus, he sleeps and dreams his life away, whether in a merry or a mournful jest. But is this a perfection? Is it a perfection in the child that it plays and so grows weary—like a man at work—and sleeps and then plays again? It is lovely in the child, and who wouldn't want to learn from a child? And when perhaps an adult does his work but is not happy in it and perhaps even vexed by it, then he may well be softened by thinking of the child and willingly learn from it and willingly, with a quiet, grateful mind, call it his teacher. But one wouldn't think twice about correcting the "teacher" if necessary, and one would be right to do so, because the adult is in all seriousness the one who is to teach the child, and it is only in the beautiful sense of a jest that seriousness calls the child the adult's teacher.

The bird does not work. In an innocent sense, his life is vanity, and, in an innocent sense, he himself takes life in vain. If this is a perfection, then it is an imperfection on the part of God that He works and has never ceased working right up to the present moment! Is it a perfection on the part of the bird that in hard times he sits there and dies of hunger and doesn't know how to do anything about it but, tossed hither and thither, lets himself fall to the ground and die? That is not how we would talk in other contexts. When the sailor gets into his boat and sets out to sea in foul weather but doesn't know how to handle it, we don't talk about his perfection! But we do admire the bold seafarer who knows how to steer and applies craft, strength, and endurance to work his passage against storm and foul weather and work his way out of danger. If, far into the morning, we see the late-rising sluggard hungrily waiting for a chance to get something to eat, do we praise him? But we do praise the busy worker, the fisherman or the cowherd, whom we see early in the morning—or, rather, whom we don't see but, early in the morning, see that he has already been there—the fisherman to tend his nets, and the cowherd to drive the cows to pasture. Work is a perfection in human beings, and by working we are like God, who also works. And so, when people work for their food, let us not foolishly say they feed themselves, but let us rather, precisely in order to remember how glorious it is to be human, say they work together with God for their food. They work with God and are thus God's coworkers. And note this: the bird isn't—he gets food enough, but he isn't God's coworker. The bird gets his food in the same way that one who tramps about the countryside gets lodging, as if the servant who works for his food called the master of the house his coworker.

The bird doesn't work—and yet he gets his food. Is this a perfection on the part of the bird? Or don't we rather say that those who don't work don't get fed? And God says the same. For when God makes an exception for the bird, it is because the poor thing cannot work. The poor little bird cannot work—is that how one talks about a perfection? It is, then, a perfection to work. It is not, as people wretchedly depict it, a hard necessity to have to work in order to live. Oh, no—it is a perfection not to be a child one's whole life long, not always to have parents looking out for one, both when they live and by what they leave you after their death. Hard necessity, which, in its own way, also recognizes a human being's perfection, is only needed in order to compel those who are unwilling freely to understand for themselves that work is a perfection and are therefore not pleased about having to work. And so, even if there was no hard necessity, it would nevertheless be an imperfection if anyone ceased from working.

It is said of the honors that a monarch can bestow that there are some who are honored by such honors, while others add honor to the honor by wearing it. So let us mention a great exemplar who really can be said to have honored work: the apostle Paul. If there was ever anyone who wanted the day to last twice as long, it was Paul; if there was ever anyone who could have made each hour greatly meaningful to many, it was Paul; if there was ever anyone who could have easily asked to be supported by his congregations, it was Paul—and yet he preferred to work with his hands. As he humbly thanked God for the honor of being scourged, persecuted, scorned; as he humbly before God prided himself on the honor of being chained up, so, too, he found it an honor to work with his own hands. With a modesty that was beautifully feminine, holy, and apostolic, he found it an honor to be bold enough to say of the gospel that he had earned not a cent by proclaiming it and had gained no money by becoming an apostle. And in relation to the lowliest, it was an honor for him to be bold enough to say that he had not been absolved from life's difficulties or been favored by being excluded from any of its advantages, since he, too, had had the honor of working with his own hands.

Ah! In the despairing, glittering, or miserable wretchedness of worldly comparison, where there is knowledge neither of true honor nor of true perfection, they talk in a different way, a cowardly and treacherous way. But out there with the bird, the anxious understand how glorious it is to work and so how glorious it is to be human. For what makes the difference is not that one person works for great rewards and another for a crust, or that one gathers an excess while another fends off poverty—no, what makes the difference is that the bird cannot work.

That, then, is how the anxious get something utterly different from anxiety to think about when they spend time with the bird. They are led to consider how glorious it is to work, and how glorious it is to be human. If work, then, causes them to forget this again, perhaps that lovely teacher the bird will fly past and remind them of what they've forgotten—if only they look up and see him.

7

The Blessedness Promised to Being Human*

If it is true that anxiety and care—especially when they have been working their way into the soul over a long time, penetrating deeply into it—also provide a particular kind of strength, then it is very likely that the friend who offers comfort will fall short in his attempts to defeat them. For it is indeed a kind of fight that is carried on between anxiety and comfort, which regard each other as enemies in the same sense as sickness and medicine: they don't hate each other straightaway but, for a while, tolerate each other. And who hasn't experienced the strength that anxiety can give a person in cleverly and forcefully defending against comfort? Such a person will be able to do what no leader is otherwise able to do by putting forward anxiety's same defense, just as fresh as before, in the very moment when it has been disarmed. Who hasn't experienced how the passion there is in anxiety can give strength to a person's thoughts and expressions that frighten even the one who is offering comfort? Who hasn't experienced how there is scarcely anyone who wants something who can wheedle someone around as much

---

* From Niels Jørgen Cappelørn et al., eds., *Søren Kierkegaards Skrifter*, vol. 10 (Copenhagen: Gad, 2004), pp. 297–307.

as the anxious can speak ravishingly in order once again to persuade themselves—and their comforters—that there is no comfort? But if that's how it is, if the anxious have become the stronger—sometimes perhaps only apparently stronger through being stiff-necked, but sometimes really stronger because of the magnitude of their trouble—is there nothing left to do? Certainly there is. One might try to get an anxious person to put himself in the place of another sufferer, since those who are unwilling to be comforted by others are often willing to share another's grief and be troubled with them on their own terms. Then the fight is forgotten, and as the anxious sadly suffer together with another, their thoughts are mollified. Those who were so well armed against comfort are now disarmed, and those who were like a fortified city are now like a city that has surrendered: by sorrowing alongside another they themselves find comfort.

It is in this way that the gospel that has been read* leads the anxious out to the field where those who, at once so weak and so strong, thought of themselves as victors over all human comfort now find themselves entirely differently situated. Consider the grass that *"today is and tomorrow is cast into the oven."* Ah! What a poor existence, what utter vanity! And even if it is not cast into the oven, "the sun rises with its heat and withers the grass; its flower falls, and the lovely form that was once seen perishes."† So the grass withers, and no one knows its place anymore.‡ No, no one knows its place anymore, no one asks about it, and, if anyone asked, it would be impossible to find it. Sorrowful existence, to exist, to have existed, and then to be thus

---

* Matthew 6: 24–34; see pp. 85–86.
† James 1:11.
‡ Psalm 103:16.

forgotten! Consider the bird—*"are not two sparrows sold for a penny?"**
Alas, a sparrow is worth nothing at all, there even have to be two of
them before a buyer will part with just a penny! What a transformation: so joyful, so happy—and now, not worth a penny. That is how
the bird dies, and how heavy it is to die thus. When the first swallow
returns in the spring, we all welcome the happy bird, but whether it
is the same one that was here last time no one knows, and no one will
be able to recognize him again!

There is indeed beauty, there is youth and delight in nature; life
is indeed manifold and teeming, there is joy and rejoicing—but there
is also something like a deep unfathomable sorrow that none of the
creatures out there suspect, and precisely the fact that none of them
suspect it is melancholy in human eyes. To be so lovely, to flower like
that, to flutter about, and to build one's nest with the beloved like
that, to live like that—and then to die like that! Is this life, or is it
death? That is what we ask when someone is sick and the sickness has
reached its critical point: Is it life, or is it death? But then one sees the
danger, one sees it right in front of one's eyes, and sees it tremblingly.
But in nature, where everything smiles so invitingly and seems so
sure! But nature's life is nevertheless always caught in this tension: Is
it life, or is it death? Is it life, eternally youthful, renewing itself—or
is it sickliness, deceitfully concealing itself so as not to be seen for
what it is, a sickliness that deceives precisely by means of the loveliness of the lilies and the meadows and the carefree flight of the bird,
while underneath it deceitfully waits to harvest the deception. That
is the life of nature: short, melodious, blossoming, but prey to death
in every moment, and death is stronger.

So then, the anxious sink into melancholy, their eyes darken,
the beauty of nature pales, birdsong falls silent as in the silence of

* Matthew 10:29.

death, and sickliness swallows it all up. But they cannot forget the bird and the lily; it is as if they want to rescue them from death by keeping them alive in memory and save them for a longer life—and therein is melancholy. And does even death's own serious reminder of death take hold of us more than the reminder offered by melancholy in the words "Is it life, or is it death?" What death says is more terrifying: "It is over." However, what melancholy says takes a stronger hold on us: "Is it life, or is it death?" Death comes in a more fearsome guise as the grim reaper, but we are grasped even more forcefully when it comes clothed in loveliness as a lily. And so, falling into the grip of melancholy, the anxious are weakened like a woman and pacified like a city that has surrendered, and comfort finds a way in.

So let us now consider how, in a serious sense, melancholy gives the anxious who go out to the lily and the bird something other than anxiety to think about and how they are led to think properly about

WHAT BLESSEDNESS IS PROMISED TO BEING HUMAN.

"No one can serve two masters; for either he will hate the one and love the other, or he will be devoted to the one and despise the other. You cannot serve God and mammon." But is this, too, a gospel saying? Indeed it is: it is how the gospel about the lilies and the birds that has just been read begins. But are these words spoken to the anxious? Indeed they are, and in speaking to them in this severe way it shows that the anxious are being treated with great respect. For when the anxious are spoken to more severely, it is a sign that they are being respected: the more someone demands of the anxious, the more they are also being respected. Severity and being demanding are precisely marks of respect. Isn't that how it is? When the doctor

sees that it is all over for the sick person, one can immediately tell
from his voice that he begins to speak as if in passing, in hushed
tones, demurring. But when, on the other hand, the doctor can
see that there's much to be achieved, and especially when the sick
themselves are capable of doing much, then he speaks severely, and
his severity is precisely a mark of his respect. That is why it is by
no means uncertain, as is indeed sometimes said, that instead of
begging to be spoken to mildly, a person will say, "Just tell it to
me straight." And when the gospel speaks severely, is it not like
a serious father saying to a child that he doesn't want to hear any
whining? Does this mean that the serious father is therefore un-
sympathetic toward what is worrying the child? Far from it. His
concern is that the child should be worried about the right things,
and so, he is like a consuming fire in relation to foolish anxieties.
And so it is with the gospel. There are many ways of talking about
the lilies and the birds. One can speak about them in a gentle way,
movingly, ingratiatingly, and as tenderly as a poet. And we, too,
may dare to talk thus, may dare to entice the anxious. But when the
gospel speaks with authority, then it speaks with the seriousness of
eternity, since there is no more time to stand about dreamily con-
templating the lily or looking longingly at the bird. There is a short,
instructive allusion to the lilies and the birds, but then the gospel
speaks seriously about what eternity demands. And as distracting
the anxious gave them, in a gentler sense, something else, so, too,
do seriousness's severe words give them something other than anxiety to think about.

"No one can serve two masters." There can be no doubt as to which
two are being spoken about here. That is why the anxious are taken
out to the fields, where it cannot be their relations to other people
that are the subject of discussion, whether they are to serve a master
like a servant or become a follower of some teacher of wisdom, but

only whether to serve God or the world. Nature does not serve two masters, it shows no hesitation or divided loyalty. The bird of the air in its poverty and the lily of the field in its humility do not serve two masters. Even if the lily doesn't serve God, it nevertheless serves only to glorify God. It does not spin, it does not work, it does not even want to be anything or to have anything for itself or to take any prey. The bird doesn't serve two masters. Even if he doesn't serve God, he exists only to glorify God, singing His praise and not asking anything for himself. And so it is throughout nature: this is its perfection—but also its imperfection, since there is no element of freedom in it. The lily, standing freely in the open air, and the bird, free under heaven, are nevertheless bound by necessity, and they have no choice.

"For either he will hate the one and love the other, or he will be devoted to the one and despise the other." And so, love of God is hatred of the world, and love of the world is hatred of God. This, then, is the terrible point at issue, either love or hate. This, then, is the place where the most fearful fight in all the world is to be fought. And where is this place? Within a person. This is why it may often have happened that someone who felt this fight within got up and sought to be distracted from it by watching the roaring of the elements and the strife there is in nature, since it seemed that such a strife was but a game, and that it didn't really matter whether it was the storm or the sea that prevailed. Why, indeed, do the storm and the sea really strive together, and what are they really fighting about? It is otherwise with the fearful fight within a person: whether the stake is millions of dollars or just a penny, the fight is about whether a person will prefer this to God—and this is the most fearful of fights because it is about what is most important of all. This penny seems to be nothing, and the fight seems to be over nothing, over a penny, and yet it is really about the most important thing of all, and

everything has been staked. Is it any more insulting to a girl if her beloved prefers a thousand dollars to having her or if he gives her over for just a penny?

Melancholy has been forgotten in the fearfulness of the struggle, but now we arrive at what is glorious in it: *that human beings have been allowed a choice*. What blessedness is promised to those who choose in the right way!

A choice. My listeners, do you know of a single word that expresses anything more glorious? And even if you were to talk on and on, year in and year out, would you ever be able to name anything more glorious than having a choice? For it is indeed true that the only true blessing consists in choosing rightly, but the power of choice is the glorious condition for that blessing. What does a girl care for having all the excellencies of the future described to her if she is unable to make her own choices? And, again, whether others praise the beloved's many perfections or name his many faults, what can she say that is more glorious than to say that he is her heart's choice? A choice—indeed, it is the jewel of great price but not destined to be buried or kept secure. For a choice that is not used is worse than nothing. It is a snare in which a person traps herself, so that she fails to become free by choosing. It is a good that you can never be rid of, it remains with you, and, if you don't use it, it becomes a curse. A choice, not between red and green, not between silver and gold—no, a choice between God and the world. Do you know of any greater objects to have to choose between? Do you know of any more overpowering and humbling expression for God's submissiveness and compliance toward human beings than that, in a certain sense, He puts Himself on a line with the world in order that human beings might have a choice? Or that God, if we may be bold enough to put such an idea into words, woos human beings, that He who has the power of eternity woos weak human beings—

for it is always the strong who woo the weak! Thus, even a girl's choice between different suitors sinks into insignificance in comparison with her choice between God and the world. A choice—and is it any imperfection in the choice that is being talked about here that a human being not only can choose but *ought to* do so? Isn't it good for a young girl if she has a serious-minded father who says to her, "My dear girl, you are free, and you may choose for yourself, but you ought to choose"? Would it be better for her to have a choice but coyly to swing this way and that and never get to the point of choosing?

No. Human beings *ought to* choose, for that is how God shows His self-respect even as He shows Himself in all other ways full of fatherly care for human beings. If God has condescended to be the one who can be chosen, then human beings ought to choose—for God is not mocked. Thus it is true that if a person desists from choosing it is the same as presumptuously choosing the world.

We are to *choose between God and mammon*. This is the eternal and unalterable condition of choice. There is no evasion, not in all eternity. No one will be able to say, "God and mammon, they are not so absolutely different: one can choose in such a way as to have them both," for this would be tantamount to not choosing. When there is a choice between two, wanting to have both is precisely "shrinking back to one's own destruction." No—oh, no. It would be presumptuously to mock God to dare think that only those who chase after great wealth choose mammon. Ah! But even someone who is willing to have just one penny without God, a penny to have all to himself, is choosing mammon. A penny is enough: the choice is made, and he has chosen mammon. The fact that it is but little is irrelevant. If you belittle a girl by choosing another, and this other is as nothing in comparison with the first, who was like some oriental queen, have you belittled her any the less? If someone bought a mere toy for a price that could have purchased something really great, has he not then belittled what is great by his choice? Is it any kind of excuse to say that instead of buying something really great he bought what even in a trivial sense is absolutely nothing? If some can't understand this, then it is because they do not want to understand that in the moment of choice God is present—not to observe but to be chosen.

It would therefore be deceptive if anyone were to say that God is so sublimely elevated that He cannot condescend to be chosen, because that would mean doing away with choice. And when choice has been done away with, because God is not present as the object of choice, neither can mammon be chosen. God's presence in the choice is precisely what makes it a choice between God and mammon. And God's being present as the object of choice is what gives the choice its eternal seriousness, for we should never forget what has been allowed to human beings, and what depends on how they choose. But that way of talking, which so sublimely wants to prevent God from letting Himself be chosen, is a way of mocking God that, very politely, tries to get Him placed out of contention instead of humbly giving thanks for what He has wanted. It is to want to be knowledgeable in a superior kind of way about the difficulties that are, so to speak, incumbent on being God. To place a crown of thorns on His head and to spit on Him is to mock God, but to make God so sublime that His existence becomes a fantasy and meaningless is also to mock God.

So then, human beings ought to choose. The fight is fearful, it is an inward battle between God and the world. The glorious danger in the condition is having a choice—but what is the blessedness that is promised when one chooses rightly or, which is the same thing, what are we to choose? We are to choose God's kingdom and His righteousness. It is for this that everything is to be renounced, entirely without regard to whether this "everything" is millions or a penny. For the one who chooses a penny instead of God chooses mammon. Only when those who, though they work and spin, are utterly like the lily that neither works nor spins; only when those who, though they sow and reap and gather into barns, are utterly like the bird who does not sow or reap or gather into barns, only then do they not serve mammon.

"SEEK FIRST HIS KINGDOM AND HIS RIGHTEOUSNESS, AND ALL THESE THINGS SHALL BE ADDED UNTO YOU."

The kingdom of God. This, then, is the name of the blessedness that is promised to human beings. It is this name and the glory of this name that is to cause all of nature's beauty and tranquility to grow pale and vanish. While melancholy, bent low, sees nature sink into perishability, the eye of faith seeks the invisible glory. As Noah, secure in his own salvation, saw a world go to ruin, so, too, does melancholy observe the downfall of the visible world; it sees every form of life that is entwined with visibility sink down, while faith, being saved, sees what is eternal and invisible.

Seek first the kingdom of God, *"who is in heaven above."* The bird doesn't seek anything. No matter how far he flies, he doesn't seek. He migrates back and forth, and his longest journey is a migration. But the one in whose soul eternity has taken hold both seeks and aspires. If visible things do not deceive him, as they deceive the one who grabs the shadow instead of the body; if temporal things do not deceive him, as they deceive the one who is always waiting for tomorrow; if the present time does not deceive him, as it deceives those who perish on the way—if none of these things happen, then the world will not satisfy his longing: rather, it will help him by repelling him in such a way that he has to seek further and go on to seek the eternal, the kingdom of God that is in heaven above. The bird never reaches that height, and even the one that flies highest flies "under heaven."

Seek first the kingdom of God *"that is within you."* The flower does not seek anything, and if it is to get anything this must be brought to it; all it does is wait, and it does so without any longing. But those whom the visible world did not deceive and whose sight it did not dim; those whom time did not lull to sleep with its monotony; those whom the present time did not enchant by means of the imagination—those are not satisfied by the world, which merely helps them by painfully keeping them awake and expectant so that they seek and seek the eternal, the kingdom of God that is within. The flower does not know such an inward, invisible glory and has immediately to reveal whatever it has: the bud quickly breaks its silence and reveals its glory, which is also soon over.

Seek *first* the kingdom of God. This is the sequence, but it is also an inverse sequence, since what human beings first get to see is precisely what is visible and perishable, which tempts and allures and seeks to entrap them in such a way that, in the end, they never get around to seeking the kingdom of God. But the right way to begin is to begin with first seeking the kingdom of God and therefore to begin by letting the world fall away. Ah! What a difficult beginning that is! We do not know exactly how to describe how this earthly life begins for each of us, since it begins without being observed, and we are excused the difficulty of making a beginning. But living for the eternal begins by first seeking the kingdom of God. There is no time to gather riches beforehand, no time to consider this question, no time even to put aside a penny beforehand, for the beginning is first to seek the kingdom of God. If you know there is something you have to do first thing every morning, then you also know that you can't give any thought to anything else that could be done prior to that; you know that if you did this prescribed task at some other time of day, then it would be out of order, because it had to be done first. And yet it is possible that such an earthly task might also be done at another time of day, but in relation to seeking the kingdom of God it has to be done first, and this is without qualification the only way in which it can be done. Anyone who wants to do it at some other time of day or at any other hour hasn't even got around to beginning, because we are to seek it first. Those who don't seek it first simply don't seek it, and it is all the same, utterly the same, whether they go in search of a penny or of millions.

"His kingdom and His righteousness." This last word describes the first, for the kingdom of God is "righteousness, peace, and joy in the Holy Spirit." There is therefore no mention here of going off to make discoveries in order to find the kingdom of God, for the kingdom of God is righteousness. If you had all the eloquent longing of the wish in depicting it, if you could subdue the world's otherwise so busy city life in such a way that everyone was waiting on your words, you would not have come one single step closer to the kingdom of God, for the kingdom of God is righteousness. Maybe you can hide yourself in a great crowd of people, so that not even the authorities know your name or your whereabouts, or you can be an absolute monarch, the sole ruler of all realms and lands, but either way you will not have come one single step closer to the kingdom of God, for the kingdom of God is righteousness. But what is righteousness? It is to seek first the kingdom of God. Righteousness is not a matter of having exceptional abilities, for it is precisely because of them that righteousness will require you to render your account when righteousness is demanded of you. Nor is it a matter

of going through the world without being noticed, for no one is so lowly as not to be able to do wrong, and just as no coin is too little to bear the sovereign's image, so no person is too lowly to bear God's image. Nor is it a matter of power and might, for no one is ever raised so high that they are higher than righteousness or that they might have to remove their crown in order to find an opportunity to act righteously. Righteousness is seeking first the kingdom of God. If you act rightly toward others and give each their due but forget God—are you then acting righteously? Isn't that kind of righteousness like when the thief deals fairly with the money he has stolen? To forget God—isn't that like stealing your entire existence? But if, before doing anything else, you first seek the kingdom of God, then you will not be acting unrighteously toward anyone, and you will certainly not have forgotten God, for how can one forget that which is always the first thing one seeks?

The beginning, then, is to seek first the kingdom of God, and righteousness is to seek first the kingdom of God. You see, that is why we said that there is no mention of going off to make discoveries in order to find the kingdom of God; quite the contrary: remain where you are, in the place assigned to you, for every kind of seeking that leaves this place behind is already a form of unrighteousness. And if it were the case that you first had to go off and do your seeking somewhere else before you began to seek the kingdom of God, then it would not be true that you had *first* to seek the kingdom of God. So while the visible world declines and sinks down in perishability, you shall nevertheless remain in your place and begin by first seeking the kingdom of God. We flee the earthquake for a safer place, forest fires drive us to unwooded regions, and floods make us seek out higher ground, but if it is the case that the entire visible world is sinking in perishability, then there is no other place for us to flee to, and that is precisely why we have to stay where we are and seek first the kingdom of God. If anything less than the entire visible world is perishing, then the kingdom of God will be like some other part of the world, and then we might well go off to try to discover where the kingdom of God may be found. But such a fruitless and self-contradictory search will either lead us to become aware that we cannot find it or, if we think that we have found it, deceive us.

But if we seek first the kingdom of God, then *"all these things shall be added unto you."* They shall be *added* unto you, for there is only one thing that is to be *sought*—the kingdom of God: neither the thousands of the rich or the few cents of the poor are to be sought, but such things will be added unto you.

"All these things" or, as another gospel puts it, "the rest." Oh, how blessed the kingdom of God must be! For if you take everything that the bird and the lily have, everything that a glorious nature has, and think of all these together, then it is all comprised in a single word: the rest, all these things. How highly the kingdom of God is to be valued, then, if we can talk like that in relation to it—so carelessly, so cursorily, so sublimely. If someone has gathered a great fortune but has a few outstanding sums owing him, then perhaps he might say that the balance—"the rest"—can be left. If a person were to be called to high office in a foreign country and set out on his journey taking everything he loved and that was important along with him but leaving various things behind, then he might say, "No, I don't need to take all these things." Ah! But everything that the bird has is this "rest," and all the glory of the lily is "all these things." Oh, how blessed the kingdom of God must be!

So then, melancholy gives the anxious something other than anxiety to think about when they go to be with the lily and the bird: they get to consider the blessedness that is promised to being human. The lily may fade and its loveliness remain unknown; the leaf may fall to the ground and the bird fly away; it may grow dark over the fields, but the kingdom of God does not change with the alternation of the seasons! So let "the rest" be needed for a long or a short time; let it come in abundance or but little; let all these things have their moment, their time to be let alone or to be possessed, their moment when they are talked about, until, in death, they are eternally forgotten. But the kingdom of God is still what is to be sought first, and it will also last through all eternities until the end, and "if that which fades away was glorious, how much more shall that which remains be glorious." And if it was burdensome to live in need, then how much easier will it be to become separated from life when one dies from need!

8

The Anxieties We Invent Ourselves*

DO NOT BE ANXIOUS ABOUT TOMORROW, FOR IT IS THE PAGANS WHO SEEK AFTER ALL THESE THINGS.

The bird does not have this anxiety.

No matter how high up in the sky he flew to look down on the world, and no matter what else he saw, he never saw "the next day." No matter how far he traveled, no matter what else he saw, he never saw "the next day." And if we say of the lily that "today it is, and tomorrow it is cast into the oven," it is a noble, simple, wise creature that, no matter how much or how directly this concerns it, is never concerned by it—it is only occupied with what concerns it all the more closely, namely, the fact that it is today. And no matter how many days the bird saw break and end, he never saw "the next day." For the bird does not see visions—and the next day is seen only by spiritual beings; nor is the bird troubled by dreams—and the next day is a persistent dream that returns over and over again; nor is the bird

---

* From Niels Jørgen Cappelørn et al., eds., *Søren Kierkegaards Skrifter*, vol. 10 (Copenhagen: Gad, 2004), pp. 79–88.

ever restless—but the next day makes every day restless. But when the bird flies far off into the distance, it is as if he arrived at his destination on the same day as he left his home. We may travel so fast by train that we get to a faraway place in a single day, but the bird is more cunning or, rather, faster still: he travels many, many days and yet arrives on the same day. No train travels as fast as that, not even if it were to travel as far. No, no one can find the time to go as quickly as the bird, and no one can go so far in such a short time as the bird. There is no yesterday for the bird and no tomorrow, he lives only in the day, just as the lily blossoms for only a day.

Naturally, the bird has no anxiety about the next day, but anxiety about the next day is precisely a trouble you yourself have invented, which is why the bird is without this kind of anxiety. And what exactly is this trouble you yourself invent? It is a trouble that "this very day," today (which has troubles enough of its own), doesn't have. And what is it to invent troubles for yourself? It is to be the cause of your own troubles. Now, the bird can also have troubles in the day in which he lives, today can have troubles enough for him, but he doesn't have tomorrow's troubles as well—because he lives only in the day. We can put this another way by saying that this is because he has no "self." "Trouble" and "today" belong together, just as "the troubles we ourselves invent" and "the next day" also belong together.

But how can the bird be our teacher in this case? Quite straightforwardly. It is quite certain that the bird is without "the next day," so be like the bird, get rid of the next day and cease to be the cause of your own anxieties—and this must be possible, since "the next day" originates in the self. If, on the other hand, you allow today to be used up by comparing it with tomorrow's troubles, then you are utterly mired in bringing about your own troubles. It is just the difference of a day—but what a colossal difference! It's easy enough for the bird to *be* rid of the next day—but to *get* rid of it. . . . Ah! But of all the enemies that by force or cunning can worm their way into a person, perhaps there is none so penetrating as this "next day," which always remains *the* next day. "To master one's own spirit is greater than to take a city,"* but if one is to master one's own spirit one must begin by getting rid of the next day. The next day is like a troll that can assume many guises, but no matter how different it looks it is nevertheless—the next day!

The Christian does not have this anxiety.

Anxiety about the next day is usually connected with earning a living, but this is a very superficial way of looking at the matter. All earthly and worldly anxiety is basically about the next day, and what makes earthly and worldly anxiety possible is precisely the fact that a human being becomes a self by combining time and eternity and, by becoming a self in this way, brings about "the next day." This, then, is where the battle is to be decided. If one merely mentions worldly and earthly troubles it is enough to conjure a monstrous notion of variety, a mass of manifold passions, a confusion of contradictions—and yet it all comes down to a battle over just one thing: the next day. The next day is like a tiny village that becomes famous because it was—and is—where the greatest of battles is to be fought, the greatest and the most decisive, namely, the battle between time and eternity. The next day is the plank across which a monstrous mass of anxieties rushes to seize the "individual's" little ship, and if the attack succeeds, then the individual is in the grip of the anxieties' power. The next day is the first link in the chain that chains a person, along with thousands of others, to that excess of anxiety that comes from evil. The next day— Indeed, it is worth pondering that a person who is sentenced to life imprisonment is said to be sentenced "for life," whereas those who worry about the next day are their own judges and sentence themselves "for life."

---

* Proverbs 16:32.

Shouldn't heaven, then, have a way of saving us from the next day, since there is no such way to be found on earth? Even if you were to die tomorrow you wouldn't escape it, since it would still be with you while you lived today. But if you are free from the next day, you have annihilated all worldly anxieties, and not only those that have to do with earning a living. For earthly and worldly things are desirable only for the sake of the next day, just as they are all insecure because of the next day, and without it they would lose both their charm and their anxious insecurity. And if you are someone who has no next day, then either you are dying, or else, by dying to things temporal, you have laid hold of the eternal. That is to say, you are either really dying or *really* living.

The gospel says, "Each day has troubles enough of its own." But can this be a gospel? It sounds more like a book of lamentations, because that's what life becomes if you conclude that, since each day has troubles enough of its own, life is nothing but trouble. We might prefer to believe that a gospel should tell us that our days are free of trouble, or that there are but a few unfortunate days. Nevertheless, this is a gospel, and it refuses to strain a midge in order to swallow a camel, since it is aiming at the monstrous figure of the troubles we bring upon ourselves, and so it assumes that people are able to deal with the other daily troubles that befall them. It therefore says, quite properly, that each day *is to have* its troubles. Admittedly, the gospel doesn't quite say this, but it does say, "tomorrow will be anxious for itself," and if it is to be anxious for itself, then it follows that you are not to be anxious about it but are to let it look out for itself. Regarding troubles, then, you are to have enough to deal with each day as it comes, and you are to let the next day look out for itself. Isn't that right? When a teacher says to a pupil, "Leave the boy next to you alone and let him get on with his own work," he's likely to add, "You've got enough to be getting on with and that *should be* enough for you." Every day is to have its troubles, which is to say that if only you free yourself from worrying about whatever troubles the next day holds and address each day's troubles as they come calmly and in the spirit of thanksgiving, you will be doing yourself a favor—namely, by becoming free of the troubles that belong to the next day. Make do with what you have, then, and cultivate the fear of God in the spirit of frugality, since each day has troubles *enough*. God will provide in this regard also; He will measure out *enough* troubles for each day, and you are not to take more than what He has measured out, for it is precisely the right amount. To be anxious about the next day, however, is to become seasick.

Everything in life depends on taking up the right attitude toward it. This is what the Christian does in relation to the next day, because it is as if it doesn't exist for him. It is well known that because the stage actor is blinded by the lights, it is as if he is looking out into deepest darkness, into blackest night. Now, one might imagine that this would disturb or unsettle him. Not at all. Ask him and you will hear, he will tell you himself, that this is precisely what he relies on; it calms him and keeps him in the spell of his art's illusion. What would disturb him, however, is if he could see just one person or glimpse a single member of the audience. That's how it is in the case of the next day. We sometimes complain about the future being so obscure, and we even lament over it. Ah! But the real misfortune is when it is not dark enough, when fear and premonition and expectation and earthly impatience catch a glimpse of the next day. Take rowers in a boat: their backs are turned to the direction of travel—and that's how it should be regarding the next day. When, helped by the eternal, we live immersed in today, this very day, we turn our backs to the next day, and the more deeply, the more eternally, we immerse ourselves in today, the more decisively we turn our backs on the next day, until we reach the point at which we don't see it at all. If we were to turn around, then the eternal would take on a confused form and transform itself into the next day. But when we work our way toward our destination (eternity) by turning our backs to it, then not only do we not see the next day, but the eternal helps us to see this very day and its tasks all the more clearly. And if the task is to work today, then that is how we must be oriented. One is always distracted and delayed by each moment impatiently wanting to see one's destination and whether one is getting any closer to it, and then double-checking on it. No. For if your resolve is serious and for eternity, then you will give yourself entirely to your work and turn your back on your destination. That is how one is oriented when one rows a boat, and that is also how one is positioned when one believes. One might almost think that believers are farther away from the eternal than anyone, since they have completely turned their backs to it and live for this very day, unlike those who stand about peering after it in order to catch just a glimpse of it. And yet believers are nearer than others to the eternal, while apocalyptic fantasists are farthest of all from it. Faith turns its back on the eternal in order to have it at its side this very day. But if—especially in earthly passion—a person turns toward the time to come, he will find himself far from the eternal. The next day will then turn itself into the kind of monstrous confused figure one finds in a fairy tale. Like the demons mentioned in Genesis that begot children from human women, the time to come is a monstrous demon that uses a human being's effeminate imagination to beget the next day.

Christians have faith, and that is how they get rid of the next day. The attitude of those who believe is almost diametrically opposed to that of those who invent troubles for themselves. For the latter almost entirely forget about the present day, because they are so anxiously preoccupied with the next day, while the believer is someone who has "presence," someone who, as the Latin implies, also has power. Those who bring troubles on themselves, however, are never present and are powerless. People often express the wish that they had been contemporary with one or another great event or great man and think that that kind of contemporaneity would develop them and make them something great. Maybe! But isn't being contemporary with oneself worth much more than any mere wish? People who really are contemporary with themselves are rare indeed. The majority are only too willing to be a hundred thousand miles or one or another age of life ahead of themselves, whether in sentiment, imagination, resolution, decision-making, wishing, longing, apocalyptically, or in some kind of theatrical illusion. But believers, those with self-presence, are contemporary with themselves in the strongest sense of the term. Moreover, being helped by the eternal to be entirely contemporary with oneself this very day not only serves one's formation and development but also yields the profit of eternity. For there never was any contemporary event or any contemporary person, no matter how honored, that was as great as eternity—and being contemporary with this, today, is precisely the task before us, while faith consists in accepting it. That is why Christians, like some of the most severe of the Church Fathers, honor a saying of Ben Sira—not interpreting it as a prudential maxim but as an expression of the fear of God: "Love your soul, comfort your heart, and drive sorrow far from you" (Ecclesiasticus 30:23).

For who indeed is as cruel as those who bring troubles upon themselves! Yet all the tortures, all these cruel inventions and cruel ways of painfully martyring oneself, are summed up in a single phrase, "the next day." And how might one deal with it? It is said that there was a library in Spain that contained a book on the back of which was written, "The best means of dealing with heretics." However, if you opened it or, rather, tried to open it, you would have discovered that it wasn't a book at all but a box in which there lay a wrap. If, then, one were to write a book titled *The Only Means of Dealing with Those Who Make Themselves Anxious*, it would be short indeed: "Let each day have troubles enough of its own." Therefore, when Christians work, and when they pray, they speak only of the present day, they pray for their daily bread "this day" and for a blessing on their work "today"; they speak of eluding the snares of the evil one "today" and of coming closer to God's kingdom "today." For if those who, when they become acquainted with terror, prayed with all their soul's passion, "Save me, Oh God, from myself and from the next day," they would not be praying in a Christian way, and the next day would already have acquired too much power over them. Christians, however, pray, "Deliver us today from evil." This is the surest way of being saved from the next day, as long as one can count on praying that way every day. If, one day, it is forgotten, the next day immediately comes into view. But Christians never forget to pray daily, and therefore they experience salvation throughout their lives, and their faith saves their courage, their joy, and their hope. That fearful enemy, the next day, exists, but Christians do not paint the devil on the wall, do not conjure evil or temptation, and do not even speak about the next day but only about this very day—and they speak about it with God.

To live thus, to fill this very day with the eternal and not with the next day, is what Christians have learned or are learning (for Christians are always learners) from their pattern. How do we see Him living without anxiety about the next day, He who, right from the first moment of His life, from when He appeared as a teacher, knew how His life would end, and that the next day would be the day of His crucifixion? Even while the people rejoicingly hailed Him as King, He knew it (oh, what bitter knowledge, in just that moment). When they shouted "Hosanna" at His triumphal entry, He knew it, He knew that they would also shout, "Crucify him"—for that was why

He had come. How, then, do we see Him living without anxiety about the next day, He who bore the monstrous weight of this superhuman knowledge? He did not suffer as human beings suffer, who, when beset by adversity and tribulation, can always believe that it might all still turn out for the best, for He knew that what lay ahead was unavoidable. He knew that every sacrifice He made in the cause of truth only hastened His persecution and end, and He therefore held His fate in His own hands: He could have ensured the people's adoring admiration of His sovereign splendor had He only been willing to compromise the truth, and, by the same token, He ensured His own end all the more by not compromising that truth one iota (oh, eternally certain path to ruin). How, then, did He live without anxiety for the next day, He who was not unacquainted with its anxiety or with any other human suffering; He who, in a moment of pain, burst out with the sigh "Would my time was come!"? In war, one speaks about covering the commander during an attack in case anyone were to attack him from behind—but how did He do it, He who, while He lived each day at a time also had to cover Himself from the enemy who was ready to fall upon Him from behind "the next day" (for He had His back turned to the next day precisely because the eternal was present to Him each present day in a quite different sense from how it is in the case of all other human beings)? How did He do it?

May we be far from seeking human admiration by presumptuously explaining what should not be explained! We do not believe that He came into the world in order to provide topics for learned investigations, but He came into the world to give us a task, to leave behind a footprint, that we might learn from Him. We have therefore posed the question in such a way as to imply the answer, remembering how He did it, and what we are to learn: the eternal was present to Him each day, and therefore the next day had no power over Him until it came—and when it came and had become the present day, it had no power over Him other than what was according to the Father's will, to which He had freely consented, and to which He obediently bowed.

But the pagans have this anxiety.

For paganism is precisely being the cause of one's own troubles. Instead of casting all their care on God, the pagans are full of troubles; they are without God and precisely for that reason are troubled and are themselves the cause of their own troubles. Since they are without God, it cannot be God who burdens them with troubles, for the formula is not "No God: no trouble—God: trouble" but "God: no trouble—No God: trouble."

"Let us eat and drink, for tomorrow we die."* Does this mean that pagans are not anxious about the next day because they say that there is no next day? No, indeed, nor do they deceive Christianity—in fact, they don't even succeed in deceiving themselves, since the way they talk about it is full of anxiety about the next day, the day in which they will be annihilated: it is an anxiety that, despite being a scream from the abyss, crazily claims to be expressing joy. They are so anxious about the next day that they wildly plunge into a state of anesthesia in order to forget it. But no matter how anxious they are, can this state ever amount to not being troubled by the next day? If those who talk like this have got rid of anything it is their understanding and their minds. "Tomorrow" is the refrain accompanying all their talk of living for the day, for the verse always ends by referring to this "for tomorrow." One is right to talk about a desperate lust for life that, precisely because it has no next day, lives entirely, as they say, for today. But this is an illusion, since this is precisely how not to live for the present day, this very day, and least of all how not to do so *entirely.* Human beings have the eternal within them, and therefore it

---

* 1 Corinthians 15:32.

is impossible for them to be *entirely* in what is purely momentary. The more they try to avoid the eternal, the farther they are from living in the present day. It is not up to us to decide whether the pagans will die tomorrow, but it is certain that they do not *live* in the present day.

"But tomorrow!" Just as Christians only ever talk about today, so do pagans only ever talk about tomorrow. They are not affected one way or the other by how things are today, whether it is a day of joy or of sorrow, of fortune or misfortune; they cannot enjoy it or use it, because they cannot tear their eyes away from the invisible writing on the wall: tomorrow. Perhaps I shall be hungry tomorrow, even if I am not so today; perhaps a thief will steal all my riches tomorrow or impugn my honor, corruption despoil my beauty, or life's envy undo my good fortune—tomorrow, tomorrow! Today I stand at the peak of good fortune—oh, but speak to me about some misfortune I must suffer today, quickly, quickly, for otherwise tomorrow may well see everything lost without limit.

What is anxiety? It is the next day. And why are the pagans most anxious when they are happiest? Because adversity and misfortune would perhaps serve to dampen the fire of their earthly anxiety. You see, earthly anxiety gives birth to and engenders anxiety, which in turn nourishes and feeds a worried state of mind—but in order to get the embers to burst into flame a draft is needed, and this is precisely what is produced by earthly desire and earthly uncertainty. These are the two currents that inflame the fire of passion in which anxiety resides.

With whom, then, do the pagans strive in their anxiety? With themselves, with their imaginations—for the next day is a powerless nothing, unless you yourself give it strength. And if you cede all your powers to it without holding back, then, like the pagans, you will in a fearful manner get to know how strong you are, and what a monstrous power the next day can be! The next day: the pagans go to meet it with souls full of dread, struggling against it like the person who is dragged before the judgment seat, vainly laboring against it like some shipwrecked sailor who stretches out his arms toward the land, or as comfortless as one who, from the land, sees his entire fortune sink down into the sea.

Thus, the pagans consume themselves, or, in other words, the next day consumes them. Alas, a human soul was extinguished *there*, someone lost his very self. No one knows how it happened. There was no dearth, no misfortune, and no adversity. No one saw the frightful power that consumed this person, but consumed he was. The pagans live like an unfortunate spirit that was unable to find rest in the grave, like a ghost—which is to say they do not live at all. In the same way that people speak about riotously turning night to day, they despairingly make this very day into the next day. That is why they do not live today and do not live to the next day. We sometimes say of the sick whom the doctor has given up on that they will not live to the next day, but the sick person is nevertheless still alive today. But it would be more accurate to say of those who invent troubles for themselves that they do not live to the next day, and that they were given up on when they gave up on the eternal. Thus, they do not live today, let alone live to tomorrow, even though they are still alive—yet to live to tomorrow one must nevertheless live today.

Like a bird that flies into a painted wall in order to perch on one of the branches and tires itself out or even dies in trying to sit on one of them, those who invent troubles for themselves lose their souls by wanting to live "the next day." Like a bird that grows tired on its journey over the great ocean and sinks toward the sea with weary wing beats and can neither live nor die, those who invent troubles for themselves grow tired on their journey across the distance separating today from the next day. To live is to be today, and when one is dead, then there is no today anymore. But those who invent their own troubles live, although not today, nor till tomorrow, and yet they live on, day after day. The Lord cannot be their light, for whether they live or die, where they are is as dark and as devoid of blessing as it is—ah, yes!—in hell.

Let us then conclude by thinking about the bird. It was a part of the gospel, and it should be a part of this address.* The bird arrives at the distant destination appointed to it on the same day; Christians are in heaven "this very day"; pagans never leave the spot. The bird is self-absorbed in a good sense and loves itself in a sensible fashion and doesn't invent nonexistent troubles; Christians love God and therefore don't invent nonexistent troubles; pagans (God forbid—and God does forbid it) are full of self-hatred and invent nonexistent troubles. The bird lives for just one day and in such a way that the next day has no existence for him; Christians live eternally, so that the next day does not exist; pagans never live and are constantly prevented from living by the next day. The bird is entirely free of anxiety; Christians have a blessing that saves them from every anxiety; the anxiety of the pagans is their punishment for inventing nonexistent troubles, for no sin punishes itself in the way that invented troubles do.

---

* See Matthew 6:25–27.

9

The Anxiety Caused by Being in Two Minds*

NO ONE CAN SERVE TWO MASTERS, FOR IT IS THE PAGANS
WHO SEEK AFTER ALL THESE THINGS.

The bird does not have this anxiety.

If the angels are God's messengers, obeying His every signal, and if He uses the winds as He does the angels, then it should be said that the bird and the lily are just as obedient, even if God doesn't use them as messengers, and even if it seems that He has no use for them. Thus, the bird and the lily have no reason to become self-important about being used by God, and they humbly feel themselves to be superfluous. But they are not therefore any the less dear to God, nor is their being superfluous the least of their good fortune. It is not unusual in humanity's busy world for the exceptionally gifted to be superfluous, because they don't fit or don't fit in with all the particular things to which the busy want to direct them or want them to be occupied with or used for. Nevertheless, their superfluity serves the

---

* From Niels Jørgen Cappelørn et al., eds., *Søren Kierkegaards Skrifter*, vol. 10 (Copenhagen: Gad, 2004), pp. 89–98.

Creator's honor more than all the important affairs of the busy. Just as Mary honored Christ more by sitting at his feet than Martha did in bustling busily about, so, too, do the superfluous beauty and joy that God has squandered on His Creation, including the lily and the bird. But precisely because they are superfluous, perfect obedience is demanded of them. All is indeed of grace, but those who understand that they are superfluous because of the degree to which they owe all to grace must be all the more obedient. Everything is indeed nothing in the hands of the Almighty, who created it from nothing, but those whose existence achieves nothing more than becoming superfluous must understand more deeply than all that they are nothing. When parents put on a party for their own children, they may indeed expect to be joyfully obeyed, or, in other words, they might expect that joy that is obedience, but if they put on a party for poor children and give them everything they would give their own, their actions all the more decidedly call for that joy whose secret is unconditional obedience.

That is precisely how the lily and the bird do nothing but serve "the Lord," without giving a thought to any other lord and without a thought for anything but Him. They are more obedient in His hand than a pliant plant in that of a gardener, more obedient to His every signal than the homing pigeon is to those of his master. Every kind of lily and bird belong to one master, but each bird and each lily obey just this one master.

That is why the bird is never in two minds. He is not—even if it might look as if he were in two minds because of how he flies hither and thither. Rather, it is the opposite; in fact, it is quite certain that he flies hither and thither for pure joy. This is not the uncertain flight of a creature in two minds but the light arc of complete obedience. The bird may indeed soon tire of his lodging and fly into the far distance, but this is not because he is fickle. Rather, it is the opposite; it is a firm and definite resolution based on complete obedience—and perhaps it is rare for any human resolution to be so definite and to stand so fast. Sometimes one also sees a bird sitting with his beak drooping down, and perhaps he does indeed have his sorrows, but he is not disconsolate. For the obedient bird is never without consolation, and his life is essentially without sorrow, precisely because he serves only one master—and this is best both for the bird and for human beings, since one becomes free of unconsoled grief by serving.

How, then, are the lily and the bird our teachers? It is quite simple. The lily and the bird serve only one master and (which is saying the same thing) they serve Him with their entire being. So then, be like the lily and the bird, serve only one master, serve Him with all your heart, with all your mind, and with all your strength,* and then you, too, will be without anxiety. You are superior to the lily and the bird and are kin to your master (whereas the lily and the bird are like the poor children mentioned above), but in obedience you nevertheless serve the same master if, like the lily and the bird, you serve Him with all your being.

The Christian does not have this anxiety.

"No one can serve two masters," or, to put it otherwise, there is only one master one can serve with all one's being. It is not like having to choose between two masters and simply choosing one of the two and serving him while remaining indifferent as to which of the two it is. That is not what it is to serve one master. No, there is only one who is master, who is "the Lord" in such a way that when one serves Him one serves one master. And it should also be clear enough that when "there is only one Lord"† and one doesn't serve one master, one doesn't serve Him. It is therefore not true that those who chose to serve mammon entirely only serve one master, since against

---

* Deuteronomy 6:5; Mark 12:30.
† Mark 12:29.

their will they are nevertheless in another master's service—"the Lord's." Those who choose a lord other than God must hate God— "for he must either love the one or hate the other." That is to say, if he loves the one, he must hate the other. But no matter how much they hate God, they can never escape from His service, and so, in the end, they don't serve only one master. Being the servant of God is not like being the servant of another human being, where it is possible to run away from one's position and to run so far that one's first master can't get one back, or perhaps even to enter some other service, so that the first master has to give up his claims. No, no matter how decisively they will it in their despair, those who choose to serve any master other than "the Lord" nevertheless continue to serve two masters.

It is this self-contradiction that is their punishment. They want the impossible, for it is impossible to serve two masters. But also, it is only possible to serve one master when one serves Him with all one's being, when one has chosen to serve "the Lord." It is almost like a temptation, almost as if the gospel wanted to indulge human beings' capriciousness by saying, "You have to choose one of these two." Ah! But this is where we need to keep a grip on the fearful seriousness of eternity, for one can only choose one of them in such a way that by choosing Him, you serve one master. Therefore, it is not true that those who commit themselves to doubt only serve one master, that is, doubt. For to doubt, as the word itself suggests, is not to be at one with yourself but to be divided in two. Nor is it true that those who, no matter how repulsive the idea is, commit themselves to villainy only serve one master, the devil. For there is no concord among thieves and just as little in a heart that has become a robber's cave. But how can it be possible to serve *one Lord if one is not in concord with oneself?*

Christians serve only one master, "the Lord," and they not only serve Him, they *love* Him, they love the Lord their God with all their mind and with all their heart and with all their strength. That is why they love him with their entire being, for only love can bring about complete unity, unifying what is different in love and, in the God who is love, unifying the personality. Love is the strongest of all bonds, because it makes lovers one with those they love—no bonds can bind more securely than this, and no bonds can bind as securely as this. The love that loves God is the bond of perfection and, in perfect obedience, makes us one with the God we love. And the love that loves God is the most beneficial of bonds: by keeping us exclusively in God's service, it frees us from anxiety. This love unifies us, it makes us eternally at one with ourselves and with the Lord who is one—and in this unity it effects our likeness with God. Oh, blessed service, thus to serve only God! And that is why it sounds so solemn when we express it in a single phrase, for such service is "divine service," and the Christian life is constant divine service. The bird never ascended so high that his life could be called divine service; he never became so *perfect* in obedience even if he was equally obedient.

Are Christians, then, more obedient than the bird? Indeed they are. For the bird has no other will but God's, whereas Christians have another will that they are constantly surrendering in obedience to God, and that is why they are so much more obedient. It is a heavy sacrifice, but it is well pleasing to God and therefore blessed. Ah! But one can talk about many different things that we can love above all else—a man or a woman, a child, a father, a fatherland, our art, or our science—but what every human being loves more than anything else, more than the child of their promise, more than the one beloved they love more than heaven and earth, is, after all, their own will. Don't lay your hand on your child, then, for God is not cruel, and don't abandon your beloved, for God is not hard-hearted. There is something else, something that lies deeper within you; it is for your salvation that it must be taken from you, even though there is nothing you hold on to more tightly, even though you harm yourself by doing so—and there is nothing that holds more tightly on to you, for a child would be more willing to be sacrificed and a lover more willingly consent to be the sacrifice. This something is your own will. Look at the bird: he is instantly at hand to obey God's will, whereas Christians, in a certain sense, come from far away and yet are more obedient than the bird. For which comes more quickly—the one who stands at your side and turns to you the moment you require it or the one who comes from afar and is nevertheless on the spot in the same moment? The bird comes as quickly as he can when God calls and all honor to it, it is a joy to see it. But Christians come infinitely more swiftly, for they come just as quickly by surrendering their own will.

That is why Christians are free from anxiety and never in two minds: because they believe; never fickle: because they are eternally resolute; never disconsolate: because they are always joyful and always thankful. That obedience is the way to achieve this they have learned and learn from Him who is the way, He who Himself learned obedience and was obedient, obedient in everything: obedient in surrendering everything (that is, the glory He had before the foundations of the world were laid), obedient in renouncing everything (even a place on which to lay His head), obedient in taking everything upon Himself (the sin of the world), obedient in suffering everything (the guilt of the human race), obediently submitting Himself to everything in life and in death.

It is in this way that Christians are perfectly to obey one master. As the bird sings without interruption to the honor of the Creator, so, too, do Christians live, or, at least, they understand and acknowledge that that is how it ought to be. But even this understanding and this acknowledgment are an expression of honor. In this way, then, the Christian life is like a song of praise to the honor of "the Lord," because it is a life resonating to God's will in a manner that is more voluntary and more harmonious than that of the spheres. This life is a song of praise, for human beings are capable of praising God only by obeying Him, and they do so best when they do it perfectly. But that is why the pitch of this song of praise is set so high and echoes so deeply—because in its humility and its joy obedience does not praise what human beings understand, but what they do not understand. And that is also why this song of praise cannot be played on the children's trumpet that is the instrument of human understanding but only on the heavenly trumpet of faith. Christians sing praises only to One and do so by their obedient accord to His will, for God does it all, and all that God does is utter grace and wisdom. Therefore, to pass over what human beings imagine they can understand as being beneficial and pleasing to them without pausing to give thanks to God is really a kind of impertinence or disobedience that Christians could never permit themselves. If Christians encounter such things, they do indeed give thanks, as they always do, but they are doubtful and mistrustful of themselves and pray to God for forgiveness in case they are giving excessive thanks simply because what happened seemed to their childish ideas to be beneficial and pleasant. For a genuine song of praise, hymn, or heavenly canticle is sung when we praise God with joyful and unconditional obedience because we cannot understand Him. This is the song of praise offered when you praise Him on the day when all the world's against you, when things grow dark before your eyes, when others find it easy to prove to you that God doesn't even exist, and when, instead of becoming self-important by *proving* that God exists, you humbly prove that you *believe* that God exists and do so by joyful and unconditional obedience. This song of praise is not something higher than obedience, but obedience is the one true song of praise; the song of praise consists in obedience, and if the song of praise is true, then it is obedience.

In relation to human beings it is a fact that by submitting to their will you can actually do yourself harm, even if, because it is blessed to sacrifice yourself for the sake of another, the harm is never that great. But how could it ever be possible for me to harm myself in any way by obeying God's will, when His will is directed toward my true good? Since that is so, should not obedience always be joyful, should I pause for even a moment to consider whether or not to be joyful, since what is being asked of me is for my own benefit?

All of Creation praises God by obeying His every gesture, but Christians praise Him with a yet more perfect obedience, an obedience that is still joyful when they understand that they do not understand God. What door has been left open, what back entrance left unguarded for being in two minds about it, for fickleness or disconsolateness to sneak their way into a Christian's soul? No, there is no stronghold as secure as that of faith. In the case of every other stronghold, even if no gate had been left open, even if no path led up to it and no path could be made, the enemy would still be able to completely cut it off from the outside world and stop all traffic to it, starving it out and forcing it to surrender. But in the case of faith, the more you cut off its traffic with the outside world (that is, with uncertainty, fickleness, and disconsolateness, which correspond better than anything to what traffic with the outside world means for a castle), the more secure the stronghold becomes. If you think you are attacking it you are wrong—you are making it more secure. It is a merely decorative and false figure of speech to say that a castle is a little world in itself—but faith's stronghold is a world in itself, its life is within its walls, and what it needs least of all, alas, what is most harmful to it, is any kind of traffic with the outside world. Cut faith off from all its connections to the outside world, starve it out: it will become all the more resistant to capture, and its life will become all the richer. And in this stronghold, alongside faith, dwells obedience.

But the pagans have this anxiety.

For paganism is precisely being in a state of division, having two wills, being without a master, or, which amounts to the same thing, being enslaved. Paganism is a kingdom that is divided against itself, a kingdom in constant rebellion, where one tyrant replaces another, but where there is never any master. Paganism is a mind in uproar: the devil of each passing moment is driven out with the help of the devil, and seven worse devils are let in. No matter how variously it expresses itself, paganism is basically disobedience, the powerless, self-contradictory attempt to want to serve two masters. Therefore it is said of it, "Woe to the sinner who walks in two ways."* One is able to tell when a congregation has been "without a priest" for many years, even though it has had many priests, and in the same way one can tell that a pagan has had many masters, or that many have been his master, and yet "no Lord" has governed his mind. There is one thing in which all pagans resemble one another, and that is their disobedience to "the Lord"; and there is one thing that no pagan does, and that is serve only one master. Perhaps they try everything else, wanting to serve as master one who is not the Lord, wanting to be without a master, or wanting to serve several masters—and the more such things they try, the worse their last is than their first.

In the first instance, the pagans are in two minds. So long as they remain in two minds it seems as if they have not incurred any blame, as if it was still possible to choose the one Lord, as if they were not anxious and their being in two minds a matter of serious reflection. Perhaps some might think that the longer a person reflects on something, the more serious his final resolve will be. Perhaps—if it ever happens. And one should never forget that there is certainly one thing that does not need to be thought about for long. In the case of

---

* Ecclesiasticus 2:12.

something trivial, a long period of reflection would be a very suspicious sign, and while life contains many such trivia, there is something in relation to which needing a long time to think about it is even more suspicious—namely, that God is, or that one must choose God. Protracted reflection is irrelevant to what is trivial, nor are long reflections or ponderings relevant to God's sublime being. Protracted reflection is in this case so far from being something serious that it is precisely evidence of a lack of seriousness, and it proves this by showing itself as being in two minds. For it is so far from being the case that we get closer to God by going on and on thinking about Him that, on the contrary, the longer we go on reflecting and postponing our decision, the farther we get from Him. To choose God is certainly the most decisive, the highest choice we will ever make, but "Alas" for those who need to think about it for a long time and "Woe" to them the longer they need. For faith is impatiently prompt, it is infinitely urgent and doesn't want to hear about anything else—it is not only closest to making its decision but is best prepared for it. Those who become guilty of the ungodly way of thinking that poses the issue in terms of whether to choose God or some other master will certainly find themselves in two minds and very probably to such a degree that they will never escape from this condition. It seems astonishing that while we say of a poor family that it's hard for them to sort themselves out, those who are so rich in ideas as to find themselves in two minds find it even harder to sort themselves out. For God is not like something you can buy in a junk shop or an item you can use knowledge and foresight to test, taking your time in measuring and valuing it so as to assure yourself that it is worth buying. Instead, the ungodly calm in which those who are in two minds want to begin their God relationship (by wanting to begin with doubt) is precisely a sign of their rebelliousness. Such an approach unthrones God so that He is no longer "the Lord," and when that has been done, it means that another master has already been chosen, that is, that one has become author of oneself—but thereby becoming the slave of being in two minds.

When one has gone on being in two minds for long enough, then fickleness (Luke 12:29) takes over the reins. Perhaps it had for a while seemed as if the state of being in two minds still contained the tension that is needed for choosing and, therewith, the possibility of choosing. That has now been used up (if it was ever there) and the pagan soul has become slack, and it becomes clear what that period of indecision really concealed. For as long as one is in two minds, a certain power is still needed to manage one's thoughts, and while one is trying to make up one's mind, one is trying to be master of one's own house by organizing one's thoughts. But now the reins of office have been taken over by thoughts that know no master but only the impulse of the moment. Impulsiveness is the master now, also in relation to the question of choosing God. At one moment, an impulse moves the pagan to think that it would be best to choose God, but then, at another, it is something else, and then some third thing. But these movements—which mean nothing—acquire no meaning and leave no trace, apart from increasing their lethargy and slackness. Imagine a sluggish pool of stagnant water in which a bubble slowly rises to the surface and emptily bursts—that is how the fickle mind bubbles with impulses and then repeats the same thing again.

And so, when one has gone on being fickle for long enough (which, naturally, leaves one drained of blood and enervated, as all ungodly rulers do), disconsolateness takes over the reins of power. Where previously the pagans had wanted to get rid of the idea of God, they now want to sink down into worldly emptiness and try to forget, to forget what is the most dangerous because also the most uplifting of all thoughts—namely, the remembrance of God or that one exists before God. For when one *wants* to sink down, what is more dangerous than what wants to raise one up? They think that they have now cured their pain, chased all imaginary ideas away, and learned to find consolation. Ah! But there it is: it is much as when someone who has sunk very low says by way of comforting himself to someone who reminds him of something higher (oh, horrible comfortlessness!), "Let me pass for what I am." The light of the spirit is extinguished, a soporific mist clouds the vision, nothing is worth taking an interest in, and yet such people don't want to die but to go on living as what they are. To dissolve in that way is horrific; it is worse than the dissolution undergone in death: it is to rot away while one lives, without even the strength to despair over oneself and one's condition. The light of the spirit is extinguished, and such disconsolate persons become crazily busy about all manner of things as long as nothing reminds them of God. They slave away from morning till night, making money, putting it aside, keeping things moving, and if you talk to them you will hear them constantly saying that this is the serious business of life. Oh, frightful seriousness, it would almost be better to lose one's mind.

What is it to be without consolation? Neither the wildest screams of those in pain nor the presumption of despair, no matter how dreadful, are identical with being disconsolate. But the self-consistency encountered in the deadly stillness of those in whom every higher possibility has been lost while they remain capable of going on living as long as no one reminds them of it—that is being without consolation. To grieve is not to be disconsolate, but to have entirely given up grieving for anything is disconsolateness. To be able to lose God in such a way that one was entirely indifferent to the loss and didn't even find life unendurable without Him—that is being without consolation; and it is also the most terrible kind of disobedience, more terrible than any act of defiance. Ah! But not even hating God, not even cursing Him are as terrible as to lose Him in this way or, which amounts to the same thing, as to lose oneself in this way. It may perhaps be in order to lose something trivial and not to bother to find it again, but to lose one's own self (to lose God) in such a way that one can't even be bothered to bend over to pick it up again or in such a way as to entirely fail to notice that one has lost it— Oh, terrible loss! It is not just that there is an infinite difference between what one has lost in the one case and what one has lost in the other, but also between *how* one loses it in each case. To lose God in such a way that repentance immediately rushes after the one who has been lost to fetch him back again; or to lose God in such a way that one is scandalized by Him, rebels against Him, or sighs for Him; or to lose God in such a way that one despairs about it—but to lose God as if He was nothing, as if losing Him was nothing!

Let us conclude by thinking about the bird, who was present in the gospel and should also be present in the address. The bird obeys God in such a way that it is open to doubt whether this isn't the same as doing what he himself wants; Christians deny themselves in such a way that this is the same as obeying God; pagans do as they want in such a way that it becomes clear that they do not obey God. The bird has no self-will to surrender; Christians surrender their own will; pagans surrender God. The bird neither gained God nor lost Him; Christians gained God as their all; pagans lost God as if He was nothing. The bird serves only one master, whom he does not know; Christians serve only one Lord, whom they love; pagans serve that master who is God's enemy. The bird obeys at once when God calls; Christians are still more obedient; but God cannot even call on the pagans, for it is as if there is no one there to call to. The obedience of the bird serves to honor God; the Christians' more perfect obedience serves to honor God yet more; the pagans' disobedience does not honor God, and they serve only to be cast out, like salt that has lost its savor.

10

Silence, Obedience, and Joy*

PRAYER

Father in heaven! In the company of others, and especially in a crowd, it is so hard to discover what it is to be human and, if one has elsewhere learned something about the matter, so easy to forget it and to forget what godliness demands of human beings. May we therefore learn it from the lily and the bird or, if we have forgotten it, learn it again from them: that, if we cannot learn it once and for all, we may do so little by little, and, for now, let the lily and the bird teach us silence, obedience, and joy.

I

CONSIDER THE BIRDS OF THE AIR,

BEHOLD THE LILIES OF THE FIELD.

But perhaps you would let the poet speak for you—and you do find it so very moving to hear the poet talk like this—when he says, "Oh,

---

* From Niels Jørgen Cappelørn et al., eds., *Søren Kierkegaards Skrifter*, vol. 11 (Copenhagen: Gad, 2006), pp. 13–48.

that I were a bird or like a bird, like the bird so free, flying far, far away over land and sea for the joy of journeying, so close to heaven and coming to, oh, so distant lands. But, alas, I feel only the bonds that tie me again and again and even nail me to the spot where daily sorrows, sufferings, and tribulations confront me: this is where I am compelled to live, my whole life long! Oh, that I were a bird or like a bird that can lift himself into the air, lighter than the weight of earthly cares, lighter than the air itself! Oh, that I had the lightness of the bird that, when he needs a foothold, can even build his nest upon the sea! Alas, but if I make even the least movement, if I but stir, I am made to feel the weight that presses upon me! Oh, that I were a bird or like a bird, without a purpose, like the little songbird that humbly sings away, even when no one listens to him, and is even able to take pride in his singing, although no one listens to it! But, alas, I don't even have a moment, I don't have anything at all for myself, but must divide myself up to serve a thousand purposes! Oh, that I were a flower, or like that flower in the meadow, blissfully in love with myself and nothing more! But, alas, my heart is split as human hearts are, and I am unable either to please myself by breaking with everything or to sacrifice everything in love!"

Thus the poet. If you listen to him fleetingly, it almost sounds as if he were saying what the gospel says as he praises the happiness of the bird and the lily in such superlative terms. But listen on. "And that is why it is almost cruel of the gospel to praise the lily and the bird and to say, 'That is how you are to be.' Alas, to say it to me, who wishes it so very, very, very truly, 'Oh, that I were like a bird under heaven, like a lily in the field.' But in reality it is impossible for me to be like that, which is why my wish turned inward and became so melancholy and yet so ardent. How cruel of the gospel to talk like that to me, as if it wants to drive me out of my mind, telling me I *should* be what I all too deeply wish to be but feel I am not and cannot be. I cannot understand the gospel, we speak a different language, and, on this point, if I were to understand it, it would kill me." That is how it always is with the "poet" in relation to the gospel. He is the same when the gospel speaks about being a child. "Oh, that I were a child," says the poet, "or like a child: 'Oh, child, so innocent and full of joy.' But, alas, from early days I have been too old, too guilty, and too sorrowful."

Astonishing. For it is actually true to say that the poet is a child. Nevertheless, the poet cannot come to terms with the gospel. For the real basis of the poetic life is despair over not being able to become what he wishes to be, and it is this despair that gives birth to the wish—but "the wish" is a comfortless discovery. True enough, wishing can comfort us for a moment, but if you look more closely you will nevertheless see that it does not give comfort. That is why we say that wishing is the comfort discovered by comfortlessness. What an astonishing self-contradiction! Indeed, but the poet, too, is just such a self-contradiction. The poet is the child of pain whom, however, his father calls the son of joy. It is pain that gives birth to the poet's wishing, this wish, this burning wish that brings joy to the hearts of others, gladdening them more than wine, more than the first buds of spring, more than the first star that one so joyously greets when, weary of the day, one longs for night, more than the last star in the heavens one bids farewell to when the day begins to dawn. The poet is a child of eternity but lacks the seriousness of eternity. When he thinks about the bird and the lily, he weeps, and as he weeps, he finds solace in weeping. So "the wish" appears and, with it, the eloquence of the wish: "Oh, that I were a bird, the bird I read about in my picture book as a child; oh, that I were a flower in the field, the flower that grew in my mother's garden." But if, with the gospel, you were to say to him that this is serious, and that seriousness is precisely letting the bird be your teacher in all seriousness, then the poet would laugh and make a joke of the bird and the lily, and perhaps he would be so amusing as to get us all, even the most serious person who had ever lived, to laugh. But he cannot change the gospel like this. The gospel is too serious for any poetic melancholy to alter it, even though this might alter the most serious of human beings so that they yielded for a moment and went along with the poet's ideas, sighing along with him and saying, "My friend, is it really impossible for you? If so, I do not dare to say, 'You ought.'" But the gospel does dare to command the poet and to tell him that he *ought* to be like the bird, and the gospel is so serious that not even the poet's most irresistible inventions can make it smile.

You "ought" to become a child again, and therefore, or to that end, you ought to begin by being able and wanting to understand the word that is directed at the child and that every child understands, a word that you ought to understand in the way that a child understands it: you *ought*. The child never asks for a reason, it daren't and nor does it need to, and these two points belong together: precisely because it doesn't dare, it doesn't need to ask for a reason; the fact that it ought to is reason enough for the child, and not all the reasons in the world would give so strong a reason for doing it. And the child never says, "I can't." The child doesn't dare to and nor is it true, and these two points belong together: precisely because the child doesn't dare to say, "I can't," it isn't true that it can't, and so it is clear that the truth is that it can. For it is impossible not to be able to do something if one doesn't dare attempt the alternative. Nothing is more certain—and the question is only whether one really doesn't dare attempt the alternative. For its part, the child never seeks any evasion or excuse, because the child understands the fearful truth that there is neither evasion nor excuse, that there is no hiding place in heaven or on earth, neither in the parlor nor in the garden, where it can hide from this "you ought." And when one fully realizes that there is no such hiding place, then it is certain that there is no evasion and no excuse. And when one knows this fearful truth, that there is no evasion and no excuse, then one naturally gives up bothering to find them, since what doesn't exist can't be found—and that means that one also gives up looking for them and does what one ought to do. It never takes a child long to think this out, for when she ought to do something and perhaps do it straightaway, there is no opportunity to take long in thinking about it. And even if she didn't have to do it straightaway, if it is nevertheless something she ought to do, and even if you gave her an eternity to think about it, the child would not need it, for the child would say, "What do I need all that time for, when I have to do it?" If, however, the child did take the time offered her, she would use it for other purposes—for games, for joy, and for suchlike things. For if a child ought to do something, then she has to do it. That's how it is, and no thinking about it is involved.

So let us then follow where the gospel points us and in all seriousness consider the lily and the bird as our teachers. In all seriousness— for the gospel is not so hyperspiritual that it has no use for the lily and the bird, but nor is it so worldly that the sight of the lily and the bird either fills it with melancholy or makes it smile.

Let us learn from our teachers, the lily and the bird,

SILENCE, OR LEARN TO KEEP SILENT.

It is certain that it is speech that distinguishes human beings from animals and, if you like, all the more from the lily. But because being able to speak is a mark of superiority, it by no means follows that there is no art in being able to keep silent, nor that it should be a lowly art. On the contrary, precisely because human beings are able to speak, keeping silent is an art, and precisely because their superiority so easily becomes a temptation, keeping silent is a great art—and it can be learned from those silent teachers, the lily and the bird.

"SEEK FIRST HIS KINGDOM AND HIS RIGHTEOUSNESS."

But what does this mean? What am I to do? What kind of striving is it of which it can be said that it seeks or desires the kingdom of God? Ought I to get a position corresponding to my abilities and powers in order to bring this about? No, you are *first* to seek the kingdom of God. Ought I, then, to give all my fortune to the poor? No, you are *first* to seek the kingdom of God. But does this, then, mean that, in a sense, there is nothing for me to do? Quite right—there is, in a sense, nothing. In the very deepest sense, you are to make yourself nothing, to become nothing before God, and learn to keep silent—and it is in this silence that you begin to seek what must come *first*: the kingdom of God.

Thus, in a godly way, one goes in a certain sense backward, toward the beginning. The beginning is not what one begins with but what one arrives at, and one reaches it by going backward. The beginning is this art of becoming silent, for there is no art in being silent in the way that nature is silent. And to be thus, in the deepest sense, silent, silent before God, is how one begins to learn the fear of God. For just as the fear of God is the beginning of wisdom, silence is the beginning of the fear of God; and just as the fear of God is more than the beginning of wisdom, since it is "wisdom" itself, so, too, is silence more than the beginning of the fear of God—it is "the fear of God." In this silence, in the fear of God, wishing, desire, and their many thoughts fall silent. In this silence, in the fear of God, the verbosity of thanksgiving falls silent.

Human beings' superiority over animals consists in being able to talk, but in relation to God this can bring about their ruin if, being able to talk, they want to talk. God is in heaven, and we are on earth, and therefore we cannot easily talk together. God is love, and human beings—as one says to a child and maybe even for its benefit—are little rascals, and therefore they cannot easily talk together. It is only with much fear and trembling that human beings can talk with God, in much fear and trembling. But to talk in much fear and trembling is also difficult for other reasons, for just as anxiety causes one to be physically unable to speak, so, too, does much fear and trembling make speech become dumb and fall silent.

The person who knows how to pray knows this, and those who don't know how to pray might perhaps learn this by praying. Perhaps there was something that was very much on your mind, something that was so important to you, something that made it so pressing for you to explain yourself to God that it made you afraid of forgetting some detail, and then, if you had forgotten something, you were afraid that God would not Himself be able to remember it—and so you focused your mind on praying with real inwardness. And what happened then, if you did indeed pray with real inwardness? Something wonderful. For as you prayed more and more inwardly, you had less and less to say, and finally you became entirely silent. You became silent, and, if it is possible that there is something even more opposed to speaking than silence, you became a listener. You had thought that praying was about speaking: you learned that praying is not merely keeping silent but is listening. That is how it is. Praying is not listening to oneself speak but is about becoming silent and, in becoming silent, waiting, until the one who prays hears God.

That is why the way in which the gospel's injunction to "seek *first* His kingdom" trains a person up by, as it were, muzzling him, and to every single question about what he ought to do answers, "No, seek *first* the kingdom of God." Thus, one can rewrite this saying as follows: Begin by praying—but not as if prayer always began with silence, which we have shown not to be the case, but because when prayer really has become prayer, it becomes silence. Seek first the kingdom of God—that means: pray! If you were to ask—and in such a way as not to leave a single point unexamined—whether this or this or this was what you had to do in order to do what was needed to seek first the kingdom of God, then you would have to be told, "No, you are *first* to seek the kingdom of God." But praying, that is, praying in the right way, is becoming silent, and that is what it is to seek first the kingdom of God.

You can learn this silence from the lily and the bird. That is to say, it is no art on their part to be silent, but when *you* become silent like the lily and the bird, you will have arrived at the beginning, which is to seek *first* the kingdom of God.

How solemn it is out there beneath God's heaven with the lily and the bird. Why? Ask "the poet" and he will answer, "Because it is silent." He so longs to go out into this solemn silence, away from the worldliness of the human world in which there is so much talking, away from all the worldly human life that illustrates only too miserably the fact that talking distinguishes human beings from animals. "No," the poet says. "If distinction is a good thing, then I would far, far prefer the silence there is out there; I prefer it—but, no, there is no comparison, such silence is infinitely preferable to human beings and their talk." For the poet believes that in the silence of nature he hears the voice of God, whereas human chatter not only makes it impossible for him to hear the voice of God but even impossible to be aware that there is any kinship between human beings and God. The poet says that being able to speak is indeed human beings' mark of distinction from the animals—if only they can learn to keep *silent*.

But to be able to keep silent is something you can learn out there with the lily and the bird, where there is silence and also, in this silence, something divine. Out there it is silent, and not only when everything falls silent in the silence of night, but also when the day is stirring as through a thousand chords and everything is like an ocean of sound, even then it is silent out there. Every single creature plays its part so well that not one of them, not all of them together, disturb this solemn silence. Out there it is silent. The wood is silent—and even when it whispers, it is silent. Even where the trees are most thickly clustered together they keep their word to one another and keep what is said to themselves—something human beings so seldom do, even when they have promised. The sea is silent—and even when it roars and is full of noise it is nevertheless silent. At first you perhaps mishear it and hear only noise, but if you were to rush off and spread the news you would have wronged the sea. If, on the contrary, you took time to listen more closely, what you would hear, astonishingly enough, would be silence, for monotony, too, is silence. When the evening silence rests on the countryside and you hear the distant lowing of the cattle or, far away, the homely voice of the farm dog, it cannot be said that this lowing or this voice disturb the silence: no, they belong to the silence and are in a secret and, to a certain extent, also a silent agreement with silence and thus augment it.

Let us now consider more closely the lily and the bird from which we are to learn. The bird is silent and waits. The bird knows, or, more precisely, he fully and firmly believes that everything happens at its proper time, and therefore he waits: he knows that it is not his business to know the day or the hour, and therefore he is silent. It will surely happen at an opportune time, the bird says—only he doesn't say it, he keeps silent, although his silence is eloquent, and his silence says that he believes this, and because he believes this he keeps silent and waits. When, then, the moment comes, the silent bird understands that it is the moment; he makes good use of it and is never put to shame. So too, in the case of the lily: it keeps silent and waits. It doesn't impatiently ask, "When is spring coming," because it knows that it will come at the opportune time, and it knows that it would by no means serve its interests well if it had permission to decide when the seasons should change. It doesn't say, "When will we get rain?" or "When will we get sun?" or "Now we've had too much rain" or "Now it's too hot." It doesn't ask beforehand what the summer is going to be like this year, whether it will be long or short. No, it keeps silent, and it waits. It is so very simple, and yet it never deceives and is never deceived. Then the moment arrives, and when the moment thus arrives, the silent lily understands that the moment is now, and it makes good use of it. Ah! Would it ever be possible for these deep teachers of simplicity so to meet "the moment" if they could talk? No—it is only by keeping silent that one meets the moment, and if one talks, if one merely says but one word, one misses the moment. The moment *exists* only in silence. That is why it so rarely happens that human beings really get to understand when the moment has arrived, or how to make good use of it— because they cannot keep silent. They do not keep silent and wait, which is perhaps the explanation for why they do not take note of the moment when it arrives for them. For although it is pregnant with rich meaning, the moment does not send any messengers on ahead to announce its advent. It comes too quickly for that, and when it does come, it isn't even a moment early. Nor, no matter how intrinsically significant it is, does the moment arrive with noise and shouting. No, it comes softly, treading more lightly than the light-footed creature, for it comes on the light foot of suddenness. It comes with stealth—and that is why one has to be utterly silent if one is to perceive "now it is there." In the next moment, it is gone, and that is why it is necessary to be utterly silent if one is to succeed in making good use of it. Nevertheless, everything depends on "the moment," and it is assuredly the misfortune of by far and away the majority of human lives that people never took note of "the moment," so that their lives only bore witness to the separation of time and eternity. And why? Because they could not keep silent.

The bird *keeps silent and suffers*. No matter how sad at heart he is, he keeps silent. Even when he gives voice to the melancholy lament of the wilderness and of the solitary places, he keeps silent. He sighs three times and is then silent. He sighs three times more, but he is essentially silent. For he does not say what it is, he does not complain, he accuses no one, but he sighs only in order to become once more silent. It is as if he is bursting with silence, so that he has to sigh in order to be able to be silent. The bird is not absolved from suffering, but the silent bird absolves himself from what makes suffering heavier (the uncomprehending sympathy of others) and from what makes suffering last all the longer (talking a lot about suffering) and from what makes suffering worse than suffering (the sin of impatience and dejection). Do not believe that it is merely a little deception on the part of the bird that he keeps silent when he suffers, while, no matter how silent he is in relation to others, he is so far from keeping silent within that he complains of his fate and accuses God and others and allows his "heart to sin by sorrowing." No, the bird keeps silent and suffers.

Alas, that is not how it is among human beings. But what is the reason why human suffering, compared with that of the bird, seems so frightful? Do you suppose it is because human beings can speak? No, for that is a mark of superiority. But it is because human beings cannot keep silent. It is a mistake when people grow impatient or, worse, desperate, and think they know what they are saying when—although this is really an abuse of speech and of having a voice—they say, or cry, "If only I had a voice like that of the storm and could express all my suffering as I feel it!" Ah! But this would be a foolish move, since the feeling of their suffering would increase in exact proportion to their power to speak of it. No—but if you could keep silent, if you had the silence of the bird, then your suffering would indeed become less.

As does the bird, so, too, does the lily—it keeps silent. Even if it stands there and suffers while it withers, it keeps silent. It is an innocent child that cannot dissimulate, but nor does it want to, and it is fortunate for it that it cannot, since the art of dissimulation is bought at a great price. It cannot dissimulate, for as it changes color it betrays the fact that it is rotting, and one can see from the pallor that comes over it that it is suffering—but it keeps silent. It would gladly stay standing and so conceal that it is suffering, but it hasn't the strength to do so, it hasn't such mastery over itself, its head sinks down, tired and bent over. The passerby—if any passerby had sufficient interest to pay attention to it—the passerby understands what this means, it is eloquent enough, although the lily keeps silent. Thus, the lily. But what is the reason why human suffering, compared with that of the lily, seems so frightening? Do you suppose it is because the lily cannot talk? If the lily could talk, and if, alas, like human beings, it hadn't learned the art of keeping silent, don't you suppose that its suffering, too, would be frightful? But the lily keeps silent. For the lily, suffering is suffering, neither more nor less. But precisely when suffering is neither more nor less than suffering, suffering is made as simple and straightforward as possible and thereby also as little as possible. Suffering cannot become any less than that, for it does indeed *exist* and is therefore what it is. But it is, however, possible for suffering to become infinitely more when it does not remain precisely neither more nor less than what it is. When suffering is neither more nor less, then suffering is only the particular thing it is and, even if it is the greatest suffering possible, is as small as it is possible for it to be. But if the actual magnitude of suffering becomes indeterminate, then the suffering becomes greater. Such indeterminacy infinitely increases suffering, and it is precisely human beings' ambiguous superiority in being able to talk that generates this indeterminacy. The definiteness of a suffering

that is neither more nor less than it is, on the other hand, can only
be found again by being able to keep silent—and such silence can be
learned from the lily and the bird.

Out there with the lily and the bird is silence. But what does this
silence express? It expresses reverence for God and the fact that He
is the One who governs, and it is to Him alone that wisdom and understanding belong. And it is precisely because this silence reverences
God and, in a manner proper to nature, worships Him that it is so
solemn. And it is because this silence is thus solemn that it is possible
to sense God in nature—and so it is no wonder that everything keeps
silent out of reverence for Him. Even if *He* does not speak, the fact
that everything keeps silent out of reverence for Him affects one as if
He were speaking.

What you can learn from the silence that is to be found out there
with the lily and the bird—and without the help of any "poet"—what
only the gospel can teach you, is that it is in all seriousness that the
bird and the lily *are* to be your teachers, and you shall seek to be as
they are and learn from them in all seriousness and become silent like
the lily and the bird.

And it is already a serious matter when, out there with the lily
and the bird, you sense that *you are before God* (that is, when you
understand the situation properly and not like the dreamy poet or
the poet who lets himself be dreamed by nature). This is something
that is mostly utterly forgotten in all the talk and chatter that goes on
when you are with others. For if just two of us talk together—and all
the more if we are ten, or more—it is so easily forgotten that you and
I, we two, are before God. But the lily, our teacher, is deep. It doesn't
let itself get involved with you; it keeps silent, and by keeping silent
it indicates to you that you are before God and are to remember that
you are before God, so that you, too, in all seriousness and in truth
might become silent before God.

And you *ought* to become silent before God as the lily and the bird are. You are not to say, "The bird and the lily may well keep silent, because they can't talk." No, you are not to say this; you are to say nothing and not to make the slightest attempt to make this lesson in silence impossible. Rather than acting seriously and keeping silent, speaking like this would be a foolish and meaningless mixture of silence and speech, perhaps making silence something to talk about—and in such a way that there was no longer silence but only talk about keeping silent. Before God, you are not to make yourself any more important than a lily or a bird. But when you are in all seriousness and in truth before God, this will follow of itself. And even if what you want to achieve in the world is something really amazing, you are to recognize the lily and the bird as your teachers and, before God, not to regard yourself as more important than the lily and the bird. And even if the whole world was not big enough to contain your plans when you set about laying them out, you are to learn from the lily and the bird, your teachers, that before God you must be able to simply fold up all your plans into a space smaller than a point and to make less fuss about them than you would about the most insignificant vacuity—and to do so in silence. And even if what you suffered in the world was as agonizing as anything that anyone had ever endured, you are to acknowledge the lily and the bird as your teachers and not to make yourself more important than the lily and the bird are in their small troubles.

This is how the gospel takes the bird and the lily seriously as teachers. It is otherwise in the case of the poet or with those who, precisely because they lack seriousness, do not become entirely silent when they are in the silence out there with the lily and the bird—but become poetical. Certainly, poetic speech is very different from normal speech and is so solemn in comparison with normal speech that it is almost like silence—but silence it is not. Nor does "the poet" seek silence in order to become silent but quite the reverse: he seeks it in order to speak poetically. Out there in the silence, the poet dreams of great acts that he nevertheless never comes to perform, for the poet is not a hero. He becomes eloquent, and perhaps he does so precisely because he is the unhappy lover of great acts, whereas the hero is their happy lover. It is what he lacks that makes him eloquent, for it is lack that makes a poet, and so, when he becomes eloquent, his eloquence is poetic. Out there in the silence, he thinks up great plans for transforming the whole world and making everyone happy, great plans that never come to anything—but, no, they become poetry. Out there in the silence, he broods over his miseries and, instead of letting the bird and the lily instruct him, lets everything, even the bird and the lily, serve his misery as an echo chamber—and the echo of his misery is his poetry, for a scream is not as such a poem, which is rather the infinite inner echo of the scream.

Thus, the poet does not become silent in the silence where the lily and the bird are to be found. And why not? Precisely because he inverts the relationship and makes himself more important in comparison with the lily and the bird, imagining that it is even a merit on his part to, so to speak, lend words to the lily and the bird and to let them speak. However, the task was in fact that he should learn silence from the lily and the bird.

But may the gospel, helped by the lily and the bird, nevertheless succeed in teaching you seriousness, my listener—and me—so as to make you utterly silent before God. And may silence lead you to forget yourself, forget what you yourself are called, forget your own name—whether it is a renowned or an ignominious or an insignificant name—in order to silently pray to God, "Hallowed be *Your* name"! And may silence bring you to forget yourself, your plans—whether they are great schemes that encompass everything or so narrow as only to concern yourself and your future—in order to silently pray to

God, "*Your* kingdom come." And may silence bring you to forget your will, your willfulness, in order to silently pray to God, "*Your* will be done." Yes, if you could learn from the lily and the bird to be utterly silent before God, there would be no limits to what the gospel could help you achieve, for nothing would then be impossible for you. But if only the gospel, helped by the lily and the bird, taught you silence, how much it would already have taught you. For, as has been said, the fear of God is the beginning of wisdom, and silence is the beginning of the fear of God. Solomon said that we should go and learn wisdom from the ant;* the gospel says we should go and learn silence from the lily and the bird.

   "Seek *first* His kingdom and His righteousness." But one expresses seeking God's kingdom first precisely by means of silence, the silence of the lily and the bird. The lily and the bird seek the kingdom of God and nothing else at all; all the rest is added unto them. But, then, how do they seek *first* the kingdom of God if there is nothing else at all they seek? Why, then, does the gospel say, "Seek *first* His kingdom," and thereby let it seem as if it meant that there was also something else to be sought, even though it is plain that the meaning of the gospel is that the kingdom of God is the only thing that should be sought? It is because it is undeniable that the kingdom of God can only be sought when it is sought first. Those who do not seek the kingdom of God first do not seek it at all. It is also because being able to seek implies the possibility of being able to seek something else, so that the gospel, since it is in the first instance external to those it addresses and who are also able to seek something else, must say, "You ought to seek the kingdom of God first." And, finally, it is because the gospel so gently and lovingly comes down to our level and speaks to us about small things so as to entice us toward the good.

---

* Proverbs 6:6.

For if the gospel immediately said, "You ought solely and exclusively to seek the kingdom of God," it might seem to us as if too much was being demanded, and, half impatiently, half anxiously and fearfully, we would retreat from it. But the gospel accommodates itself to us. There we are, looking at all the things we might seek—and then the gospel turns to us and says, "Seek first His kingdom." Then we think, "Well, since I am allowed to seek other things, too, I will begin by seeking the kingdom of God." If we really begin to do so, then the gospel knows what will happen next, namely, that we will be so satisfied and filled with this kind of seeking that we will simply forget about seeking anything else. In fact, we will be so far from wanting to seek anything else that it will have become true that we solely and exclusively seek the kingdom of God. That is how the gospel behaves, and that is how an adult talks to a child. Imagine a child who is really hungry. As the mother puts the food on the table and the child gets to see what is set out for him, he might become so impatient as to say, "What's the good of those measly crumbs? Once I've eaten them, I'll be just as hungry as before." Perhaps he will be so impatient that he refuses to start eating, "because those measly crumbs won't do anything for me." But the mother—who knows that the whole thing is a misunderstanding—says, "There, now, little friend, just eat that up first, and then we can see about getting a bit more." So the child sets to—and what happens? The child is full up before he has eaten the half of it. But if the mother had immediately corrected the child and said, "But there's more than enough," she would certainly not have been wrong, but her behavior wouldn't have exemplified the wisdom that is proper to bringing children up, as, in the event, she did. So it is with the gospel. The gospel doesn't make it a matter of importance to correct its readers or to scold them. What is most important to the gospel is to get us to do as it would have us do. That is why it says, "Seek first." Thereby it, so to speak, shuts the mouths of all those who would raise objections to it, silencing them, and getting them really to begin with this seeking. And then this seeking so fills us up that it indeed becomes true that we find ourselves solely and exclusively seeking the kingdom of God.

Seek first the kingdom of God, become like the lily and the bird—that is, become utterly silent before God—and then the rest shall be added unto you.

II

"NO ONE CAN SERVE TWO MASTERS; FOR EITHER HE WILL HATE THE ONE AND LOVE THE OTHER, OR HE WILL BE DEVOTED TO THE ONE AND DESPISE THE OTHER."

My listener! You know how there is often talk in the world about an "either-or," and how this either-or arouses considerable attention, dealing in the most diverse ways with diverse issues: hoping, fearing, busily active, tense but inactive, and so on. You also know that in this same world it has also been said that there is no either-or, and this wisdom, too, has aroused almost as much attention as the most meaningful either-or. But out here, in silence, with the lily and the bird, is there any doubt that there is an either-or? And is there any doubt as to what this either-or concerns? And is there any doubt that, in the deepest sense, it is the only either-or?

No, there can be no doubt about it, out here in this solemn silence that is not merely a silence under God's heaven but a solemn silence before God. There is an either-or: either *God*—or, yes, well, the rest doesn't matter, for whatever else anybody might choose, if they do not choose God they have missed out on the either-or or have been themselves lost through their either-or. So either *God*—notice how no emphasis at all falls on what follows, except that it is opposed to God. Thus, it is really God who, by being the object to be chosen, constrains the decision being made in the choice to the point of its being in truth an either-or. If, light-mindedly or with a heavy heart, anyone could think that where God is one of the options, there are really three things to choose among, then they have lost God, and for them there really is no either-or. For either-or also disappears with God, that is, when the idea of God disappears or is distorted. But how could this happen to anyone in the silence to be found among the lilies and the birds?

So then, either-or: either God; or, as the gospel explains it, *either* love God *or* hate Him. Yes, when you are surrounded by noise, or when you are distracted, this seems almost like an exaggeration: there seems to be far too great a distance between loving and hating for anyone to have the right to bring them so close together, into a single breath, a single thought, in just two words, without any subordinate clauses or parentheses to harmonize them or even the least punctuation mark to stop them following immediately on each other. But just as a body in a vacuum falls infinitely rapidly, so, too, does the silence out there with the lily and the bird, that solemn silence before God, make these two contradictory terms, either love or hate, repel each other and come together in one and the same instant or even come into existence in the same instant. And as little as there is any third element in a vacuum that might delay the falling body, so is there no third element in this solemn silence before God that could keep loving and hating back from falling into a state of shared difference.

Either God—or, as the gospel explains it, either be devoted to Him *or* despise Him. In the company of others, at work and at play, and when one goes about with the many, there seems to be a great distance between being devoted to a person and hating him. "I don't care to go about with that person," we say, "but that doesn't mean that I despise him, by no means." And that is indeed how it is in association with the many, where we have to do with one another in a general social way without any essential involvement with them and with a greater or lesser indifference to them. But the smaller the numbers, the less our social circle is in general terms, the more either-or begins to become the rule for our relationships—and association with God is in the deepest and most unconditional sense unsocial. Take two lovers, a relationship that is also unsocial, precisely because it is so inward. As far as their relationship is concerned, it is a matter of either being devoted to each other or despising each other. And now, in silence before God among the lilies and the birds, where there is no one at all present, where there is no one else to be with other than God, here it is a matter either of being devoted to Him or of despising Him. There is no excuse, there is no one else present, and there is, in fact, no occasion when you can be devoted to another without despising God—for in the silence it becomes clear just how close God is to you. The two lovers are so close to each other that, as long as the other is still alive, the one cannot be devoted to anybody else without *despising* the other. That is the kind of either-or that this relationship involves. For whether an either-or of this kind (either devotion or hate) is at issue depends on how close the two parties are to each other. But God, who certainly never dies, is even closer to you, infinitely closer than two lovers are to each other, for He is your Creator and preserver, He it is in whom you live and move and have your being, and He it is by whose grace you receive all things. So it is no exaggeration to say that either you are devoted to God or you despise Him. It is not as when someone poses an either-or for the sake of something insignificant. Such a person is someone of whom it is rightly said that he has no idea, but that is not at all the case here. For partly it is a matter of God being God, and partly it is because the issue is not something indifferent, as when one has to choose between a rose and a tulip. But God brings the choice into relation to Himself and says, "Either *me* . . . either you are devoted to me, unconditionally, in everything, or you despise me." God could scarcely talk of Himself otherwise. Should God—or should God be able to—talk about Himself as if He was anything but unconditionally Number One, as if He were not unique, not unconditionally everything but simply a something, a someone, who hoped to be also taken into account? God would have had to have lost Himself to speak like that, to have lost all idea of who He is, and He would no longer be God.

So then, in silence with the lily and the bird, there is an either-or: either God . . . and this to be understood as meaning either love Him or hate Him, either be devoted to Him or despise Him.

What does this either-or mean? What is God demanding of us, for either-or involves a demand, as when the lover demands love, or when one person says to another, "either-or"? But God does not relate to you as a lover, nor you to Him as a lover. The relationship is another; it is that of creature to Creator. What, then, does He demand with this either-or? He demands obedience, unconditional obedience. If you are not unconditionally obedient to Him in everything, then you do not love Him, and if you do not love Him, then—you hate Him. If you are not unconditionally obedient to Him in everything, then you are not devoted to Him, or, if you are not devoted to Him unconditionally in everything, then you are not devoted to Him, then—you despise Him.

This unconditional obedience—that if you do not love God, you hate Him, and if you are not devoted to Him unconditionally in everything, you despise Him—this unconditional obedience is something you can learn from those teachers to which the gospel directs you, the lily and the bird. It is said that by learning to obey, you learn to command, but it is yet more certain that by being oneself obedient, one can teach obedience by one's own example. So it is with the lily and the bird. They have no power by which to compel the learner, they have merely their own obedience by which to compel attention. The lily and the bird are "the obedient teachers." Is this not a peculiar figure of speech? *Obedient* is normally a word one applies to the pupil who is required to be obedient. But here it is the teacher who is to be obedient! And what does he teach? Obedience. And how does he teach? By means of obedience. If you could be as obedient as the lily and the bird, then you, too, would be able to teach obedience by your own example. But since neither you nor I are obedient in this way, let us learn from the lily and the bird the meaning of

OBEDIENCE.

Out there with the lily and the bird, there is silence, we said. But this silence, or, what we sought to learn from it, how to become silent, is in truth the primary condition for being able to obey. When everything around you is solemn silence, as it is out there, and when you are silent within, then you feel, and you feel with infinite emphasis, the truth of what it is to love the Lord your God and to serve Him alone. Then you feel that it is "you," you who are to love God in this way, you alone in the whole world, you, all alone in this solemn silence, so alone that every doubt, every objection, every excuse, every evasion, every question, and, in short, every voice is silenced within you—that is, every voice but God's, who, encompassing you and within you speaks silently to you. If you have never experienced such silence about you or within you, then you have never learned and will never learn obedience. But if you have learned silence, then you will have no problem in learning obedience.

Pay attention to the natural world around you. Everything in nature is obedient, unconditionally obedient. Here, God's will is

indeed done on earth as it is in heaven. Everything in nature is unconditionally obedient. Here, it is not simply because of the fact that,
since God is the Almighty, nothing, no matter how small, happens
without His will, as is also the case in the human world. No, here it is
because everything is unconditionally obedient. Nevertheless, there
is still an infinite difference on this point. For it is one thing that not
even the most cowardly or the most defiant acts of human disobedience, whether by an individual or by the whole human race, can
achieve anything at all against His will, but it is quite another that
His will is done because everything obeys Him unconditionally, and
there is no other will but His in heaven or on earth—which is how it
is in nature. In nature, it is the case that, as Scripture says, "not even a
sparrow falls to earth without His will,"* and this is not only because
He is the Almighty, but because everything is unconditionally obedient and His will is the only will. Not the slightest object, not a word,
not a sigh, is to be heard there. The unconditionally obedient sparrow
falls unconditionally obediently to the earth when it is His will. In
nature, everything is unconditionally obedient. The sighing of the
wind, its echo in the woods, the babbling of the brook, the murmuring of summer, the whispering of the leaves, the rustling of the
grass, every sound, every sound you hear is an expression of nature's
attentiveness, of unconditional obedience. That is why God can be
heard in it, in the same way that you can hear Him in the music of the
spheres that expresses the obedience of the celestial bodies. The glee
of the rushing wind, the gentle yielding of the clouds, the easy flow
of the sea and the ocean's unmoving mass, the speed of the lightning
flash and the great crash of thunder that follows—it is all obedience.
When the sun rises right on time and sets right on time, when the
wind surges back and forth at a sign, when the water ebbs and flows

* Matthew 10:29.

at the appointed hour, and when the seasons are in complete agreement as to just when to change—all of it, all of it is altogether obedience. Yes, if there was a star in the heavens or a speck of dust on earth
that wanted to assert its own will, they would be annihilated in that
very same moment, as easily in one case as in the other. Because all
of nature is, in this perspective, nothing: it is nothing but the unconditional expression of God's will, and in the moment that it ceases to
be that it ceases to exist.

Let us then consider the lily and the bird more closely, and do so
in a human way, so as to learn obedience from them. The lily and the
bird are unconditionally obedient to God, and they are masters in
that art. As befits those who are masters of their art, they know how
to hit the mark unconditionally, something that most human beings,
alas, either miss or in some way bungle. For there is one thing that
neither the lily nor the bird can understand: half-measures—something that most human beings, alas, understand best. Just a little bit
of disobedience, just so much as to make their obedience no longer
unconditional, is something the lily and the bird are incapable of,
and they don't want to understand it. That even the very, very smallest act of disobedience should in truth merit any other name than
contempt for God is something the lily and the bird do not do and do
not want to understand. What wonderful sureness, to be able to hit
the mark like that and to live one's life so unconditionally. Ah! But
how deep these teachers are, for is it at all possible to find assurance
in anything but the unconditional, since what is conditional is intrinsically insecure? So I might do better to put it somewhat differently
and not so much admire the sureness with which they unconditionally hit the mark but rather say that it is precisely the unconditional
that gives them the admirable assurance that makes them teachers of
obedience. For the lily and the bird are unconditionally obedient to
God; in obedience they are so simple or so sublime *that they believe*

that everything that happens is unconditionally God's will, and that they have nothing else to do in this world than to either do God's will in unconditional obedience or, in unconditional obedience, submit to God's will.

Even if the place that is assigned to the lily is as inauspicious as possible—and one can easily foresee that its whole life will be superfluous to requirements and it will never be seen by a single person who might find pleasure in it—even if the place and the environment (and I have not forgotten that I am talking about the lily) are so "desperately" inauspicious that they are not only not sought but even avoided, even then the obedient lily obediently accepts its circumstances and springs up in all its loveliness. We human beings, if we were in the lily's place, would say, "It is a burden scarcely to be endured that, if one is a lily and as lovely as a lily, one should be assigned to a spot in such a place where one will blossom in an environment that is as unfavorable as possible and that seems to be calculated to annihilate any impression of one's loveliness. No, it is not to be endured! It is a self-contradiction on the part of the Creator!" That is how a human being or, rather, we human beings would think and talk if we were in the lily's place—and our misery would make us wither away. But the lily thinks in another way, it thinks like this: "I myself have not been able to decide my place or my circumstances, so this means that it is not in the least my concern. That I stand where I stand is God's will." That is how the lily thinks, and that things really are as the lily thinks, that it is God's will, can be seen in the fact of its loveliness—for not even Solomon in all his glory was thus attired. Oh, but if there was a difference between one lily and another in terms of loveliness, this lily would have to get the prize, since it has one loveliness in addition. For there is no art to being lovely when one is a lily, but it is something else to be lovely in such circumstances, in an environment that does all it can to frustrate one, to be oneself so completely and to remain as one is in such a way that one mocks the power of that environment (although, no, the lily does not mock anyone, for it is entirely carefree in its loveliness). For the lily is true to itself, despite its environment, because it is unconditionally obedient to God. And because it is unconditionally obedient, it is unconditionally carefree, which is something that only those who are unconditionally obedient can be, especially under such conditions. Its being wholly and entirely obedient and its being unconditionally carefree—two features that can be correlated directly and inversely—is why it is lovely. Only by being unconditionally obedient can one hit upon the "place" where one is to take up one's position with unconditional accuracy. And when one hits upon it unconditionally, one understands that it is a matter of unconditional indifference whether or not the "place" is a dunghill.

Even if it turned out as unfortunately as possible for the lily, and the moment when it was to burst forth was so unfavorable that it could be seen beforehand as almost certain that it would be snapped in the very same moment, so that its coming into the world would be its going hence—even so, it would seem to it that it came into the world only in order to go hence, and that this was lovely. The obedient lily can be as it is and be obedient, it knows that such is God's will, and it bursts forth. If you saw it at that moment, there wouldn't be even the slightest sign that its unfurling was also its undoing. It burst forth so fully developed, so rich and so beautiful, and it went hence in unconditional obedience, so rich and so beautiful, and the whole thing lasted but a moment. A human being or, rather, we human beings, if we were in the lily's place, would in all likelihood despair over the thought that our coming into the world and our going hence were one and the same, and our despair would then prevent us from becoming what we were capable of becoming, even if only for a moment.

It is otherwise in the case of the lily. It was unconditionally obedient, and therefore it became what it was in its loveliness, it realized all that it was possible for it to be, undisturbed, unconditionally undisturbed by the thought that that same moment would be its death. Ah! But if there was a difference between one lily and another in terms of loveliness, this lily would have to get the prize, for it has one loveliness in addition: that it was lovely despite its certainty that it would perish in that very moment. And truly, seeing ahead to one's end and having the courage and the faith to come into the world in all one's loveliness is something that only unconditional obedience can do. As has been said, human beings would be disturbed by the certainty of their end. And because of that, they would not realize the possibilities that had been granted them, even though it was but the shortest of lives that had been measured out for them. "To what purpose?" they would say. "Why?" they would say. Or, "What good does it do?" they would say. Thus, instead of developing all their possibilities, they would be the agents of their own downfall even before the moment had arrived and, unlovely, would limp through life. Only unconditional obedience can hit the mark of "the moment" with unconditional accuracy, and only unconditional obedience can make use of "the moment" without being disturbed by the following moment.

Even if, when the moment for his migration arrives, the bird thinks that he is certain that things are so good where he is that his journey would mean letting go of a certain good for something uncertain, the obedient bird nevertheless sets out on his journey at that very moment. Simple as he is, his unconditional obedience helps him to understand just one thing, but he understands it unconditionally, and now is unconditionally in the moment. When he is affected by life's harshness, when he is tested in difficulties and things go hard for him, when each morning for many days he finds his nest has been wrecked, the obedient bird starts over each day, working with the same enthusiasm and care as he did the first time. Simple as he is, his unconditional obedience helps him to understand just one thing, but he understands it unconditionally: that this is his work, and that each has to do what is allotted him.

And what if the bird experiences something of the world's wickedness? Take the little songbird, singing away to the glory of God and having to deal with a badly behaved child who finds it funny to laugh at him and, if possible, ruin the solemn occasion; or a solitary bird that has found a place he loves and a much-loved branch on which he especially loves to sit, perhaps also dear to him on account of treasured memories, and then some human being comes along who takes pleasure in throwing stones at him or in some other way chasing him away. Ah! A human being is almost as tireless in wickedness as the bird is tireless in seeking his way back to his love and to the old place, even though he has been driven away and frightened off. The obedient bird is as he is, unconditionally so in everything that happens to him. Simple as he is, his unconditional obedience helps him to understand just one thing, but he understands it unconditionally: that everything of that kind he experiences does not really concern him and therefore does so only improperly, or, rather, it really does concern him, but it is also unconditionally the case that he must be true to himself in unconditional obedience to God.

That's how it is with the lily and the bird from which we are to learn. You are therefore not to say, "It's all very well for the lily and the bird to be obedient, since they can't do anything else or do anything in any other way. It's not much of an example of obedience when one does one's duty out of necessity." But you are not to speak like this; you are not to say anything at all. You are to keep silent and obey, so that if it is in fact the case that the lily and the bird do their duty out of necessity you, too, may succeed in doing your duty out of necessity. For you, too, are subjected to necessity. God's will shall be done in any case, so strive to do your duty out of necessity, by doing God's will in unconditional obedience. God's will shall be done in any case, so see to it that you do your duty out of necessity by being true to yourself according to God's will in unconditional obedience. Do so with such unconditional obedience that you can truthfully say of yourself in relation to doing and to being true to yourself in God's will, "I can do no other, I cannot do it any other way."

That is what you should strive for, and you should reflect that, however it may be in the case of the lily and the bird, if it is really more difficult for a human being to be unconditionally obedient, then there is also a further danger for us, that, if I dare say so, makes it even easier for us: the danger of abusing God's patience. For have you ever really seriously thought about your own life or human life, the human world that is so different from nature, where everything is unconditionally obedient? Have you ever posed such questions to yourself and been able to feel without a shudder the truth involved in God calling Himself "the God of patience,"* meaning that He, the God who says "either-or" (that is, "either love me or hate me; either be devoted to me or despise me"), has patience enough to bear with you and me and all of us? Imagine if God was a human being. How very, very, very long ago He would have grown weary and fed up with me (to take myself as an example) and with having to deal with me and, albeit for very different reasons, would have said, as a human parent might say, "This child is both ugly and sickly and stupid and dim, and even if there is nevertheless some good in it, there is so much bad that it cannot be endured." No, no human being can endure it, only the God of patience can do so.

Think of the innumerable multitude of human beings now living. We talk about how patient one has to be to teach little children, but how much patience God must have to teach this innumerable multitude! And what makes the need for patience infinitely greater

---

* Romans 15:5.

is that those who have God as their teacher suffer in varying degrees from the illusion that they are great big grown-up people, an illusion from which the lily and the bird are utterly free, which is why unconditional obedience comes so easily to them. A human teacher might well say, "All that's needed is for the children to imagine that they are grown-ups—it would exhaust one's patience and drive one to despair; no one could endure it." No, no human being could endure it, only the God of patience can do so. That, you see, is why God calls Himself the God of patience—and He surely knows what He is talking about. It is not as if He just felt like calling Himself that, since He does not now feel one thing, now another, as the impatient person does. He has known from all eternity—and He knows from thousands and thousands of years of daily experience—He has known from eternity that so long as time endures, and so long as the human race exists, He will have to be the God of patience; otherwise human disobedience will be unendurable.

In relation to the lily and the bird, God is the fatherly Creator and preserver: only in relation to human beings is He the God of patience. It is true enough that this is a comfort, a much-needed and indescribable comfort, which is why Scripture says that God is the God of patience—and of comfort. But it is also a frightfully serious matter that human disobedience is the cause of God being the God of patience, a frightfully serious matter that human beings are capable of taking God's patience in vain. We have discovered a divine attribute that the lily and the bird, which are always unconditionally obedient, do not know about; or, to put it another way, God has been so loving toward human beings as to let it be revealed to them that He has this attribute and is patient. Thus, in a certain sense—but, oh! what a frightful responsibility—God's patience in a certain sense corresponds to human disobedience. It is a comfort, but on the condition of a frightful responsibility. Human beings can dare to believe that even if everybody else gave up on them, and even if they are not far from giving up on themselves, God is still the God of patience. This is a treasure beyond price— Ah! But use it well: remember that it has had to be saved up; for the sake of God in heaven use it well, for otherwise it will plunge you into even greater wretchedness and become the opposite of what it is—no longer a comfort but rather a frightful accusation against you. For if it seems to you that saying one should be devoted to God unconditionally and in everything and that if one doesn't do this then one "at once" despises Him is to speak too rigorously—although it is no more rigorous than the truth of the matter—to take His patience in vain is certainly to despise Him, and that is by no means putting it too rigorously.

Take care, then, that you follow the direction pointed out by the gospel and learn obedience from the lily and the bird. Do not be frightened off, and do not despair, when you compare yourself with these teachers. There is nothing to despair about, for you *ought to* learn from them, and the gospel comforts you: first, by telling you that God is the God of patience, and then by adding that "You are to learn from the lily and the bird, learn to be unconditionally obedient like the lily and the bird, learn how not to serve two masters, for no one can serve two masters, since he will either . . . or."

But if you can learn to be unconditionally obedient from the lily and the bird, then you will have learned what you should learn, and you will have learned it from the lily and the bird (and if you have learned it thoroughly, then you will have become more perfect than they, who are no longer your teachers but your image). You will have learned to serve only one master, to love Him and to be unconditionally devoted to Him in everything. Then, too, will the prayer—that is assuredly already answered—be answered through you when you pray, "Your will be done, on earth as it is in heaven." For your unconditional obedience makes your will one with God's will, and thus

God's will, as it is in heaven, will be done through you on earth. Similarly, you will be heard when you pray, "Lead us not into temptation," for if you are unconditionally obedient, there is nothing ambiguous in you; and if there is nothing ambiguous in you, then you are in a state of unbroken simplicity before God—and if there is one thing that not all of Satan's cunning or temptation's snares can surprise or get a grip on it is simplicity. Ambiguity is what Satan's sharp eyes are looking out for as his prey, but it is never found among the lilies and the birds; it is what temptation is aiming at, sure of its prey, but it is never found among the lilies and the birds. Where there is ambiguity, *there* temptation lies, and it is all too easy for it to be the stronger. But where there is ambiguity, there, too, lies another form of disobedience, one that lies beneath the surface, a subterranean disobedience. That is why there is not a trace of ambiguity in the lily and the bird, because they are unconditionally obedient at the deepest level, in every respect, and from the ground up. And it is precisely because there is nothing ambiguous in the lily and the bird that it is impossible to lead them into temptation. Where there is no ambiguity, Satan is powerless. Where there is no ambiguity, temptation is as powerless as a fowler with his net when there are no birds to be found. But if there is just the tiniest, tiniest hint of ambiguity, then Satan grows strong, and temptation closes on its prey. He is sharp-sighted, the evil one, whose snare is called temptation and whose prey is called the human soul. Properly speaking, temptation does not come from him, but there is nothing ambiguous, nothing at all, that can conceal itself from him—and once he has discovered it, temptation is there to do his service. But those who are hidden in God by means of unconditional obedience are unconditionally safe. From their safe hiding place, they can see the devil, but the devil cannot see them. "From their safe hiding place"—for as sharp-sighted as the devil may be in relation to ambiguity, he is in the same degree blind when looking at simplicity: he becomes blind, or it strikes him blind. But it is not without a shudder that those who are unconditionally obedient watch him. This glittering gaze looks as if it could penetrate the earth, the sea, and the heart's deepest secrets, and indeed it can, and yet, despite this gaze, he is blind. For he who spreads out temptation's net is blind in relation to those who are hidden in God by means of unconditional obedience and there is no temptation for them, for "God tempts no one.* Thus, the prayer "Lead us not into temptation" is answered, that is, let disobedience never lead me to risk leaving my hiding place, and if I nevertheless do become guilty of some act of disobedience, do not drive me straightaway from the hiding place, outside of which I will be led into temptation. And if, through unconditional obedience, we remain in our hiding place, then we are also "delivered from evil."

No one can serve two masters, for he will either love one and hate the other or will be devoted to one and despise the other. You cannot serve God and mammon, God and the world, good and evil. So then, there are two powers, God and the world, good and evil, and the reason why human beings can only serve one master is that even if one of these two powers is infinitely stronger than the other, they are at war with each other in a matter of life and death. It is a terrible danger that human beings have to face by virtue of being human—a danger that, in their unconditional obedience or blissful innocence, the lily and the bird escape, since neither God and the world nor good and evil fight over them—the danger wherein "humanity" is placed between these two terrible powers and given the power of choosing between them. It is this terrible danger that means that one must either love or hate, and that not loving means hating. For these powers are so hostile toward each other that the slightest inclination toward one is seen by the other

---

* James 1:13.

as unconditionally opposed to it. But what if we forget this terrible danger we are in (a danger, let it be noted, against which forgetting about it truly serves no useful purpose)? If we forget that we are in this danger, if we think that we are not in danger, if we even go so far as to say "peace" and not "danger," then what is said in the gospel must seem to us to be a silly exaggeration.

But, alas, it is precisely because we are so deeply immersed in the danger, so lost, that we have no idea either of the love with which God loves us (which is the love that makes God demand unconditional obedience) or of the power and cunning of evil and of its weakness. Ah! But human beings are from the very beginning too childish to be able to and to want to understand the gospel. When it says "either-or," this seems to them to be an exaggeration. How can the danger be so great that unconditional obedience is needed? And that unconditional obedience has its basis in love is something human beings cannot get their heads around at all.

What, then, does the gospel do? The gospel, which is wise in the matter of a good upbringing, does not let itself get involved with us in a quarrel about ideas or words, so as to *prove* to us that it is right. The gospel knows very well that this is not how to go about it, as if human beings were first to understand what it says and then had to decide to obey it unconditionally. Rather, it is the reverse: it is by unconditional obedience that human beings first get to understand what the gospel is saying. That is why the gospel speaks with authority and says, "You *ought*." But in the same moment it grows gentle, so much so as to touch even the hardest. It is as if it takes you by the hand, in the same way that a loving father does with his child, and says, "Come, let's go out to the lily and the bird." Once out there, it continues in the same vein: "Consider the lily and the bird, give yourself up to them, lose yourself in them. Doesn't the sight of them move you?" Then, when the solemn silence out there among the lilies and the birds moves you deeply, the gospel explains matters further and asks, "But why is this silence so solemn? It is because it expresses the unconditional obedience by which everything serves just one master, turns in service to just one, united in complete unity, in one single act of divine worship. So let yourself be grasped by this great idea, for everything is but one idea, and learn from the lily and the bird." But don't forget that you *ought* to learn from the lily and the bird, and you ought to become as unconditionally obedient as they are. Reflect on the fact that it was the human sin of not wanting to serve one master—or wanting to serve another master or wanting to serve two or more masters—that disrupted all the beauty of this world in which everything had previously been so very good. It was human sin that fragmented this united world. And reflect on the fact that every sin is an act of disobedience, and every act of disobedience a sin.

III

"CONSIDER THE BIRDS OF THE AIR: THEY NEITHER SOW NOR REAP NOR GATHER INTO BARNS"—THEY ARE NOT ANXIOUS ABOUT TOMORROW. CONSIDER "THE GRASS OF THE FIELD, WHICH TODAY IS."

Do this and learn

JOY.

Let us then consider the lily and the bird, these two joyful teachers. "Joyful teachers," yes, for you know that joy is communicative, and therefore there is no one better able to teach joy than those who are themselves joyful. Those who are teachers of joy really have nothing else to do than to be joyful or to be joy. No matter how much effort they put into communicating joy, if they are not joyful themselves the lesson will be imperfect. So there is nothing easier to teach than joy— Alas! All one needs to do is to be always and in truth joyful. But this "Alas!" signifies that this is not so easy; that is, it is not so easy to be always joyful—although nothing is more certain than that when one is, it is easy enough to teach joy.

But out there with the lily and the bird, or out there where the lily and the bird teach joy, there is always joy. And the lily and the bird are never embarrassed in the way that human teachers sometimes are when they have written down what they wanted to teach on a bit of paper and left it in their library or, in brief, do not always have it on them. No, *there*, where the lily and the bird teach joy, there is always joy—it is in the lily and the bird themselves. What joy when the day begins to break and the bird wakes early to the joy of the day ahead; what joy—albeit in another tonality—when evening draws near and the bird joyfully hurries home to his nest; and what joy in the long summer days! What joy when the bird joyfully begins his song, for he is not like the joyful laborer who sings on his way to work, since the bird's real work is to sing! What new joy when the neighbor, too, begins to sing, and then the next-but-one, and then the whole choir join in—what joy! And when, finally, it is as if there is an ocean of notes, echoing from wood and valley, from heaven and earth, an ocean of notes in which the one who started it off now tumbles over himself with joy—what joy, what joy! And so it is the bird's whole life through. He always and everywhere finds something or, rather, enough to make him joyful. He doesn't waste a single moment but would regard every moment in which he wasn't joyful as wasted. What joy when the dew falls and refreshes the lily that, being thus cooled, gets itself ready to rest. What joy, when, fresh from its bath, the lily cheerfully dries itself off in the first rays of the sun! And what joy in the long summer days!

Oh, just look at them—look at the lily, and look at the bird, and look at them together! What joy when the bird hides himself by the lily, where he has his nest and where he is so indescribably at home, while he jokes and plays the fool with the lily to pass the time! What joy when, from high up on his branch or even higher, from high in the sky, the bird happily keeps an eye on his nest and on the lily, which smilingly turns its eye up toward him! Oh, blissful, happy existence, so rich in joy! And is the joy perhaps any the less, because in a petty sense it is such small things that make them joyful? No it is not, and this kind of petty way of understanding it is a misunderstanding, alas, a very grievous and distressing misunderstanding. For it is the fact that it takes so little to make them joyful that proves that they themselves are joy and joy itself. Is it not so? For if one found joy in something that was nothing at all and yet was in truth indescribably joyful, then that would be the best proof of all that one was oneself joyful or was joy itself. And that is how the lily and the bird are, these joyful teachers of joy who, precisely because they are *unconditionally joyful*, are joy itself. For those whose joy depends on certain conditions are not themselves joy; their joy is a conditional joy and is conditional in relation to its conditions. But the one who is joy itself is unconditionally joyful, just as, conversely, the one who is unconditionally joyful is joy itself. Ah! But the conditions we human beings need before we can be joyful cause us much trouble and anxiety, and even if we got all the conditions we asked for we might nevertheless not be unconditionally joyful. But, say, you deep teachers of joy, isn't it true that it can't be any other way? For to have to be helped to be joyful, even if one had all the conditions one wanted, would mean that it was impossible to be joyful more than in a conditional way or otherwise than in a conditional way. Setting down conditions and being something in a conditional way correspond to each other, and, no, only those can be unconditionally joyful who are joy itself, and only by being unconditionally joyful can one be joy itself.

But is there no way of saying briefly how it is that joy makes up the content of the teaching offered by the lily and the bird, or what the content of their teaching in joy is? In other words, what thought does their teaching express, and can it be stated briefly? Indeed it can, it's easily done, for no matter how simple the lily and the bird may be, they are certainly not thoughtless. So then, it's easily done, although let us not forget that an inordinate abbreviation is already involved in this regard, since the lily and the bird are themselves what they teach, and they themselves express that which they are giving instruction in. In distinction from the direct, or first, way of being original—as when the lily and the bird have, in the very strictest sense, firsthand knowledge of what they teach—this is an acquired originality. And when this acquired originality is found in the lily and the bird, it is once again something simple. For whether a teaching is simple does not so much depend on whether it uses simple everyday expressions or lofty and learned ones. No, what makes for simplicity is when those who teach are themselves what they teach. That is how it is in the case of the lily and the bird. But their instruction in the joy that their lives also express is, in all brevity, as follows: there is a today that *is*—and, yes, this *is* is infinitely stressed; there *is* a today—and there is no anxiety, absolutely none, about the next day or the next day after that. This is not light-minded on the part of the lily and the bird but is the joy of silence and obedience. For when you keep silent in the solemn silence that exists in nature, then there is no next day. And when you obey as Creation obeys, there is no next day—"the next day," that unblessed day invented by chatter and disobedience. But when, thanks to silence and obedience, there is no next day, then, in silence and obedience, today, today *is*—and then there is joy as it is found in the lily and the bird.

What is joy, or what is being joyful? In truth, it is to be present to oneself. But to be present to oneself in truth is to *be* today, in truth to *be today*. And to the same degree that it is true that you *are* today, and in the same degree that you are entirely present to yourself in being today, in that same degree will misfortune's "next day" not exist for you. Joy is the present time, where the entire stress lies on *the present time*. That is why God is blessed, for in all eternity He says, "Today"— He who is eternally and infinitely present to Himself in being today. And that is why the lily and the bird are joy, because silently and obediently they are entirely present to themselves in being today.

"But," you might say, "it's easy for the lily and the bird." The answer is: *you* should not come along with any *buts* but should rather learn from the lily and the bird how to be so entirely present to yourself in being today that you, too, are joy. But, as said, no *buts*, for in all seriousness you *ought to* learn joy from the lily and the bird. Still less should you become self-important in such a way that, since the lily and the bird are simple, and, perhaps, in order to make your being human felt, you get witty and, speaking about some particular tomorrow, say, "It's easy for the lily and the bird, for they don't even have a tomorrow to worry about—but human beings not only have to worry about what they are going to eat tomorrow but also about what they had to eat yesterday and haven't yet paid for!" No, no witticisms that might naughtily disrupt the lesson! But learn, at least begin to learn, from the lily and the bird.

Can anyone really be serious in thinking that what the bird and the lily are joyful about, or that what it is to be like them, is nothing worthy of joy? So the fact that you came into the world, that you exist, that "today" you have what you need in order to exist—that you came into the world; that you became a human being; that you can see (just reflect on the fact that you can see); that you can hear; that you can smell; that you can taste; that you can feel; that the sun shines on you and shines for you, and, when you grow weary, the moon comes up and the stars are lit; that winter comes and all of nature changes its garb and takes on a strange new role, and does so to please you; that spring comes and the birds return in numerous flocks, and do so to give you joy; that the green shoots spring up and the woods grow beautiful and present themselves as a bride, and do so to give you joy; that autumn comes and the birds take their departure, not because they count themselves as precious but, no, so that you will not grow bored of them; that the wood puts away its finery for the sake of the next time, that is, so that it will be able to give you joy the next time—is this nothing to be joyful about? Ah! But if I dared to scold—but, out of respect for the lily and the bird I don't dare, and so, instead of saying that this is nothing to be joyful about, I say that if this is not something to be joyful about, then nothing is. Reflect on the fact that the lily and the bird are joy, and yet they have, in this perspective, much less to be joyful about than you, who also have the lily and the bird to be joyful about. Learn from the lily, then, and learn from the bird, for they are masters in the art of existing, of *being today*, of *being joy*. If you cannot look with joy on the lily and the bird who are joy itself, and if you cannot look with joy on them in such a way as to want to learn from them, then you are in the same situation as the child of whom the teacher says, "He doesn't lack ability, for the lesson is so easy that lack of ability can't come into it—it must be something else, perhaps only a lack of interest that one doesn't need to take too seriously for now and treat as if it were unwillingness or even contradictoriness."

That is how the lily and the bird are teachers of joy. And yet the lily and the bird also have their sorrows, as the whole of nature has sorrows. Doesn't all Creation groan under the perishability to which it is subjected against its will? For everything is subjected to perishability! No matter how securely the star sits in the heavens, it will one day change its place and fall, and the one that never changed its place will nevertheless change it when it plunges down into the abyss. All the world and everything in it will be changed as one changes a garment when it is cast off, prey to perishability! And even if the lily avoids the fate of being cast straightaway into the oven, it must nevertheless wither after having beforehand suffered one thing and another. And even if it was granted to the bird that he should die of old age, he must one day die and be separated from those he loves after having beforehand suffered one thing and another. Ah! But all things are perishable, and everything will one day become what it is: prey to perishability! Perishability, perishability, this is *the sigh*—having to be subject to perishability is what a sigh means, it is to be locked up, to be bound, imprisoned; and what a sigh says is: perishability, perishability!

And yet the lily and the bird are unconditionally joyful, and here you see properly the truth of the gospel saying that you *ought to* learn joy from the lily and the bird. You could not ask for better teachers than those who, although they bear the burden of an infinitely deep sorrow, are nevertheless unconditionally joyful and are joy itself.

How the lily and the bird deal with this looks almost like a miracle: in deepest sorrow to be unconditionally joyful; to *be* when tomorrow is so frightful, that is, to be unconditionally joyful today—how can it be done? It can be done quite simply and in all simplicity; the lily and the bird do it all the time, and yet they manage to get rid of this tomorrow as if it didn't exist. There is a saying of the apostle Paul, who had taken the lily and the bird to his heart, and, simple as they are, they take it quite literally— Ah! But that's just how they help us, by taking it quite literally. There is a tremendous power in this saying when it is taken quite literally, although when it is not taken literally according to the letter, it becomes less and less powerful until, finally, it becomes a meaningless figure of speech. But unconditional simplicity is needed to take it unconditionally and entirely literally. This saying is "Cast *all* your care *on God*."* Look—the lily and the bird do so unconditionally. Helped by their unconditional silence and their unconditional obedience they cast *all* their care from them, like the most powerful catapult hurling its charge and with the kind of passion with which one throws off what one most loathes. They cast it off, and they do so with a sureness that hits the target as surely as any artillery and with a faith and a confidence like that possessed only by the most practiced hand—and *on God*. In this very instant—and this very instant is from its first moment, today, instantaneous with the moment in which it came into existence—in this very instant it is unconditionally joyful. Oh, marvelous skill! To be able all at once to lay hold of all your care and to be able to cast it off so skillfully and so surely hit the mark! Yet this is what the lily and the bird do, that is why in this very instant they are unconditionally joyful. And this is as it should be, for God is the Almighty, he carries the weight of the whole world and all its cares—including those of the lily and the bird—infinitely lightly. What indescribable joy! That is, the joy that God is almighty.

Learn, then, from the lily and the bird, learn the skill of the unconditional. True enough, it is a marvelous piece of artistry, but that is precisely why you ought to pay even closer attention to the lily and the bird. It is a marvelous piece of artistry, and, like the "art of meekness," it contains a contradiction, or, rather, it is a work of art that resolves a contradiction. The verb *to cast* makes one think that a certain force is being deployed, as if one had to gather all one's forces and with a tremendous effort powerfully "cast" one's sorrows away. And yet, "power" is precisely not what one should use. What is to be used, and used unconditionally, is "compliance"—and yet one

---

* 1 Peter 5:7. Kierkegaard here erroneously ascribes the saying to Paul.

is to cast off one's cares! Moreover, one is to cast off *all* one's cares, and if one doesn't cast off *all* one's cares and keeps much, some, or just a little of them back, then one doesn't become joyful, let alone unconditionally joyful. And if one doesn't unconditionally cast them *on God* but somewhere else, then one doesn't get unconditionally rid of them, and they will somehow or other come back again, often in the guise of a still greater and still more bitter sorrow. For casting off your cares but not casting them on God is "distraction," but distraction is a dubious and ambiguous method of dealing with care. If, on the other hand, you unconditionally cast all your care on God, this is to become "collected," and yet—this is indeed a wonderfully contradictory work of art—it is a *collection* in which you are unconditionally *quit* of all care.

Learn, then, from the lily and the bird. Cast all your care on God! But do not cast off joy. On the contrary, hold fast to it with all your might and with all the forces at your disposal. If you do this, then the accounts are soon drawn up, and you will always get to keep some joy. For if you cast off all your care, all that is then left to you is what you have of joy. But this is barely enough. Learn more from the lily and the bird, then. Cast all your care on God, do it entirely, unconditionally, as the lily and the bird do it. Then you will be as unconditionally joyful as the lily and the bird are. And this is unconditional joy: to worship the almightiness with which the almighty God bears all your cares as lightly as if they were nothing. And, as the apostle goes on to add, it is also unconditional joy when, in worship, you dare to believe "that God cares for you." Unconditional joy is precisely joy over God, over whom and in whom you can always, unconditionally, be joyful. If you are not unconditionally joyful in this relationship, then the fault is unconditionally in you, in your inability to cast all your care on Him, in your being unwilling to do so, in thinking yourself so clever and being so self-opinionated. In short, it lies in your not being like the lily and the bird. There is only one care in relation to which the lily and the bird cannot be our teachers, a care about which we shall therefore not talk here, namely, sorrow over sin. But in relation to all other cares, the situation is that if you do not become unconditionally joyful, then you are responsible for it, because you were not willing to learn from the lily and the bird and by unconditional silence and obedience became unconditionally joyful before God.

But one more thing. Perhaps you will join "the poet" in saying, "Indeed, if one could build one's dwelling place beside the bird, secretly, in the solitude of the forest, where the bird and his mate make a pair, but where there is no other society; or if one could live together with the lily in the peaceful fields, where every lily fends for itself and there is no society—how, then, could one not cast all one's care on God and be or become unconditionally joyful? For it is precisely 'society' that is the problem, namely, that human beings are the only beings that torment themselves and others with the unhappy fantasy of society and of social happiness and do so in the same degree that society gets ever bigger and bigger to the ruin of each individual and itself." However, you are not to talk like that. No, think about the matter more carefully and admit with shame that, properly speaking, it is the inexpressible joy of love that makes it impossible for society to disturb the birds—him and her, this pair—despite their cares or the solitary person's self-contented joy. For there is in fact a society there. Look more closely and admit with shame that what really constitutes the unconditional silence and the unconditional obedience with which the bird and the lily are unconditionally joyful over God is what makes the lily and the bird equally joyful and equally unconditionally joyful in solitude and in society. Learn, then, from the lily and the bird.

If, then, you could learn to be entirely like the lily and the bird, and if I, alas, could learn it, then, both in you and in me, the prayer that is the last prayer in the Lord's prayer would come true: a prayer that, in this regard, is a model for all prayer—namely, by praying itself into joy and into greater and unconditional joy and finally having nothing more to pray for or to desire but, unconditionally joyful, to end in worship and praise—that is, "For the kingdom, the power, and the glory are yours." Indeed, *His* is the kingdom—and therefore you are to keep unconditionally silent lest you disrupt things by drawing attention to yourself and letting it be known that you are there; instead, let the unconditional solemnity of silence express the fact that *His* is the kingdom. And *His* is the power—and therefore you are to obey unconditionally and unconditionally accept all that you are, for His is the power. And *His* is the glory—and therefore in everything you do and in everything you suffer you have unconditionally but one thing left to do: to give Him the glory, for the glory is His.

Oh, unconditional joy! His is the kingdom, the power, and the glory—forever and ever. "Forever": eternally. Behold this day, eternity's day, it never ends. Therefore hold with unconditional firmness to the fact that His is the kingdom, the power, and the glory forever and ever, eternally, in order that "today" might be for you the day that never ends, a today in which you can become eternally present to yourself. So let the heavens fall and the stars change their places and all things be overthrown, let the bird die and the lily wither— the joy you have in worship and you in your joy will nevertheless *today* survive the end of all things. Consider, even if it is not true for you, that just by virtue of being human it is nevertheless true for you as a Christian that, Christianly speaking, the peril of death is so meaningless that it is a matter of "even today you will be with me in paradise."* So rapid, then, is the transition from time to eternity—the greatest possible distance—that even if it were to involve the end of

---

* Luke 23:43.

all things it would still be so rapid that even *today* you are in paradise if, Christianly, you *remain in God.* For if you remain in God, whether you live or die, whether it goes well with you or badly, as long as you live and whether you die today or only after seventy years, and whether your death is in the ocean's deepest depths or you are blown into thin air, you are never outside God, you *remain*—that is, you are present to yourself, in God, and therefore, even on the day of your death, you are today in paradise. The bird and the lily live only for a day, but even a very short day is nevertheless joy, because, as has been argued, they truly *are today* and are *present to themselves* in this today. And you, if you are granted the longest of days, to live today and still today to be in paradise, is this not something to make you unconditionally joyful—you who ought, as indeed you can, far, far exceed the bird in joy—is this not something you can be assured of every time you pray this prayer, and something you get closer to every time you inwardly pray this joyous prayer? "For the kingdom, the power, and the glory are yours—forever and ever. Amen."

Part III

LOVE:
At the Feet of the Savior

11

The Look of Love*

"LOVE HIDES A MULTITUDE OF SINS."

Epistle: 1 Peter 4:7–12.

IN PRAISE OF LOVE

What is it that makes a person great, admirable among creatures, and well pleasing in God's eyes? What is it that makes a person strong, stronger than the whole world, or so weak as to be weaker than a child? What is it that makes a person firm, firmer than a cliff, or yet so soft as to be softer than wax? It is love. What is older than everything? It is love. What is it that outlives everything? It is love. What is it that cannot be taken away but itself takes it all? It is love. What is it that cannot be given but itself gives everything? It is love. What is it that stands fast when everything falters? It is love. What is it that comforts when other comforts fail? It is love. What is it that remains when everything is changed? It is love. What is it that abides when what is imperfect is done away with? It is love. What is

---

* From Niels Jørgen Cappelørn et al., eds., *Søren Kierkegaards Skrifter*, vol. 5 (Copenhagen: Gad, 1998), pp. 65–77.

it that bears witness when prophecy is dumb? It is love. What is it that does not cease when visions come to an end? It is love. What is it that makes everything clear when the dark saying has been spoken? It is love. What is it that bestows a blessing on the excess of the gift? It is love. What is it that gives pith to the angel's speech? It is love. What is it that makes the widow's mite more than enough? It is love. What is it that makes the speech of the simple person wise? It is love. What is it that never alters, even if all things alter? It is love.

Only that which never turns into anything different from what it is is love. Paganism, too, praised love, its beauty and its power. But such love could become something different, something seen as worthy of almost greater praise. Love was beautiful, more beautiful than anything else, but revenge was also sweet, sweeter than anything else. And paganism's idea of love and of heaven was so poor, seeing self-interest at work in everything in heaven and on earth, that it believed the same power that chose to give human beings pleasure in love jealously kept to itself the right of vengeance, because this was still sweeter. No wonder, then, that revenge lay hidden in every form of love in paganism, and that it could never dispel anxiety but only forget it. No wonder, then, that the enemy worked quietly away while love slept in peace, or that anger secretly kept its watch and waited for its chance. No wonder, then, that it could suddenly burst out with utter ferocity. No wonder, then, that it filled the soul of the pagan who thirsted after its forbidden sweetness and felt that he thereby experienced his kinship with the powers of heaven! No wonder, then, that, just as no one was considered happy until his last hour had come—because even then it might happen that a person could be mocked for *having* been happy—so, too, was no love considered happy until then. No wonder, then, that sorrow mingled itself in every joy, or that even in the moment of joy the idea of what might happen in the following moment passed anxiously before his eyes with its deathly message! How might such a pagan ever overcome the world? But if that was impossible, how might the world even be won?

What is it that never alters when everything else alters? It is love—and only that which never turns into anything different from what it is is love. The pious Israelite also bore witness to love—but his love was the child of alteration and change, and he knew how to hate his enemy. Even if he left vengeance to the Lord, because it was to Him that vengeance belonged, he himself was not unacquainted with its sweetness. And it is also sweet to know that the Lord's vengeance is more fearful than any merely human revenge. Human beings may curse their enemies, but the Lord curses the ungodly and their descendants through many generations. No wonder, then, that anxiety always kept one eye open, even when love was most carefree. No wonder, then, that even when love dreamed least of it, wrath sat silently calculating what had been given and what received, about mine and thine! No wonder, then, that no love was considered happy until the last hour had come, because only then could one know whether love's *uncertain* demand had been fulfilled.

What is it that never alters when everything else alters? It is love—and only that which never turns into anything different from what it is is love. For love gives everything and therefore has nothing left to demand; it demands nothing and therefore has nothing to lose; it blesses and blesses again when it is cursed, it loves its neighbor, but the enemy is also its neighbor; it leaves vengeance to the Lord, because it believes that He is capable of yet greater mercy.

It is this love that the apostle Peter is talking about in the reading we have heard, and as the apostle testified to this love many times and in many ways, so here he witnesses to its power when he says, "Love hides a multitude of sins."

It is this saying, this testimony, that we are now going to consider more closely as we reflect on *how love hides a multitude of sins.*

HOW TO SPEAK OF LOVE

But how should we speak about this? Should we speak in such a way as not to allow ourselves time to dwell on the words, because the mere sound of them was enough to reproach us, to make us mourn for, or to awaken a striving toward the goal that every human being ought to be striving toward? Should we speak in such a way that—if it were possible—we might get each individual determined to buy the opportune moment, so that the saying might move those whom it encountered standing idly about to enter the race or encourage those who were already on the way to hasten more quickly toward perfection? Should we speak thus—as if we were speaking to those who were not yet perfect? Should we remind you how rarely one finds a person who has never known or who has completely forgotten "the world's childhood teaching" that revenge is sweet? Should we remind you that all of us, if we are honest, only too often catch ourselves in detailed, penetrating, and experienced explanations of the grievous truth that revenge is sweet? Should we remind you how rare it really is to find someone who left vengeance to the Lord, because they were assured that He had a milder explanation of the guilt and would pass a more merciful judgment on it, since He is greater than any human heart? On the contrary—how often every honest person has to admit that he did not refrain from revenge because of being able to leave it to the Lord! Should we remind you how rare it really is to find a person who forgave in such a way that his enemy really repented and thereby became his neighbor, a person whose forgiveness really abrogated the scales of justice and made no distinction between the one who was called early in the day and the enemy who was called only at the eleventh hour, even if the one had owed only fifty cents and the enemy five hundred? Should we remind you how rare it really is to find people who love in such a way that their ears don't pick up any malicious whispers when things go well for their enemies, because their hearts know nothing of envy, or who love in such a way that "their eyes do not show that they regret having forgiven" when good fortune favors their enemies, or who love in such a way that when things go badly for their enemies, they forget that they are enemies? Should we warn against what people don't on the whole regard as very serious, namely, a certain kind of snide cunning that knows how to secretly find out what people have done wrong and that, even if it isn't used to pass judgment on or injure them by its intrusiveness, nevertheless ruins them?

Should we exhort each person here to seek that Christian love, because each of us so often stands in need of forgiveness? Should we exhort each person here to judge themselves and thereby forget to judge others? Should we warn against judgment and prejudice, because no one can entirely see into another's heart, or because it has sometimes happened that instead of the divine wrath consuming those against whom it had been invoked the Lord looked graciously and mildly on them in secret? Should we warn each person here not to zealously call wrath down on others, because refusing to be reconciled will store up a yet more dreadful wrath against those who invoke it on the Day of Judgment?

Is that how we should speak? It may well be advantageous to be spoken to like that sometimes, but it is very difficult for the speaker to do so without becoming guilty of what he is speaking against, namely, judging others. In fact, even when the discourse speaks of judging oneself, it is very difficult to avoid becoming entangled in new misunderstandings and thereby unsettling others. For these reasons, we have chosen an easier task. We shall dwell on the words themselves and, as every other kind of love has been praised in the world, we shall give an account of and praise the love that has the power to perform the miracle of forgiving a multitude of sins. And we shall speak as if to those who are perfect. If some of you don't feel that you are perfect, the discourse makes no distinctions. We shall allow ourselves to find repose in the apostolic saying that is no deceptive poetic figure or some rash outburst but a faithful thought, a valid testimony, which, in order to be understood, has to be taken literally.

THE LOOK OF LOVE

Love hides a multitude of sins. An old saying tells us that love makes us blind. This is not intended to imply any imperfection in the lover or something about how he is in himself, since it was only when love took up its abode in his soul that he became blind, and the more love took possession of him, the blinder he became. Or did love become less perfect when, after having first deceived itself by not wanting to see what it nevertheless did see, it ended by really not seeing it? For who was best at hiding something—the person who knew that it was hidden or the one who had even forgotten that? An old saying says that "to the pure all things are pure,"* and this is by no means intended to indicate an imperfection on the part of those who are pure or something that will gradually disappear. On the contrary, the purer one is, the purer everything one sees becomes. Or was it an imperfection on the part of the pure that, having first saved themselves from being sullied by impurity by not wanting to know what they nevertheless did know about, they finally ceased to know about it?

It is not just a question of what one sees, but what one sees depends on how one sees. For looking at an object is not just a matter of receptivity or discovery but is also productive, and to the extent that it is productive, what is decisive is how those who are doing the looking

---

* Matthew 5:8.

are in themselves. When one person sees one thing and another sees another, even though they are both looking at the same situation, one discovers what the other hides. To the extent that the object under consideration belongs to the external world, the observer is perhaps less important; or, more accurately, what is necessary for being an observer is not something that affects one's deeper being. But the more what is being examined belongs to the realm of spirit, so much the more does it matter *how* the observer is in his innermost being. For the things of the spirit can be acquired only by means of freedom, and what is acquired by means of freedom is also what we ourselves bring forth. In that case, it is not the external but the internal difference that counts, and it is from within that everything that makes us impure and the way we look at impure things proceeds. What we see with the external eye is irrelevant, but "an evil eye issues from within a person."* But an evil eye discovers much that love doesn't see, because an evil eye sees the Lord acting unjustly, even though He is good. When wickedness dwells in a heart, the eye is readily offended, but when purity dwells in a heart, the eye sees the finger of God, for the pure see God always, "but those who do evil do not see God."†

It is therefore what is within us that decides what we discover and what we conceal. When sinful lust dwells in a heart, the eye discovers a multitude of sins and makes them even more numerous. The eye is the light of the body, but when the light that is in a person is dark, how great the darkness then becomes!‡ When anxiety about sin dwells in a heart, the ear discovers a multitude of sins and makes them even more numerous. And what use is it to such a person if he is blind, for a rogue shuts his eyes and listens with his roguish ears

---

* Mark 7:21–22.
† 3 John 1:11.
‡ Matthew 6:22–23.

(Ecclesiasticus 19:24). When love dwells in a heart, the eyes are shut so as not to see the sins that have been openly committed, still less do they see hidden sins. For "the one who winks the eye has wickedness in his mind" (Proverbs),* and the one who understands the wink is by no means pure. When love dwells in a heart, the ears are closed to what is being said in the world and to bitter mockery. For the one who says "Racha" to his brother must answer to the Council,† but the one who understands what it means when he hears it said is by no means perfect in love. When hastiness dwells in a heart, a person is quick to discover a multitude of sins. Such a one understands very well what has been only half said, and, even if it is as if it were spoken at a great distance, such a one quickly seizes upon a word that has scarcely been uttered. When love dwells in a heart, a person is slow to understand and does not hear a hasty word, nor does he understand it when it is repeated. Such a person puts what has been said in a good place and puts a good construction on it. He doesn't understand long speeches full of anger and mockery, because he is waiting for the word that will give a point to what is said.

When fear dwells in a heart, a person easily discovers a multitude of sins and sin's treachery, deceit, and scheming, for

EACH HEART IS A NET, EACH ROGUE LIKE A CHILD, EACH
PROMISE LIKE A SHADOW.

But the love that hides a multitude of sins is never deceived. When miserliness dwells in a heart, when it gives with one eye and keeps seven eyes on what it is going to get back (Ecclesiasticus 20:14), it readily discovers a multitude of sins. But when love dwells in a

---

* Proverbs 10:10.
† Matthew 5:22.

heart, the eye is never deceived. For love, when it gives, does not keep its eyes on the gift but looks always to the Lord. When envy dwells in a heart, then the eye has power to draw out something impure even from what is pure. But when love dwells in a heart, then the eye has the power to love forth the good, even in what is impure. Such an eye does not see what is impure but only the purity that it loves and loves forth by loving it. There is indeed a power in the world that talks in such a way as to translate "good" by "evil," but there is also a power that comes from above and that translates what is evil into what is good—and that is the love that hides a multitude of sins.

When hate dwells in a heart, then sin lurks at the door, and its manifold desires are lying in wait, but when love dwells in a heart, then sin will have fled far away and cannot be seen. When strife, envy, anger, quarreling, duplicity, and factions dwell in a heart, there is no need to go far to discover a multitude of sins, nor does one need long to give them expression. But when joy, peace, patience, mildness, faithfulness, goodness, gentleness, and abstinence dwell in a heart, it is no wonder that even if a person were to stand in the midst of a multitude of sins, he would be like a stranger or foreigner who didn't know how things were done in this country. And if he had to explain it all, then this would surely be in such a way as to hide the multitude of sins!

But perhaps that's not how it is. Perhaps we would seem smarter if we said that there is a great multitude of sins in the world, and it is exactly the same whether love discovers them or not. Should we then let the apostolic saying and the love that it describes be accounted as no more than an elegant piece of phraseology that can't stand up to scrutiny? But the kind of smartness that proceeds in that way—does it understand love as well as it understands the multitude of sins? Would it be willing to concede the opposite case: that the multitude of sins is just as great whether it is able to use the understanding to learn about them or not? Isn't it actually rather gratified by its own cunning in being able to discover and track down our hidden sins? But then there would be a kind of equivalence: the understanding discovers a multitude of sins, and love covers them. The one is no truer than the other. Is there a third way of knowing about sin other than knowing about it through the understanding or lovingly being ignorant of it? Such knowledge would surely be inhuman. For it is not merely a piece of rhetoric to say that love hides a multitude of sins: it is true, and the power of Christian love may not be as great in terms of prestigious feats as other kinds of love are, but it is greater in its quiet miracles.

Happy the one who saw the world in all its perfection when everything was still very good; happy the person who was with God to witness the glory of Creation; but more blessed is the soul of one who is God's fellow worker in love and blessed is the love that hides a multitude of sins.

THE MANIFOLD NATURE OF SIN—AND OF LOVE

Love hides a multitude of sins. Sin's multitude—what a fearful expression, and one that readily reminds us of another common expression: the manifold of Creation. It is an expression that makes us think of the numberless troop of generations, the uncountable swarm of living beings that no one can number, because no number would be large enough and because there is no moment in which one could begin to count, since innumerably more are being brought to birth in every moment! Isn't that how it is with the multitude of sins, for, as it is said, to those who have shall also be given, and they shall have in abundance, and sin, too, is very fruitful, one sin giving birth to many more and thus becoming more and more multitudinous? But love hides a multitude of sins. If love did not shut its eyes, if it did not hide the multitude of sins by the manner in which it beheld them, how would it then dare to try to bring a halt to the power of sin? Therefore, love hides a multitude of sins by having already hidden them in advance.

A wise man of old said, "Refrain from quarreling, and you will diminish sin" (Ecclesiasticus 28:8). But the one who diminishes sin has hidden sin's multitude, and hidden it twice over, by not sinning and by restraining another from doing so. And yet the one who refrains from quarreling only restrains another person from sinning for a moment, since perhaps that person will go off and look for a quarrel elsewhere. But those who convert sinners from the error of their ways are those of whom the apostle James says that they hide a multitude of sins.*

But is it possible to count all the ways in which love hides multitudes of sins? Aren't they even more multitudinous than the multitude of sins? When it sees the broken reed, it knows how to hide multitudes of sins in such a way that the reed is not broken under its burden. When it sees the smoking wick, it knows how to hide multitudes of sins in such a way that the flame is not snuffed out. When it has triumphed over a multitude of sins, it knows how to hide that multitude and make everything ready to celebrate the sinner's reception, like the father of the prodigal son who stood with open arms, waiting for the one who had gone astray, forgetting everything and causing him, too, to forget it all, thus once more hiding a multitude of sins. For love does not weep even over a multitude of sins, since to do so would mean to see them—but it hides the multitude of sins. And when sin resists, love becomes yet more manifold; it never grows tired of faithfully being so unequally harnessed, never tired of believing all things, hoping all things,

---

* James 5:20.

bearing all things. When sin hardens itself against love and wants to be rid of it, when it repays good will with abuse, mockery, and scorn, love does not repay abuse with abuse but blesses instead of cursing. When sin enviously hates love, when it wickedly tries to make love itself sin, it finds no guile in it but only prayer and admonition. But when prayer and admonition serve merely to inflame sin and become a new occasion for a multitude of sins, love is speechless but no less faithful; it sets about its saving work as faithfully as a woman, in the same way as a woman does, "without a word" (1 Peter 3:1). Sin thought it had achieved its aim, and that they would now go their separate ways—but, behold! love remained by its side. Sin wanted to repel love and force it to go a mile with it—but, behold! love went two. It struck love's right cheek—but, behold! love offered the other cheek, too. It took love's shirt—but, behold! love gave its cloak as well. Sin already senses its own powerlessness, it cannot hold out, it wants to tear itself free, it wounds love as deeply as it can, since even love, it thinks, cannot forgive more than seven times—but, behold! love can forgive seventy times seven, and sin grows tired of having to be forgiven more quickly than love grows tired of forgiving.

Yes, just as sin has the power to keep going until it has extracted every better feeling from a person, so is there a heavenly power that starves multitudes of sins out of a person. This power is the love that hides a multitude of sins.

Is it not so? Would we do better to praise a clever person who knew how to make a multitude of sins look even more dreadful? Should we not rather ask this clever person how he got to know all this? Indeed, if sin could persuade love that it was correct, then love would never be able to begin and would never achieve anything. But that is why love begins by hiding a multitude of sins and therefore ends where it began, by hiding a multitude of sins.

BLESSED IS THE ONE WHOSE SIN IS FORGIVEN, AND MORE
BLESSED THE LOVE THAT HIDES A MULTITUDE OF SINS.

LOVING THE INNOCENT AND THE GUILTY

Love hides a multitude of sins. If love had triumphed in the world, then the multitude of sins would indeed be hidden and everything would be perfected in love. If love's hosts were numerous in the world, if their numbers were equal to those of the enemy, then they could go to it, one to one. How, then, could love fail to triumph, since it is the stronger? But if, on the other hand, love's servants are but a little flock and each of them but a solitary person, will love really be able to hide a multitude of sins? And if we wanted to understand the apostolic word as speaking about something other than love's pious ignorance and its jealousy for its own cause, wouldn't it then be a beautiful but futile saying? Should we regard the apostolic saying as a piece of inspired folly and instead praise the clever person who says, "Life follows strict laws, and if love is a next-door neighbor to ungodliness in the hour of need, ungodliness gets no benefit from it"? Would the understanding just as reasonably concede the opposite, namely, that it is irrelevant to love if ungodliness lives next door? Will the understanding deny that the innocent must often suffer with the guilty in life? Let us interrogate the understanding.

An old pagan who, in pagan times, was renowned and praised for being a wise man was sailing in the same ship as an ungodly person. When the sea became perilous, the ungodly one raised his voice in prayer, but the wise man said to him, "Keep quiet, friend, for if heaven discovers that you are on board, the ship will go down." Is it, then, true that the guilty can bring about the downfall of the innocent? Isn't it rather the opposite? Perhaps the understanding merely lacks the courage to believe it, and while it is clever enough—comfortless as that is—to uncover all that is wretched in life, it lacks the heart to grasp

the power of love. Isn't that so? For the understanding always makes a
person timid and feeble-spirited, while love sets the spirit free, and it
is for that reason that everything an apostle says is free-spirited. What
would have happened on that ship if, instead of an ungodly person,
there had been a pious man, an apostle perhaps? Isn't that what, in
fact, happened? A pagan ship was once sailing from Crete and heading
toward Rome when it got into difficulties, and many days passed when
neither sun nor stars could be seen. On this ship was an apostle, Paul,
who stood forth and said to those on board, "Men, I exhort you to be
of good cheer, for not one soul will be lost."* Should ungodliness really
have greater power than love? Should the fact that an ungodly person is
on board have the power to affect how it is for others, while an apostle
has no such power? Doesn't the Lord rather say that the days of tribulation will be shortened for the sake of the elect?

Is it an unworthy idea of God to believe that love hides a multitude of sins? In all our talking and thinking, aren't we perhaps
forgetting that God in heaven is not stopped in His tracks by any
disappointment, that His thoughts are living and present, penetrating all things and judging the counsels of the heart? Would anyone
be right to remind us that if we wanted to praise love, we would do
better to limit ourselves to what is true by saying that it is beautiful
and lovely that love would like to hide a multitude of sins and turn
wrath aside, but it is going too far to say that love actually does hide a
multitude of sins? But haven't those who talk like that forgotten what
we do not forget: that love prays for others' sins? Haven't they forgotten that the prayer of the righteous can accomplish much?

When Abraham spoke privately with the Lord and prayed for
Sodom and Gomorrah, didn't he then hide a multitude of sins?† Or

---

* Acts 27:21–22.

† Genesis 18:23–33.

is the person who says that this prayer actually served as a reminder of a multitude of sins to be praised for their acuity? Such a one might say that Abraham's prayer hastened the judgment, just as his own life was already a judgment that, if it had any power to make a difference, would have made the judgment all the more fearful. But how did Abraham pray? Let us put it in human terms. Wasn't it as if he drew the Lord into his thought processes, bringing the Lord to forget the multitude of sins by counting the number of the righteous, whether there were fifty, forty, thirty, twenty, or just ten innocent people? Didn't Abraham then hide a multitude of sins? And doesn't the downfall of the city rather demonstrate the opposite or demonstrate anything other than the fact that there were not even ten innocent people in Sodom? Yet who was Abraham in comparison with an apostle, and what was his free-spiritedness in comparison with an apostle's?

A human life is so great that, if we have lived righteously, we will be set in judgment over angels; but more blessed is the love that hides a multitude of sins.

We have praised the power of love to hide a multitude of sins, and we have spoken as if speaking to those who are perfect. If some don't feel perfect, the discourse makes no distinctions. So let us one last time dwell on this love by looking at the image in which it is made visible to the soul. If looking at yourself in this mirror convinces you of how unlike it you are, if it is the same for all of us—the discourse makes no distinctions.

When the Scribes and Pharisees had taken a woman in flagrant sin, they took her to the Temple and brought her face to face with the Savior.* But Jesus bent down and wrote on the ground with His finger. He who knew all things also knew very well what the Scribes

---

* John 8:3–11.

and Pharisees knew before they told Him. The Scribes and Pharisees were quick to discover her guilt, which was easy to do, since her sin was flagrant. They also discovered another sin, the one they made themselves guilty of when they cunningly sought to snare the Lord. But Jesus bent down and wrote on the ground with His finger. Why did He bend down? Why did He write on the ground with His finger? Did He sit there like a judge, paying close attention to the prosecutor's speech, attentively bending over to note down the point of the charge so as not to forget it and to be able to judge with due severity? Was this woman's sin the only one that the Lord noted in writing? Or didn't He who wrote on the ground with His finger rather write so as to delete the charge and forget about it? There she stood, the sinful woman, surrounded by those who were perhaps more guilty than she was, yet who loudly accused her. But love bent down and didn't hear the accusation that went right over its head, carried away on the wind. It wrote with its finger to delete what it itself knew—for sin discovers a multitude of sins, but love hides a multitude of sins. Yes! Love hides even the multitude of sins to be found in sin's own eye, for by a single word the Lord silenced the Scribes and Pharisees, and no accuser was left, no one to condemn her. But Jesus said, "Nor do I condemn you. Go and sin no more—for punishment gives birth to new sins, but love covers a multitude of sins."

12

Love and Sin*

Epistle: 1 Peter 4:7–12.

THE NATURE OF APOSTOLIC SPEECH

Just as the content of an apostolic address makes it essentially different from every other human address, it is also different in many ways with respect to its form. In order to individualize its message, it does not command its listeners to stop or invite them to rest, nor does it command the speaker to stop or allow him to forget his work. An apostolic address speaks with concern, with ardor, burningly, aflame, altogether and utterly moved by the powers of the new life—calling, crying out, beckoning; its exclamations are forceful; it is brief, abrupt, and shakes the listener as it is itself shaken, as much by fear and trembling as by longing and a blessed expectation. In every part, it testifies to the powerful restlessness of the Spirit and the deep impatience of the heart. How should one who is running find time for long discourses that would require him to stand still? How should the one who is striving to become all things to all people find time for

---

* From Niels Jørgen Cappelørn et al., eds., *Søren Kierkegaards Skrifter*, vol. 5 (Copenhagen: Gad, 1998), pp. 78–86.

long-winded reflections, since they would slow him down in taking up his spiritual weapons? How should the one who is steering under hope's full sail toward what is perfect find any time for human complexification?

But if an apostolic address is always impatient, like a woman giving birth, there are two considerations in particular that inflame it yet more. One is the idea that the night is past and the day has broken, and that, since the night has been quite long enough, what is now needed is to make good use of the day. The other is the idea that the time is coming when one will no longer be able to work, for the days are numbered, the end is at hand, and the end of all things is drawing near.

The text that has been read also testifies to this apostolic ardor and begins with a "therefore," which, in the text of the apostolic letter, relates back to what has immediately preceded it: "The end of all things is drawing near." This saying not only explains this "therefore" but also what, humanly speaking, might perhaps need explaining in the text, since it goes on to show how different this apostolic impatience is from the overhastiness of a man who has got himself heated up about something. For doesn't it seem remarkable that the beautiful admonition to have an inward love for one another above all things and the accompanying and so significant word of comfort, "love hides a multitude of sins," are directly followed by the apparently arbitrary admonition to "practice hospitality ungrudgingly"? And yet it is precisely this admonition that proves the apostle's authority and wisdom. If it was a man who had got himself heated up by saying that "the end of all things is drawing near," would he have added an admonition like this? Wouldn't it be self-evident that it had become superfluous? For wouldn't the point of what he was saying be to empty people out of their houses, so there wouldn't be anyone left who needed a house, and, if there were, there wouldn't be any shortage to choose from? But an apostle is not impatient in this way, and his restlessness is higher than all human composure. The apostle loves his congregation too much to pusillanimously keep quiet about the terrible fact that the end of all things is drawing near, but, on the other hand, he knows how to straightaway call the congregation back to order and in such a way as to make them forget their terror, as if everything was peaceful and secure and there were the kind of opportunities one might wish for to prove one's love to the neighbor in life's ordinary circumstances. Talking about the fact that the end is drawing near is therefore no fruitless storm cloud that goes around causing confusion everywhere but a kind of anxiety that clears the air and makes everyone milder and more inward and more loving and quicker to purchase the opportune moment—but also strong enough not to be wiped out by the thought that the opportune moment had passed. The apostle who is speaking is not someone intoxicated by dreams but someone who thinks and speaks soberly.

But "the end of all things is drawing near." This is a terrifying saying, even in the mouth of a light-minded person, not to mention on the lips of an apostle. Peter therefore also adds a word of comfort that is strong enough to overcome the anxiety: "Love hides a multitude of sins." But perhaps there's no need for this? Perhaps the end of all things means it's all over? Is there any hiding place other than the one offered to everyone, to the just and to the unjust? Are not those who lie in the bosom of the earth well hidden and in safekeeping? Might anyone fail to understand the apostle on this point, because he does not explicitly name the day on which the question of such a love will be asked? Or have both words of terror and words of love lost their meaning, because the end of all things didn't come about in the way that had been anticipated? Is an apostle an idle fellow who has the power merely to predict the end of all things in general without it concerning either himself or anyone in particular and not even to do so in such a way as to satisfy the curious? No—surely, what was uppermost in his mind was the fact that the end of all things was near also meant that his and his congregation's days were numbered.

And, in fact, this really did happen both to the apostle and to his congregation, for it is something that repeats itself continuously from one generation to another, and what happens next is also repeated— for every human being must die and come to Judgment. But armor is needed also on Judgment Day, and it is this, and its perfection, that the apostle is describing. For this armor is love, the one thing that will not be done away with, the one thing that remains with a person throughout life, that remains in death, and that will triumph in the Judgment. For love is not like a deceitful friend who first entices you and then stays with you only so as to be able to mock you. No, love abides with us, and when everything grows confused, when our thoughts accuse us, when our anxieties rise up to declare us guilty, then love faces them down and says to us, "Be patient. I shall remain with you and bear witness for you, and my testimony will yet over-come these confusions." In fact, even if love led you astray, even if it was afterward unable to acquit you, it would nevertheless say, "Will I leave you in the hour of need? No. Even if everyone abandoned you, and even if you abandoned yourself, I, who led you astray, will abide with you, and I can comfort you by the fact that it was I who did it." Imagine if it were not so. What power would then be able to get someone to venture such terrifying things as love does? And how terrible would it be if love did not understand how to explain itself and make itself understood by the one concerned, even if no one else understood it?

So let us consider the apostolic saying more closely. The apostle is speaking to those who are imperfect, for how should someone who is perfect have a multitude of sins that need to be hidden! But those who are imperfect, those who are crushed—those he comforts with the thought that love hides a multitude of sins. This is not to light-mindedly falsify what the apostle is saying, nor is it to cleverly deceive ourselves and betray what is being said by implying that those who love are perfect. Those who do not see in themselves a multitude of sins that need to be hidden will have no use for the saying. Nor will those who do not let themselves be comforted by it have any benefit from it. For the comfort consists precisely in this: that the same heart that contains a multitude of sins can also be love's dwelling place, and this love has the power to hide a multitude of sins.

Let us, then, seek the comfort that the apostle offers by thinking *how love hides a multitude of sins.*

LOVE AND CONSCIOUSNESS OF SIN

But how is this possible? Isn't it precisely love that leads a person to realize how multitudinous their sins are? Hasn't it often come to pass that people have lived lightly and without a care in youthful opti-mism without becoming conceited about their own perfection but also without feeling themselves burdened or brought to a halt by the consciousness of what would make life difficult—until love took hold of them? How they had been living previously didn't seem so good, then, since love—in so many ways—had discovered their imperfec-tions and weaknesses. And were those who took a rational approach to life any better off? They despised the light-mindedness of youth and, instead, kept a watch on themselves and strove to get rid of their failings. Thanks to this striving, they also acquired a kind of self-satisfaction. They were unafraid of being tested by rational argu-ment, they saw honor as their due, and they challenged the world to do its worst—but then love took them in its sights, and, see, having lifted their heads so proudly and subjected others to their gaze, they now had to lower their eyes, because they had discovered a multitude of sins. In this way, those who were able to endure reason's rigorous judgment could not bear the mildness of love. But this is not how it was with the righteous. They were strict on themselves and didn't want to be like others. They knew that those who want to be constant must work hard and renounce much, but they also knew that they had triumphed in this fight, that they had gained insight into the wisdom that there is righteousness in heaven, for they considered themselves righteous. Then love looked down on them, and, see, those who had comforted themselves with their ability to give each their due, to give to humanity what is humanity's right, and to God what is God's, those who already in this life looked forward to going through their accounts on the Day of Judgment now discovered a multitude of sins and were incapable of reckoning up even a thousandth of them.

So it is not just that love can thus, in a single moment, discover what has been hidden. No—it is as if love increased the multitude of sins still to come. For, because love had aroused their self-concern, what such people had so lightly mastered when they were full of self-confidence now seemed difficult to them. Where they had previously had no intimation of temptation, they were now tempted, and they felt a fear and trembling they had never before known. And it was easy for them to be assured as to the veracity of this, since the temptation vanished as soon as they once more became convinced of their own righteousness.

HOW LOVE HIDES SINS

Is it, then, possible that the same power that discovered a multitude of sins, the same power that pours love's concerns into a human heart, almost multiplying the multitude—is it possible that this same power can hide them in the same person? But what use would it be if it didn't? What is love, after all? Is it a nighttime dream that comes in one's sleep? Is it a kind of daze in which everything is forgotten? Should we think contemptuously of love by imagining that it is in such ways that it hides a multitude of sins? If that were so, then we would do better to stick with youth's light-mindedness or manly self-examination or human self-righteousness. Is wisdom to be bought, understanding to be bought, peace of mind to be bought, the blessedness of heaven to be bought, and life itself to be bought with the pangs of birth—but love to know no birth pains?

Love is no dream, but if we insisted on calling it that, then we would do better to say that its first pangs are a restless and anxious dream that finishes with an awakening to the love that hides a multitude of sins. Because love takes all. It takes a person's perfection, and if someone wants to hold on to this, then love is hard on them. But it also takes a person's imperfection, their sin, and their sorrow. It takes a person's strength but also their suffering—for what terrible sufferings are not hidden by love and made to be as if they didn't exist in the light of love's joy over having saved another soul? But what love takes, it hides—and when it takes all, it hides it all; and, having taken all, it gives something in return that has a power of concealment that passes all understanding. Human beings have often thought that there were other means capable of taking away and thereby concealing what they wanted to have hidden. However, a pagan of ancient times already said that a person cannot ride away from sorrow, since it sits behind him on the horse. These words are often repeated, as if they offered deep insight into the human heart. And yet, what if that ancient pagan riding though life with sorrow behind him on the horse had had no need to look behind him? Love doesn't look back—for how might the eye that loves have time to look at what is behind it, since, if it did, it would in that same moment lose sight of its object? Or how might ears that love have time to listen to accusations, since, if they did, they would in that moment cease to hear love's voice? And if the eye did squint backward or the ear listen out, then they would reveal a petty heart—and love would not be to blame for this, since it makes love angry. For those who want to think of their own perfection do not love, and those who want to keep account of their imperfections do not love. Indeed, if they believed themselves to be so imperfect as to be excluded from love, then they would reveal the fact that they didn't love, for they would be counting their imperfections as if they could weigh in the balance against perfection. But love takes all, and those who exclude themselves will either be pleased with themselves but displeased with love or will grieve over themselves and still not take pleasure in love.

THE COURAGE OF LOVE

But to love someone in this way requires the courage to want to love. For the secret of earthly love is that it bears the impress of God's love; otherwise it would be merely stupid or a shallow form of flattery, as if one person were so perfect in relation to another that he was able to arouse such anxiety or really take everything from the other. For to love God in such a way calls for a humble free-spiritedness, since the love of God awakens in a person like a wailing newborn baby and not like the child who knows its mother and smiles at the sight of her. But when the love of God wants to hold fast to the Lord, the enemy rises against it in terrifying ways, and the power of sin is mighty in engendering anxiety. But love does not shut its eyes in the hour of danger. Instead, as an old hymn puts it, it offers itself in order to press

THROUGH THE DARTS OF SIN TO THE REST OF PARADISE.

And the farther off it is when it catches sight of the darts of sin, the more terrifying they appear. Yet the closer it presses to them, the less it sees them, and when they have all lodged in its breast, wounded as it is, it doesn't see them anymore but only sees love and the blessedness of paradise.

When Jesus was one day sitting at table in the house of a Phari-see, a woman came into the house.* A woman would not be invited to such a dinner, this one least of all—for the Pharisees knew that she was a sinner. If nothing else had been able to terrify her and stop her in her tracks, the Pharisees' proud contempt, their silent ill will, and their righteous indignation might well have frightened her off: "But she stood behind Jesus at his feet, weeping, and began to wash his feet with her tears and dry them with her hair, to kiss his feet and anoint them with ointment." There was a moment of anxiety—but what she suffered in solitude, her grief, the accusation in her own breast, was yet more terrifying. It was easy to see, because it was in agreement with what could be seen in the Pharisees' expressions. And yet she went on and, as she moved against the foe, she moved herself to peace—and when she had found rest at Christ's feet, she lost herself in love's work. As she wept over it all, she finally forgot what she had been weeping about at the beginning, and her tears of repentance turned to tears of adoration. Her many sins were forgiven, because she loved much.

There have been those who, having wasted their lives in the ser-vice of pleasure, finally lost themselves and scarcely knew themselves anymore. This is the devious and dreadful deceit of pleasure: that it brings about self-deception, leaving only a light-minded, transient sense of one's own existence, presuming to deceive God's own knowl-edge of the creature. But this woman was granted the grace of, as it were, weeping herself out of herself and weeping herself into love's repose—for much is forgiven those who love much. And this is love's blessed deceit, "that the one who is forgiven much, loves much," as if to need forgiving for much was an expression of love's perfection.

---

* Luke 7:37–50.

LOVE AND JUDGMENT

Yet even if love were capable of diverting an accusing gaze away from the multitude of sins, so that, lost in love, a person no longer saw them (because love was hiding them)—is that person, then, saved forever? Is there nothing that can stop her in her tracks and suddenly bring to mind what love was hiding? Is there no external judgment to which human beings must submit? And, in this case, does love have the same power as before, so that not even the judge discovers the multitude of sins, because love is hiding them? But can a judge be deceived? Doesn't he pierce every veil and reveal all? Can a judge be bribed? Is he not rather unbendable in pursuing the demands of justice? Can the world's judgment be mistaken? Offer it your love—but that doesn't stop you being guilty; bring it the best feelings of your heart—but that doesn't stop you being guilty; offer it your tears of repentance—and justice demands its own righteousness.

But love's judgment is also incorruptible. Offer it gold, and it will scorn you. Offer it power and might, and it will belittle you. Offer it all the glory of the world, and it will judge you for loving the glory of the world. Proclaim your marvelous deeds, and it will judge you because they were not done in love. For judgment demands what judgment demands, and the world's judgment demands what belongs to the world, but love's judgment turns its eye from what is lacking. Love's judgment demands what belongs to love, for the one who judges demands, and the one who demands is seeking, but the one "who hides sin's multiplicity seeks love" (Proverbs 17:9), and the one who finds love hides the multitude of sins—for the one who finds what he is seeking conceals what he did not seek.

Isn't this apostolic saying a comfort, then, giving a spirit of freedom to judgment? Isn't it just the comfort that's needed, because it passes all understanding? The understanding is great in its power to recall everything, and it regards love as foolish in hiding a multitude of sins. But do we want to rob ourselves of comfort by using the understanding to measure love and divide it up as a recompense for particular sins only and, thus, continue in our sins? Do we want to exclude ourselves from love, for when we are within love, who is there to accuse us? Or is it not the same love that hid sin's multiplicity from a person who, for love's sake, hides a multitude of sins? Indeed, even if love had not completely triumphed in a person, even if anxiety revealed what her love was not strong enough to hide, love will nevertheless come to the aid of the love that is in her on the Day of Judgment, chasing away the fear and hiding a multitude of sins.

When Jesus sat one day at table in the house of a Pharisee, a woman entered into the same house. She was bowed down, for she bore a multitude of sins. The world's judgment on her was clearly legible in the faces of the Pharisees, nor was it mistaken: her grief and her tears hid nothing but revealed it all, and there was nothing to discover but a multitude of sins. Yet she did not seek the world's judgment, "but she stood behind Him, at his feet, weeping." Then love discovered what the world had hidden—the love that was in her, and since this love had not yet triumphed in her, the Savior's love came to her aid, so that "the one to whom five hundred denarii had been remitted will love most." He made the love that was in her stronger, so that it was able to hide the multitude of her sins—yet this love was already there, since "her many sins were forgiven because she loved much."

Blessed are those whose hearts testify that they have loved much; blessed are those of whom God's all-knowing Spirit bears witness that they have loved much; they have comfort now and to come, for love hides a multitude of sins.

13

Learn from a Woman*

Luke 7:37–50.

That a woman is portrayed as a teacher or as an exemplar of devotion
will surprise no one who knows that devotion or godliness is essentially womanly. Even if "women are to keep silent in the assembly"†
and in that respect should not teach, keeping silent before God is
precisely a characteristic of true godliness, and this, then, is what you
are to learn from this woman.

It is therefore from a woman that you also learn a faith that is
humble in relation to the extraordinary, a humble faith that does not
unbelievingly or doubtingly ask, "Why?" "What for?" or "How is it
possible?" but humbly believes, as Mary did when she said, "Behold,
I am the Lord's handmaiden."‡ She *said* it, but, take note, to say it
is really to keep silent. It is from a woman that you learn the right
way to listen to the Word: from Mary, who, although she "did not

---

* From Niels Jørgen Cappelørn et al., eds., *Søren Kierkegaards Skrifter*, vol. 12 (Copenhagen: Gad, 2008), pp. 263–273.
† 1 Corinthians 14:33–34.
‡ Luke 1:38.

understand what was said to her," nevertheless "kept all these words in her heart."* She didn't begin by demanding to have it explained but silently kept the Word in the right place, for it is in the right place when the Word, the good seed, "is preserved in a holy and honest heart."† It is from a woman that you learn the quiet, deep, godly sorrow that keeps silent before God: from Mary, for, although it did indeed happen as had been prophesied that a sword pierced her heart, she despaired neither at the prophecy nor at what happened. It is from a woman you learn how to care for the one thing needful: from Mary, Lazarus's sister, who silently sat at Christ's feet with what her heart had chosen, namely, the one thing needful.

You can similarly learn from a woman how to sorrow rightly over sin: from the sinful woman whose sins have long, long since ceased to be and have been forgotten, but who is herself eternally unforgettable. How could it be otherwise than that one should learn from a woman in this matter? For in comparison with women, men have many thoughts, although it is questionable whether in this regard it is entirely to their advantage, since they also have many half-thoughts in addition. Men are certainly stronger than the weaker sex, than women, and are better equipped for fending for themselves, but, once again, woman has just one thing—one thing—yes, it is precisely this that is her element: oneness. She has one wish, not many wishes—no, just one wish, but she has committed herself entirely to it. She has one thought, not many thoughts—no, just one thought, but, thanks to the power of passion, it is prodigiously powerful. She has one sorrow, not many sorrows—no, just one sorrow, but it lies so deep that just this one sorrow is indeed infinitely greater than many; just one sorrow, but one that is also so deeply internalized: sorrow over her sin, for she is a sinful woman.

---

* Luke 2:50–51.
† Luke 8:15.

For what is seriousness? Men may well be more serious thinkers, but in relation to feeling, passion, and decision, and in relation to not obstructing oneself and one's decision-making with thoughts, resolutions, and conclusions or not disappointing oneself by coming to the edge of making a decision without actually doing so, women are more serious. But especially in a godly sense, and still more especially with regard to sorrowing over sin, being serious means being capable of making a decision.

So let us then turn our attention to the sinful woman and to what we can learn from her.

First, we can learn to become like her by being indifferent to everything else on account of an unconditional sorrow over our sins, yet in such a way that one thing remains important, unconditionally important: finding forgiveness.

My listeners, we see careworn people often enough in life, anxious people who now worry about this and now about that and sometimes about all sorts of things at one and the same time. We see people who are anxious without really knowing what they are anxious about. But rarely enough do we see someone who cares about just one thing and cares so unconditionally for this one thing that everything else becomes indifferent to them.

Yet it is to be seen, even if it is not usual. I have seen, as perhaps you, too, have, someone who was unlucky in love and to whom everything then became indifferent, whether forever or for a long time. But this is not sorrow over sin. Or there are those whose bold plans are ruined all at a stroke by some unexpected obstacle and to whom everything then became indifferent, whether forever or for a long time. But this is not sorrow over sin. Or there are those who struggled with time when it became long, and who struggled for a long time; they endured and kept on enduring, even till yesterday—but today the power of renewal failed them, and they sank down and everything became indifferent to them. But this is not sorrow over sin. Or there are those whose destiny it is to be heavy-hearted, and, being heavy-hearted, they observe everything as alien to them and indifferent and, just as the air can sometimes be so light that one cannot breathe, everything is too light for them, because their hearts are heavy. But nor is this sorrow over sin. And there are those whose terrifying lust for life leads them to heap up transgression on transgression, year after year, who spend most of their time sinning, until they reach the point at which they are burned out and everything becomes indifferent to them. But it is certainly true to say that this is not sorrow over sin: there were plenty of sins, but it is not sorrow over sin. There is one thing that is entirely commonplace, and you can find it in each and every one of us; you can find it in yourself as I find it in myself: sin and sins. But something that is rarer is sorrow over sin.

Yet I have seen, as perhaps you, too, have, someone who unconditionally sorrowed over one thing, over his sin. It followed him everywhere, or, rather, it hounded him—during the day and in his dreams at night, at work and when he vainly sought relaxation after work, in solitude and when he vainly sought to be distracted by socializing with others; it wounded him from behind when he turned toward the future, and it wounded him in front when he turned toward the past; it taught him to wish for death and to fear life and, then again, to fear death and to wish for life, so that without taking his life it took his life from him and made him as fearful of himself as of a ghost. It made him indifferent to everything, absolutely everything—but, note well, this kind of sorrow is despair. There is one thing that is entirely commonplace, and you can find it in each and every one of us; you can find it in yourself as I find it in myself: sin and sins. But a true sorrow over one's sin is something very rare—which is why it is indeed requisite that every Sunday, the opening prayer in the church service bids us "to learn to sorrow over our sins." All honor to those in whom such true sorrow over sin is found, so that everything else becomes infinitely indifferent to them, for this is merely the negative expression of what gives them strength—namely, that there is one thing that has become unconditionally important to them. And that everything else has become unconditionally indifferent may be a mortal sickness, but it is one that is nevertheless so far from being unto death that it is precisely to life, for life is to be found in the one thing that has become unconditionally important to them—that is, finding forgiveness. All honor to them, they are very rarely to be seen. But, my listeners, we often enough see people for whom what is unimportant has become important, and even more often do we see people for whom all sorts of things have become important, but rarely do we see someone for whom just one thing is important, and still more rarely do we see someone of whom it can be said that the one thing that she regards as unconditionally important really is in truth the one really important thing.

Pay attention to the sinful woman, then, so as to learn from her.

Everything had become indifferent to her, and she didn't care about anything except her sin, or, rather, every other care she had was as if nonexistent, because her sorrow had become unconditional. This, if you like, is how there is a blessing tied to having just one sorrow: that one is no longer troubled by anything else, and this is a mark of having just one sorrow.

That is how it was with the sinful woman. But how different she was from what we usually see in life! If we (that is, not someone free from sin or guilt, for none of us is) also have other worries and are anxiously bowed down by them, then we will perhaps be confused and count this sense of being weighed down as being anxious over our sin. We seem to think that all that is required is that a person should be anxious, whereas what is demanded is that we *ought to* be anxious about our *sin* and ought *not to be* anxious about anything else. But we get confused and do not notice that if it was our sin we were sorrowing over, let alone sorrowing over it to the exclusion of everything else, we would not even feel our other anxieties at all and would use the opportunity to express a true sorrow over sin by the fact that we bear these anxieties more lightly. Perhaps we don't understand it like this and rather wish to be absolved from our other worries in order to be able simply to sorrow over our sin. Ah! But then we scarcely understand what it is that we are wanting and will be more likely to experience the whole matter as much too demanding. For when God executes a severe punishment on a person by letting him experience the consequences of his sin, it is sometimes as if He acted like this or said to Himself, "I shall free this person of every other anxiety. Everything shall smile on him, everything will be compliant, everything he puts his hand to will succeed, so that he will all the less succeed in forgetting but will rather sense all the more strongly what really troubles him." So the excuse that is frequently heard—that one has too many other worries to be able to sorrow over one's sin in the right way—just isn't true. No, these "other worries" are precisely the opportunity for expressing genuine sorrow over one's sin by bearing these other worries more lightly. These "other worries" do not sharpen but ease our burden, since they give no scope for thought to go astray but instantly set us a task with regard to expressing sorrow over our sins—namely, the task of bearing these other worries more patiently, more humbly, and more lightly.

Everything else had become indifferent to the sinful woman, everything temporal, earthly, worldly: honor, respect, good times, the future, her family, friends, and how others judged her. And she bore all her worries, whatever we call them, lightly, almost as if they were nothing, for only one thing unconditionally occupied her in her anxiety—her sin. It was this she was sorry about and not its consequences (the shame, the dishonor, the humiliation); no, she did not confuse the sickness with the remedy. Ah! How rare is the person who would be willing to accept the forgiveness of sins on condition of being willing to undergo the punishment of becoming entirely revealed to others, so that they could see right into the soul and all its secret guilt! Ah! How rare it is that someone becomes so unconditionally indifferent. Instead, the sin for which we condemn ourselves, and which we pray to God to forgive us, is perhaps the very sin that we might conceal with a neurotically anxious fastidiousness, in case anyone else gets to see it.

To the sinful woman, on the contrary, everything had become indifferent: the hostility of the situation, the objections of those at the feast, the cold superiority or cruel mockery of the Pharisees. Indeed, the place she had come to was like an invulnerable castle, secured precisely against the possibility of her gaining admittance—if it had not been the case that everything else had become indifferent to her. Perhaps no other woman, no woman who had not been conscious of being a sinner and therefore would not have faced so great a danger, would have dared to do it, but she dared it, she, to whom everything had become indifferent.

But no, that is not quite accurate. She dared to do it because one thing had become unconditionally important to her: finding forgiveness. It was there that it was to be found, and so she dared to do it. This is what got her up on her feet and drove her forward, while the fact that everything else had become indifferent to her was what caused her to scarcely notice the opposition. You will say that it was "the courage born of despair." Maybe, but, in truth, she was very far from being in despair—otherwise the person to whom one thing is unconditionally important (when that one thing is the unconditionally important thing) would be in despair. She had the strength of despair—this was what made her indifferent to everything and stronger than the hostility of the situation, so strong that she did not sink beneath the weight of shame, did not flee the mockery; she, however, the one who had such strength, was not in despair but had faith. And so she entered in, indifferent to everything else. But her unconditional indifference aroused no attention and no fuss, for she believed and was therefore so quiet, so reserved, so humble, so insignificant in her infinite indifference to everything that she attracted no attention to herself as she made her entrance. Nor was expressing her absolute indifference to everything the least bit important to her, since only one thing was infinitely important to her: finding forgiveness. Yet if this one thing had not been important to her to such a degree as to make everything else unconditionally indifferent, then she would not have found the way into that Pharisee's house, where forgiveness was to be found.

Next you can learn from the sinful woman what she herself understood: that, with regard to finding forgiveness, she herself was able to do absolutely nothing.

If we consider her behavior from first to last, we have to say that she did absolutely nothing.

She did not wait to go to that house where she would find the Savior and salvation; she did not wait until she felt herself worthy. No, for then she would have long remained absent and perhaps never come there or gone in. She resolved to go straightaway, unworthy as she was—the mere feeling of unworthiness drove her in such a way that the decision to go was instantaneous. Thus, she herself did nothing or understood that there was nothing she could do. Can this be described more strongly than by saying that it was precisely the feeling of unworthiness that determined what she should do?

And so, she makes ready to go but not by thinking about what she is going to say or anything like that. Oh, no: she buys an alabaster jar with ointment to take and so follows the scriptural injunction: "When you fast, anoint your head and wash your face, so that no one shall see that you are fasting but only your Father who is in secret."* Thus, she goes festively to the feast; and, truly, who could guess what her errand is or what her going into that house means to her! Yet she entirely understands that she herself can do nothing. Instead of giving herself over to self-torment, as if she might thereby become more well-pleasing to God and get closer to Him, instead, she *wastes*—that's what Judas thought—she *frivolously* wastes—that's what those who torment themselves would think—she wastes what in an earthly sense belongs to the festivities: she takes with her an alabaster jar with ointment, festally requisite at such a feast.

She enters in. She is entirely aware that she herself can do nothing. Therefore, she doesn't give herself up to the passion of self-accusation by her cries, as if that might have brought salvation closer or might have made her more well-pleasing. She does not exaggerate—and, in truth, no one is able to indict her on that account. No, she does nothing. She is silent. She weeps.

She weeps. Perhaps someone will say that she did, then, do something. But, no, she can't hold her tears back—and if it had struck her that these tears might be regarded as doing something, then she would even have been able to hold them back.

And so, she weeps. She has sat herself down at Christ's feet, and there she sits, weeping. But let us not forget the festivities any more than she has forgotten them, precisely because she is entirely aware that with regard to finding forgiveness, she is able to do absolutely nothing. Let us not forget the festivities—or the ointment that she has brought with her. She does not forget about it and understands it as her proper task to anoint Christ's feet with ointment and to dry them with her hair, weeping.

---

* Matthew 6:17–18.

If you do not already know, can you guess what this picture means? Indeed, since she doesn't say anything, it is in a certain sense impossible to do so. And, for her, anointing His feet (as required by the festivities) and weeping (which corresponds to something entirely different) all flow into one. But she is the only one who is really concerned by what it means, she who is entirely aware that she herself is able to do absolutely nothing with regard to finding forgiveness—and He who, as she fully understands, is unconditionally able to do everything.

Then she hears Him speaking with those who are at the feast. She fully understands that He is talking about her when He speaks about the difference between sinners, about how one had owed five hundred denarii and another fifty, and that it is reasonable that if both are forgiven, the first will love more than the second. She well understands how both the one case and the other—God be praised—apply to her, but she also understands entirely that she herself is able to do nothing. Therefore, she does not mix in the conversation, she keeps silent, keeping her eyes to herself or on the task she is occupied in, anointing His feet, washing them with her hair, weeping. Oh, what a powerful and true expression for doing nothing—to be as if absent even though one is there, even though one is oneself what is being talked about.

Next she hears Him say, "Her many sins are forgiven her." She hears it, but now He says more: he adds, "*Because* she loved much." I assume that she didn't hear this at all, for perhaps it would have troubled her that there was a "because," and that it was attributed to her, and perhaps it would also have made love anxious to be praised like that. I therefore assume that she didn't hear it or perhaps heard it but misunderstood what was said and believed that He had said "because He loved much." Then what had been said would have meant that His infinite love, because it was so infinite, had caused her many sins to be forgiven, something she could fully have understood, so much so that it was as if she herself had said it.

Then she returns home, a silent character throughout the whole performance. Who could guess what this occasion has meant to her, this occasion when she had gone with sin and sorrow and gone away with forgiveness and joy?

So then, what does this woman, from whom we are to learn, do? Answer: nothing. She does absolutely nothing. She practices the high, rare, extremely difficult, and genuinely womanly art of doing absolutely nothing or of understanding that with regard to finding forgiveness one can oneself do nothing. "How easy!" Indeed—if it were not for the fact that the easiness of it is the difficulty. It is true that the one who conquers himself is greater than the one who takes a city,* and, in relation to God and in relation to receiving the forgiveness of one's sins, the one who stirs up a commotion in order to do something is not as great as the one who can become entirely silent in order in godly fear to let God do everything, entirely aware that in this regard one can do absolutely nothing, and that everything, everything a human being might be able to do—whether it is the holiest or the most astonishing act—is in this regard nothing. Even if it were in other respects something that, humanly speaking, is really good and not the miserable self-deception of a treacherous heart, it would be so far from contributing in the remotest way to earning the forgiveness of sins that it would rather be the occasion for a new debt of gratitude toward the infinite grace for having furthermore let it come off successfully. No, indeed! What a miserable aberration or fearful presumption if anyone even remotely fell to thinking like that! No, with regard to earning the forgiveness of sins, or being *before* God, a human being can do absolutely nothing. And how might it even be

---

* Proverbs 16:32.

possible, since even in relation to the least thing that a human being can do, we can, humanly speaking, do nothing without God!

Finally we learn from the sinful woman—not directly from her, indeed, but by thinking about our circumstances in comparison with hers—that we have a comfort she did not have.

Perhaps someone will say that it was easy for her to believe in the forgiveness of her sins, since it was told her from Christ's own mouth. What, over many centuries, has been experienced by thousands and thousands, what has been handed down from one generation to another through many generations as a matter of experience, "that one word from Him heals for endless ages"—how could she not have felt it and experienced it when she heard the healing word from His own mouth?

To be sure, a rather widespread misunderstanding prevails on this point, because we are deceived by the imagination into not seeing the matter as if it were really present and therefore forget that precisely the fact of being contemporary with Christ made it, in a certain sense, all the more difficult. But, self-evidently, those who, despite all the difficulties and dangers, really believed did have an advantage over all later generations in hearing the word from Christ's own mouth. It is not as it is when we read about it, reading how in general there is forgiveness of sins in Christ, for if I heard it said to me by Christ, then it would be impossible to have any doubt that He meant me, that He said it in order for me to receive the gracious forgiveness of my sins, just as it would be impossible to doubt that it was Christ's word.

But there is another side to the matter. There is a comfort that, while Christ lived, didn't yet exist, and that He Himself was unable to offer anyone. This is the comfort of his atoning death as the pledge that our sins are forgiven us. In the flesh, Christ was above all an exemplar to His contemporaries. Even though He was the Savior and His life a life of suffering in such a way that it can be said that even during His earthly life He bore the sins of the world, what was most striking was that He lived as an exemplar. And, since Christianity is not the kind of teaching that is the same whoever proclaims it but is as the one who proclaims it and is true according to the truth of the life of the one who proclaims it, no human being could keep up with Him: all must fall away, even the apostles.

But then He dies, and His death alters everything, infinitely. It is not as if His death did away with the meaning of what He had previously exemplified, but His death brings about the infinite comfort, the infinite advance payment that enables the seeker to make a beginning: this is that infinite satisfaction has been made, so that the doubter and the renunciant are offered the highest pledge—none more reliable could possibly be found—that Christ died to save us, that Christ's death is the atonement and makes full satisfaction. The sinful woman did not have this comfort. She heard from His own mouth that her many sins were forgiven her, that is true, but she did not have the comfort of His death as those who came afterward did. Imagine that at a later time, the sinful woman might have been afflicted by doubt as to whether her many sins had really been forgiven her. If she were no longer able to hear it directly from Christ Himself, she would have found rest in thinking she could hear Christ say, "Just believe it, for you heard it from my own mouth." But when those who live many centuries after Christ are afflicted by doubt as to whether their sins, too, have been forgiven them, they will find comfort in thinking they can hear Christ say to them, "Just believe it, I have given my life to earn the forgiveness of your sins, so just believe it, a greater assurance is impossible." Christ could indeed say to His contemporaries, "I shall give myself up as a sacrifice for the sin of the world and also for yours," but isn't it easier to believe this when He has done it and has given Himself up? Is it a greater comfort when He says that He will do it or when He has done it? No love is greater than this—than that one lays down his life for another. But when is it easiest to believe it, and when is the comfort greatest: when the lover says, "I will do it," or when he has done it? No, it is only when he has done it that doubt is impossible, as impossible as can possibly be, and it is only when Christ has been sacrificed as the atoning sacrifice that there is a comfort that makes it impossible to doubt the forgiveness of sins, as impossible as can possibly be, for it is a comfort that is only given those who believe.

14

A Parable of Love*

PRAYER

*Lord Jesus Christ, in order that we might rightly pray to you for every-
thing, we begin by praying for one thing: help us to love you much, increase our love, inflame it, and purify it. Such a prayer you will hear, for
you are not love in the sense of being the object of love in such a way as
to be indifferent to whether anyone loved you or not, for that would be
cruel. Nor are you love in such a way as to stand in judgment, jealous of
who loves you and who does not, for that would be wrathful. No, that is
not how you are, for then you would also fill us with fear and anxiety—it
would be terrible to "come unto you," fearful "to remain in you"—nor
would you be that perfect love that casts out fear. No, mercifully, lovingly,
or in love, you are love in such a way as to love forth the love that loves you,
and to increase its love until it loves you much.*

"THEREFORE, I SAY TO YOU, HER MANY SINS ARE FORGIVEN
HER, BECAUSE SHE LOVED MUCH."†

---

* From Niels Jørgen Cappelørn et al., eds., *Søren Kierkegaards Skrifter*, vol. 11 (Copenhagen: Gad, 2006), pp. 273–280.
† Luke 7:47.

My listener, you know who is being talked about here: it is that woman who was called "a sinful woman." "When she learned that He was at table in the Pharisee's house, she brought an alabaster flask of ointment, and standing behind Him at His feet, weeping, she began to wet His feet with her tears and wiped them with the hair of her head, and kissed His feet, and anointed them with ointment."

Yes, she loved much. There are many opposed forces that oppose one another in life and death such that one of them will be annihilated if it draws near another. It is like that for the sinner, man or woman, who draws near to the Holy One and is revealed to Him in the light of His holiness. Night does not flee in greater terror from the day that will annihilate it, and if there are such things as ghosts, no spirit retreats in greater terror from the dawn than the sinner tremblingly withdraws before the Holy One, who, like the day, reveals all things. The sinner flees for as long as he can, and for as long as he can he seeks to evade this way that leads to death, this encounter with the light—and he is inventive in a truant's excuses and evasions and deceptions and explanations. But she loved much—and what is the strongest expression for loving much? It is to hate oneself—*she went in to encounter the Holy One.* She, a sinful woman! A woman! Modesty is what a woman needs most of all, she needs modesty more than life itself, and she would rather lose her life than lose her modesty. True enough, this modesty should have prevented her from sinning in the first place, but then it is also nevertheless true that when a woman returns to herself again, her modesty is all the stronger, crushing her and annihilating her. Perhaps it was this that made her journey toward annihilation easier, because she was already annihilated. And yet, humanly speaking, was there any chance of leniency? Even a sinner who has honestly admitted or knows within himself that he is annihilated might become lenient toward himself if he were to become revealed as he was in a face-to-face encounter with the Holy One—that is to say, he would be lenient to himself to the extent that he still nevertheless loved himself somewhat. But she—is there any leniency for her, any at all? No, there is no leniency. She hated herself: she loved much.

She went in to the Holy One in the house of the Pharisee, where many Pharisees had gathered, ready to judge her, also on account of her vanity, her sickening vanity—especially on the part of a woman— at shoving her way in with her sin; she who should have hidden herself from the eyes of all, in some hidden corner of the world. She might have wandered the whole world over and never found anywhere where she could encounter so severe a judgment as that which the proud Pharisees were waiting to pass in the house of the Pharisee. Moreover, there is perhaps no suffering so precisely calculated to torture a woman as the cruel mockery that the proud Pharisees were waiting to inflict on her in the house of the Pharisee. But she—is there, then, no compassion that she might be spared such cruelty? No, there is no compassion. She hated herself: she loved much.

She went in to the Holy One in the house of the Pharisee, *to the feast*. To the feast! It makes you tremble, and, trembling, you hesitate to follow her further. You can easily be convinced as to why it should make you tremble if you consider that all of this happened at a feast: not in a "house of mourning" but in a "house of festivity." A woman comes into a feast; she brings with her an alabaster flask with ointment—this is indeed in keeping with a feast. She sits at the feet of one of the guests—and weeps. This is not in keeping with a feast, and the truth is that this woman is a disruptive presence. But she herself, this sinful woman, did not find it disturbing. Certainly she did not refrain from trembling, but she did not draw back because of her trembling but went on into the feast—and to confession. She hated herself: she loved much.

Sin's heavy secrecy weighs on a person more heavily than any- thing else, except for the one thing that is still heavier: having to go to confession. The secrecy of sin is more fearful than any other kind of secrecy, except for the one thing that is still more fearful: owning up to it. Human compassion has therefore sympathetically discovered a way of soothing and supporting this difficult birth. For sinners are given the opportunity to confess their sin in a holy place, where everything is quiet and seriously solemn, and, within it, a yet more hidden part is reserved for such confession, where everything is as quiet as the grave and a lenient judgment is to be passed on the soul that is ready to die to the world. In the fact that the person who hears the confession is hidden, human compassion has found a way of easing the burden. Otherwise, having to see him might make it too heavy, too heavy for the sinner to unburden his conscience. Finally, human compassion even discovered that such confession wasn't even necessary, nor such a hidden confessor, and that confession need only be before God, who is in secret and who nevertheless knows all things, so that the confession could remain hidden within one. But at a feast—and a woman! A feast is no hidden, out-of-the-way place, nor is its light a half-light, nor is its mood like that of a graveyard, nor are those who are listening silent or invisible. No, if concealment and twilight and being out of the way and all of that help ease the way to confessing one's sin, a feast would be the cruelest place of all to do it in! Where is the cruel person who discovered this method, so that we might move Him with our prayers to show her some leniency? Nothing that cruelty ever invented is as cruel as this, but she was the one who discovered it, she alone, the sinful woman! Normally, the cruel tormentor is one person and the person who is tortured is another, but she herself discovered the torture, she was herself the cruel tormentor, she hated herself: she loved much.

Yes, she loved much. "She sat at Christ's feet, wet them with her tears, and wiped them with the hair of her head." What she is expressing is: I am capable of literally nothing; He is unconditionally capable of everything. But this is indeed what it is to love much. When one thinks that one is capable of achieving something, one may well love, but one doesn't love much, and to the extent that one thinks one can achieve more, one loves so much the less. She, on the other hand, loved much. She didn't say a single word, not even to vouch for herself. Ah! All too often such expressions are deceptive, and one needs to make a further affirmation that what one has vouched for is really so. She affirms nothing, she acts: she weeps, she kisses His feet. She does not think about how to staunch her tears—no, she has nothing to do but weep. She weeps, and it is not her eyes but His feet she dries with the hair of her head. She is capable of literally nothing, He of unconditionally everything: she loved much. Oh, eternal truth, that He was capable of unconditionally everything; oh, what an indescribable truth was in this woman; oh, what an indescribable power of truth was in this woman who so powerfully expressed powerlessness and being capable of literally nothing: she loved much.

Yes, she loved much. She sits weeping at His feet. She has entirely forgotten about herself, forgotten every thought that might inwardly disturb her; she is quite still, as still as the sick child that is quietened at its mother's breast where it cries itself out and forgets about itself. For it is no help to forget such thoughts and still to remember oneself: if one is to succeed, one must forget oneself—and that is why she is weeping, and as she weeps, she forgets herself. Oh, blessed tears that give the blessing of forgetfulness! She has entirely forgotten herself, forgotten her surroundings with everything there that might have disturbed her, for, since they were almost designed to remind her in fearful and painful ways about who she was, it would be impossible to forget such surroundings if one did not forget oneself. But she weeps, and as she weeps she forgets herself. Oh, blessed tears of self-forgetfulness, such that as she weeps she is not even once reminded of what she is weeping about, so completely has she forgotten herself. But the true expression for loving much is precisely to forget oneself completely. As long as one remembers oneself, one can indeed love, but one doesn't love much, and to the extent that one remembers oneself, one loves so much the less. She, however, has completely forgotten herself. But the greater the incentive that the moment offers to remember or think about oneself, if one nevertheless forgets oneself and thinks of the other, so much the more does one love.

It is like this in loving relationships between two people, even if these do not entirely resemble what is being talked about here, although they can nevertheless throw some light on it. Those who, in the moment when they are most preoccupied with themselves and in the moment that is most precious to them, forget themselves and think about the other love much. The one who is himself hungry but forgets about himself and gives the little he has (which is only enough for one person) to another loves much. The one who is in peril but who forgets about himself and gives the other the only life belt loves much. So too, in the case of those who, in the moment when everything within them and everything around them not only reminds them of themselves but forces them against their will to remember themselves—when they nevertheless forget themselves they love much, as she did.

"She sits at his feet, anoints them with ointment, dries them with the hairs of her head, kisses them, and weeps." She says nothing, so she is in no way what she says. Rather, she is what she does not say, or what she does not say is what she is, she *is* a sign, like an image: she has forgotten speech and language and the restlessness of thoughts and, what is even more restless, this self: she has forgotten herself, she, the lost one who is now lost in her Savior, lost in resting at His feet, like an image. And it is almost as if the Savior Himself saw her and saw the matter like this, as if she was not an actual person but an image. It is certainly in order to heighten the impact of the application of His words on those who are present that He does not talk to her: He does not say, "Your many sins are forgiven you, because you loved much," but he talks *about* her, saying, "Her many sins are forgiven her, because she loved much." Even though she is present, it is almost as if she is absent; it is almost as if He has turned her into a picture, a parable; it is almost as if He has said, "Simon, I have something to say to you. Once upon a time there was a woman, a sinful woman. When one day the Son of Man sat at table in the house of a Pharisee, she also entered in. The Pharisees mocked and judged her, because she was a sinful woman. But she sat at his feet, anointed them with ointment, dried them with the hair of her head, kissed them, and wept. Simon, I will tell you something: her many sins were forgiven her, because she loved much." It is almost like a story, a holy story, a parable—and yet it is really happening at this very moment in this place.

But *"her many sins were also forgiven her."* And how could this be expressed any more strongly or more truly than by it all being forgotten and she, the sinful woman, being transformed into a picture? If He had said, "Your sins are forgiven you," how easy it would have then been for her to be reminded of herself again had she not previously been strengthened by the infinite forgetfulness expressed in the words "her many sins were forgiven her." "She loved much," and therefore she completely forgot herself; she completely forgot herself, "therefore her many sins were forgiven her"—forgotten, yes, almost as if they had been drowned along with her in forgetfulness. She is transformed into a picture, she becomes a memory, although not of a kind that might remind her of herself. No, this memory of her, which she herself forgot when she forgot herself, has even forgotten what she was called. This didn't happen gradually but straightaway, and the name she is remembered by is: the sinful woman, neither more nor less.

What if someone says that there was something selfish in this woman's love? The Pharisees were also taken aback that she approached Christ and drew conclusions that were unfavorable to Him, namely, that He was no prophet—and she it was who had exposed him to this because of her love, that is, her selfish love. What if someone says that there was something selfish in this woman's love, and that because it was based on need she basically only loved herself?

If anyone were to talk like that, I would answer, "Naturally there was," and I would add, "May God help us, there is still no other way." And then I would add, "God forbid that I should ever be so bold as to want to love my God or my Savior in any other way, for if there were no self-love of this kind in my love, then I would be able to imagine that I could love Him without needing Him, and God preserve me from such presumption!"

My listeners, this woman was a sinful woman. The Pharisees judged her, and they also judged Christ for letting Himself get involved with her, judging that He was therefore no prophet, let alone the Savior of the world—precisely when He was showing himself to be the Savior of the world. This woman was a sinful woman, and yet she became an exemplar. Blessed are those who are like her in loving much! The forgiveness of sins that Christ offered her while He lived continues to be offered in Christ from one generation to another and to all. To all and to each in particular is said, "Your sins are forgiven you." All receive, and each individual receives, at the altar a pledge that their sins are forgiven them. Blessed are those who are like the sinful woman in loving much! For even if it is said to all it is nevertheless only true when it is said to those who are like that woman who loved much. It is true that your sins are forgiven you in Christ, but this truth, which is also spoken to each individual, is in another sense not yet true but must be made true by each individual.

In this way, that woman is an eternal picture. By her great love she made herself, if I dare put it like this, indispensable to the Savior. For the forgiveness of sins that He earned was made true by her, by her who loved much. You can turn this around any way you like, but you will end up saying the same thing. You can praise her for being blessed by having her many sins forgiven her, and you can praise her for being blessed for loving much, and you will basically be saying the same thing—as long as you take note that the one she loved much was specifically Christ, and when you also don't forget that Christ is grace and the giver of grace.

What kind of test was it in which her love was tried? In relation to what can we say that she loved more or in relation to what that she loved less? Is the test whether she loved Christ more than father or mother, gold or possessions, honor or reputation? No, the test in which this woman was tried is the test of loving your Savior more than your sin. Ah! But perhaps there have been those who loved Christ more than father or mother or gold or possessions or honor or life but who nevertheless loved their sin more than their Savior. They did not love it in the sense of wanting to continue in it or to go on sinning but in the sense of not rightly confessing it. In a certain sense, this is something fearful, but it is true, and everyone who has any knowledge of the human heart will confirm it—namely, that there is nothing a person hangs on to with such a desperate grip as his sin. Therefore, a completely honest, deep, utterly true, and entirely unremitting confession of sin is a perfect act of love, for such a confession is what it is to love much.

The address now draws to a close. But is it not true, my listeners, that even if the Pharisees judged it highly inappropriate for that woman to force her way into the feast, she is by no means in the wrong place today, between the confessional and the altar? Oh, forget about the one who has been speaking, forget about his artfulness, if indeed he has shown any; forget about his errors, which were maybe many; forget what has been said about her—but do not forget her. She will lead you on your way, she who loved much and whose many sins were therefore forgiven. She is far from being some frightening picture, but, on the contrary, she incites us more than any speaker could do to heed the invitation that leads us to the altar: "Come unto me, all you that labor and are heavy laden," for there she goes at our head, she who loved much, she who therefore also found rest for her soul in loving much—whether we think of this in terms of her many sins being forgiven her or think that it was because she loved much that she found such rest and her many sins were forgiven her.

15

Luke 7:47 *

PRAYER

Lord Jesus Christ, you did not come into the world in order to judge it, but because you were the love that was not loved, your life judged the world. We call ourselves Christians, we say that we know no one to turn to but you—but to whom can we go when it is precisely your love that stands like a judgment against us, because we love little? There is no comfort for us if we cannot turn to you, and we would have to despair if you were really to refuse to mercifully accept us, forgiving our great sin against you and against love, accepting us who have sinned so much and loved so little.

"ONE WHO IS FORGIVEN LITTLE LOVES LITTLE."

Written by the altar is the invitation "Come unto me, all you that labor and are heavy laden, and I will give you rest."† A person accepts the invitation and goes to the altar—but when he returns from it, he encounters another saying, one that could be written over the inside

---

* From Niels Jørgen Cappelørn et al., eds., *Søren Kierkegaards Skrifter*, vol. 12 (Copenhagen: Gad, 2008), pp. 285–292.
† Matthew 11:28.

of the church door, to be read not by those entering the church but only by those leaving it. This is the saying: "Little is forgiven those who love little." The first saying invites us to the altar, the second justifies it—it is as if it said, "If you did not receive forgiveness for your sins at the altar, every last one of them, then it is down to you; the altar is not to blame, but you are, since you only love a little."

When you pray, it's difficult to arrive at the amen in the right way. The person who has never prayed thinks that it's easy enough to get to the end, but those who have felt the longing to pray and begun to do so may well have found that it always seemed as if there was something more in their hearts, as if they couldn't say everything they wanted to say or couldn't say it in quite the way they wanted to, so that they can't arrive at the amen. In exactly the same way it's also hard to receive the forgiveness of sins offered at the altar in just the right way. The gracious forgiveness of all your sins is promised you. Just listen to that, take it quite literally: the forgiveness of all your sins. That means that, in a godly sense, you are to leave the altar as lightheartedly as a newborn child who is weighed down by nothing, nothing at all—in fact, even more lightheartedly, since there was much that had weighed on your heart. There is no one who keeps you back at the altar, no one—unless you yourself do so. So cast off all your burdens, and the memory of them as well, in case you keep them in your memory—and cast off even the memory of having cast them off, so that you don't keep a trace of them there. Cast off even the memory of having cast them off in case that leads you to retain them. Cast everything off of you. There is nothing you have to be doing except believingly casting it all off and casting off everything that weighs on you and burdens you.

What could be easier? Generally, the hard thing is to take on a burden—but to dare to cast it off? And yet how difficult it is. Yes, even rarer than one who takes the whole burden on himself are those who, having been assured of a gracious forgiveness for their many sins and having received the pledge of that forgiveness, accomplish the apparently so easy task of feeling themselves unburdened of every sin, the smallest and the greatest alike. If you could see into people's hearts, you would certainly see how many go up to the altar oppressed and sighing under their heavy burdens. And if you could see into their hearts as they went from the altar, you would possibly see that there really wasn't one who had been entirely unburdened—and perhaps you would sometimes see one who went away even more troubled, troubled by the thought of not having been a worthy altar guest, because he had not experienced any solace.

We shall not keep this secret from one another, we shall not talk to one another in such a way that our talk doesn't acknowledge how things really are and depict everything as being so perfect that it doesn't really touch us real human beings. No, indeed—for how, then, could our talk help anybody? On the contrary, when the discourse makes us out to be as imperfect as we are, then it helps us to keep constantly striving. It neither produces intoxicated dreams in which we imagine to ourselves that everything could be decided once and for all, nor does it cause us silently and dejectedly to throw it all over, because it didn't happen as we had wanted it to this time or as we had prayed and longed for it to be.

In this brief, prescribed moment, then, let us think about this saying: "One who is forgiven little loves little"—a *word of judgment* but also a *word of comfort*.

And you, my listener, do not be disturbed by the fact that in this moment, when you are about to go to the altar, I perhaps speak to you as if I am assuming or demanding too much. Do you think that the speaker at such a moment ought to talk in a different manner, perhaps using all available means to soothe the individual and inspire confidence? Although if it afterward became clear that the sacred act hadn't entirely brought about joy or been a blessing for one or another person, then one might talk in another way! Oh, my friend, is it not true that, on the one hand, it is not just one or another individual who does not find what he is seeking at the altar but rather just one or another who really does? And then, on the other hand, is it not the case that a person is better supported in finding what is highest by being concerned, concerned in an inward sense, than by going forward overconfidently or with a careless cheeriness? There is indeed such a thing as a longing for God, a confidence in God, a comfort in God, a hope in God; there is love; there is good cheer—but nevertheless what is perhaps the surest way to find Him is a godly sorrow. Sorrowing for God is no passing mood that swiftly vanishes. It is perhaps deepest when one is nearest to Him, and one who is sorrowful in such a way is most afraid for himself the closer he draws to God.

"One who is forgiven little loves little." This is a word of judgment.

Generally, people see it like this: justice requires severe judgment, whereas love is mild, it does not judge, and, if it does, its judgment is mild. Oh, no—love's judgment is the most severe judgment of all. What was the most severe judgment ever pronounced on the world? Was it the Flood? Was it the ruin of the tower of Babel? Was it the destruction of Sodom and Gomorrah? Or wasn't it rather the yet more severe judgment pronounced in Christ's innocent death, love's own sacrifice? And what was the judgment? It was that love was not loved.

So it is here. The word of judgment does not say that the one who is forgiven little had sinned so much that his sins were too great and too many to be forgiven. No, the judgment is that he loves little. It is therefore not justice that rigorously refuses forgiveness and acquittal from sin. It is love that, mildly and mercifully, says, *"I* forgive you for everything—and if you are forgiven only a little, then it is because you love only a little." Justice sets strict limits and says, "No further! The measure is exact and there can be no forgiveness for you"—and that is how it is. Love says, "Everything is forgiven you, and if you are forgiven only a little, then it is because you love only a little"—but then a new sin has been committed, a new guilt added: the guilt of being forgiven only a little and of being guilty for this not on account of past sins but of lack of love. If you want to learn fear, then learn it—not from the severity of justice but from the mildness of love! Justice looks on us in judgment in such a way that we cannot endure its look, but when love looks upon us, even if we try to avoid its gaze and lower our eyes, we are nevertheless aware that we are seen. For love works its way into life in a far more inward way than justice. It penetrates into the very source of life. Justice confirms the great gulf between itself and the sinner by pushing him away, while love stands by his side, not accusing, not judging, but forgiving and acquitting. Justice speaks to the sinner in a voice of judgment that he cannot endure; he tries to stop his ears. But even if he wanted to, it would be impossible for him not to hear love, whose judgment, whose fearful judgment is: your sins are forgiven you. A fearful judgment indeed, the words of which are nothing less than terrible, and yet just for this reason the sinner cannot refrain from hearing what the judgment is.

Where can I flee from justice? If I took the wings of the morning and fled to the farthest sea, it is there; and if I hid myself in the abyss, it is there; and so in every place—but, no, there is one place I can flee to: to love. But when love judges you, the judgment (oh, horror!) is: Your sins are forgiven you. Your sins are forgiven you—and yet there is something, something in you (for where else could it find a hiding place, since love forgives everything?), that makes you aware that they have not been forgiven you. What could the horror of even the most severe judgment be in comparison with such a horror? What is the severest judgment the world can impose, what is a curse, in comparison with this judgment: your sins are forgiven you. In comparison with this, the justice who says, as you yourself say, "No, they are not forgiven," is almost mild. What is the suffering of the fratricide who, when he became a fugitive and outcast, feared that everyone would recognize him by the mark with which justice had marked him—what is this suffering in comparison with the agonies of that unfortunate person who experienced the forgiveness of sins as judgment and not as salvation? What fearful severity! That it is love, forgiving love, that, not by judging—no, for it itself suffers in doing it—is nevertheless transformed into judgment! That it is love, forgiving love, that does not want, as justice does, to expose the guilty but, on the contrary, wants to protect the guilty by forgiving and acquitting them—that it is nevertheless this love, which itself suffers in doing it, that exposes guilt even more fearfully than does justice!

Think about this phenomenon: those who make themselves guilty. According to justice, it is because people make themselves guilty that they cannot be forgiven. In saying this, justice has in mind their many sins, for justice cannot forget anything. Love says, "You have made yourselves guilty," but doesn't think about the many sins. No, love wants to forget them all; it has forgotten them all. And yet, says love, you have made yourselves guilty. Which is the more dreadful judgment? Surely it is the latter, which sounds almost crazy—because the accusation does not involve the many sins but the fact that they are forgiven, that they are all forgiven. Imagine a sinner who is sinking down into the abyss and, with his very last breath, cries out in anxiety, because he has at last admitted that the justice he had mocked all his life long was in the right in saying that he had made himself guilty. This is dreadful—but there is one thing even more dreadful: that is when it is not justice that addresses him but love, love saying, "You have made yourself guilty." Justice does not let itself be mocked, and, truly, nor does love. The judgment of love is more severe than the severest judgment that justice passes on the greatest sin: "Little is forgiven him, because he loves but little."

"One who is forgiven little loves little." This is a word of judgment but also of comfort.

I do not know, my listener, how you transgressed, or what your guilt or your sin may be. But there is one sin we are all guilty of in a greater or lesser degree: that we love but little. So take comfort from this saying, as I take comfort from it. And how do I take comfort from it? I comfort myself by reflecting that it says nothing about the divine love but only about mine. It does not say that the divine love has now become weary of being love, that it has changed or become weary of virtually squandering itself on the ungrateful human race or on my ingratitude with such indescribable mercy. It does not say that it has become something else or a lesser love, a love whose ardor has cooled because of the ungrateful human race or my ingratitude. No, the saying says nothing at all about that. So take comfort, as I take comfort. How? By considering that the reason why this is not said is that God's holy word does not lie. Therefore, it is not by accident or out of malice that nothing is said about this, but because it really is true that God's love has not grown weary of loving. No. If this is not said, it is because it really isn't so. And if it had been said—but no, it couldn't be said because God's word does not lie.

Oh, what a blessed comfort for the deepest sorrow! What if God's love had truly changed and you hadn't heard about it but, troubled that you had hitherto loved only a little, resolved devoutly to ignite the love that was in you, and, at the very moment when it burst into flame, you were ready to fan it further? And what if, at this moment, despite feeling ashamed of how imperfect your love nevertheless was, you wanted to draw near to God in order, as Scripture says, to be reconciled to Him, but you discovered that He had changed!

Imagine a girl who is in love. She anxiously admits to herself how little she has loved up until now, "but now," she says to herself, "I am going to love with all my heart"—and she does. The anxious tears she sadly cries over herself ought to be able to quench the fire, but, no, they are themselves too fiery, and it is these very tears that cause the fire to burst into flame. But in the meantime, the one she loved had changed and no longer loved her. Oh, that would be a sorry predicament! Oh, and just one such sorrow can be enough for a human being—none of us can bear more. And so, if we had to admit how little we had previously loved God and became anxious lest God had in the meantime changed—then, why then, I would despair, and I would despair at once, for there would be nothing more to hold out for, either in time or in eternity. And that is why I take comfort from this saying. I do not allow myself any escape from it, and I put all the excuses and all the glosses I might put on my behavior aside. I lay bare my breast, and when I am to be wounded by the word that strikes home in judgment, judging that "you loved but little"— Oh, strike ever deeper, ever deeper, you healing pain! And even when the judgment is "You didn't love at all," there is a sense in which I feel no pain but only an indescribable blessedness. For my condemnation, the judgment on me and on my worthless love, I contains nothing but this: that God has not changed from being love.

That is how I am comforted. And I find a comfort in the saying that you, my listener, probably also find, precisely when you hear it in such a way as to be wounded by it. For it does not say that those who are forgiven little *loved* little. No, it says, they *love* little. Oh, when justice judges, it makes a reckoning, it draws a conclusion that takes into account all that is past and says, "He loved little." In saying that, it declares that the matter is once and for all decided: we two must part and have nothing more in common. The saying, the word of love, on the contrary, says that those who are forgiven little love little. They love little. They *love*—that is to say, that is how it is now, now in this moment. Love says no more than this. Infinite love, how true you are to yourself even in your smallest utterance. They love little now, in this "now." But what is the now, what is the moment? Quickly, quickly, it passes, and now, in the next moment, now everything has changed—now they love, and, even if it is not yet much, they are trying to love much. Now everything has changed, only not "love." Love is unchanged. Unchanged, it is the same love that lovingly waited for them, that lovingly refrained from reaching a decision about them, forbearing from seeking to divorce them but instead remaining with them. And now it is no longer justice that by way of conclusion says, "They loved little," but it is love that with joy in heaven says, "They loved little, but that was then—now it has changed, now, now they love much."

But doesn't this, then, mean that the forgiveness of sins is *earned*, if not by works, then by love? When it is said that the one who is forgiven little loves little, doesn't it mean that it is love that decides whether one's sins are to be forgiven and to what extent? And doesn't that mean that the forgiveness of sins is *earned*? No, it does not. Earlier in the same gospel passage (at the end of verse 42), Christ talks about two debtors, of whom one owed a lot, the other a little. Both were forgiven, and so He asks, "Which of the two ought to love the most?" And the answer is: the one to whom much was forgiven. Now, look closely and see how we have not come into the unhappy regions of merit, but how everything remains within love. When you love much, much is forgiven you—and when much is forgiven you, you love much. Look, this is how salvation blessedly recurs in love! First, you love much and much is forgiven you—and, oh, look how love grows even stronger, and how the fact that so much has been forgiven you loves forth love again and you love much because much has been forgiven you!

It is the same with love as it is with faith. Imagine one of those unfortunates whom Christ miraculously healed. In order to be healed they had to have faith; so they have faith—and they are healed. Now they have been healed—and their faith becomes still stronger, and so they are saved. It is not as if they first of all had faith and were then healed, and then it was all over. No, the fulfillment itself even increases faith, and after the fulfillment, their faith becomes even stronger than it was before they were healed. So it is with loving much. The love that loves much is strong, divinely strong in weakness, the love that forgives so much. But love is even stronger the second time around, when the same love loves a second time and loves because much has been forgiven.

My listener, you remember how this discourse began. It is possible to disturb solemn occasions in two ways: either by talking about something inappropriate, even if it is otherwise both important and meaningful, or by talking in a disturbing way about what is most on a person's mind in such a moment. "One who is forgiven little loves little"—this could seem disturbing at just this moment, the moment before you go up to the altar at which you will receive the forgiveness of your sins. Ah! But as what is upbuilding always inspires dread at first, and as all true love is always restless at first, and as the love of God is always sorrowful at first, so what seems disturbing is not always so. What is truly calming is always unsettling at first. But compare these two dangers: the danger of being pacified by a false confidence and the danger of being unsettled by being reminded of what is unsettling—but unsettling in what way? What is unsettling here is that one can also be forgiven for having previously loved but little. There is something extraordinary about being unsettled. It is true that those who allow themselves to be molded by it do not appear to be as strong as those who know nothing of it. But, in the end, it is those who, precisely by being weak, are nevertheless perhaps the strongest. In the very end, they achieve through weakness what the strongest were unable to achieve.

So may God bless this unsettling address; that it may have unsettled you for the good; that, at the altar, you may calmly understand that what you receive there is the gracious forgiveness of all your sins.

16

1 Peter 4:8*

PRAYER

Lord Jesus Christ, birds have their nests and foxes their holes, but you had nowhere to lay your head, you were homeless in all the world, and yet you are the hiding place, the only hiding place to which the sinner can flee. And still today you continue to be the hiding place, and when the sinner flees to you, hides in you and is hidden in you, then he is well protected for eternity, for "love" hides a multitude of sins.

"LOVE HIDES A MULTITUDE OF SINS."

When we are speaking about human love, what we have said elsewhere is true, and in two respects. First, that those in whom there is love, those who love, hide a multitude of sins by not seeing the neighbor's errors. Or, if they see them, they are like those who do not see them—they hide them from themselves and from others, and love, in a sense that is even more beautiful than when one is in love, makes them blind, blind to the neighbor's sins. Then, second, those

---

* From Niels Jørgen Cappelørn et al., eds., *Søren Kierkegaards Skrifter*, vol. 12 (Copenhagen: Gad, 2008), pp. 295–302.

in whom there is love, those who love, even if in other respects they are at fault or have imperfections, and even if their sins are manifold, love; the love that is in them will hide the multitude of their sins.

When it is Christ's love being talked about, then the saying can be understood in only one way, for the fact that He was love did not serve to cover over what was imperfect in Him, the Holy One in whom there was no sin and in whose mouth there was no deceit. Of course it didn't, since all there was in Him was love, love in His heart and nothing but love in every one of His words, in all His works, in His whole life, in His death, right to the end. Ah! But love is never so perfect in a human being, which is why—or, rather, why, despite this—we have the benefit of it. When we lovingly hide a multitude of sins, then love does for us in return what we do to others: it hides our sins. That is why we ourselves need the love we show to others and how we gain an advantage from the love that is in us. Nevertheless, to the extent that this love manifests itself outwardly, it hides a multitude of sins even if, unlike Christ's self-sacrificial love, it does not embrace the whole world but only a very few. Ah! But even if it is rare enough for a person to be loving, then it is no surprise, one might be tempted to say, when people strive for that which they themselves need—love—and to that extent to be loving is in a certain sense to be looking out for oneself. But Christ did not need love. Imagine if He had not been love; imagine if He had only wanted to be what He was, the Holy One, but without love; imagine if, instead of saving the world by hiding a multitude of its sins, He had come into the world in order wrathfully to judge it—imagine all this, so that you can all the more inwardly consider that there is a unique sense in which it can be said of Him and of Him alone that His love hid a multitude of sins, that *this* was "Love"; that, as Scripture says, there is only one who is good, namely, God,* so that

---

* Matthew 19:17.

He alone was the lover who hid a multitude of sins—not just of some individuals but of the whole world.

Let us, then, in the brief time allotted speak about this saying, that *love* (Christ's love) *hides a multitude of sins.*

It is true, isn't it, that you have felt the need, and felt it today, of a love that can hide sins—your sins—which is why you are going today to the Lord's altar. It is all too true that, as Luther said, everyone has a preacher who accompanies them, eating with them, drinking with them, waking with them, sleeping with them, and who, in short, is always around them and always with them, wherever they are and whatever they are doing—and that this preacher is called flesh and blood, lusts and passions, habits and inclinations. But it is also undoubtedly true that there is a confidant in everybody's innermost being who is just as meticulous in accompanying them, and this is their conscience. Perhaps some people might succeed in concealing their sins from the world and foolishly be pleased that they had done so or, nevertheless, and more accurately, acknowledge that it is a miserable weakness and cowardice not to have had courage enough to be open about it all. But no one can conceal his sins from himself. It is impossible, for the sin that was also entirely and unconditionally hidden from oneself would not be a sin, just as little as if it were hidden from God. But this cannot be the case, since as soon as we come to know about ourselves and with regard to every part of that self-knowledge, we also know about God, and God knows about us. And the reason why this confidant and preacher who follows a person everywhere is so powerful, so accurate, and always so close and so incorruptible is because he has an agreement with God. He is with us waking and sleeping— Ah! If only his preaching doesn't make us sleepless! He is with us in the midst of the world's tumult— Ah! If only his voice does not turn the world's tumult into silence! He is with us when we are alone— Ah! If only he doesn't succeed in preventing us from feeling alone in even the most isolated places! He is with us in our daily work— Ah! If only he doesn't make us feel alienated from it like someone who is distracted! He is with us in the midst of festivities— Ah! If only he doesn't make them seem like a gloomy prison house! He is with us in the holy places— Ah! If only he doesn't hold himself back from coming there! This confidant and preacher follows us, knows what we know, knows what we are doing or leaving undone now, in this very moment, just as he also knows about what is now long, long ago in the past—although not long forgotten, for this confidant makes sure that it is not forgotten, and he has a fearful memory. No one can escape this confidant as little as the man who, in that pagan tale, sought to ride away from the sorrow that sat behind him on the horse, and, to change the image somewhat, as little as it helps "the deer to rush forward in order to flee the arrow that is lodged in his breast, for the more furiously he rushes forward the more firmly the arrow takes hold."

But today you are so far from wanting to make the useless attempt to flee, or to avoid this confidant and preacher, that you have given him leave to speak. For while it is certainly the priest who speaks from the pulpit when he preaches, the true preacher is nevertheless that confidant within. The priest can preach only in general terms, but the preacher within is quite the opposite: he only speaks and only ever speaks about you, to you, and in you.

I do not want to try to frighten you, and I myself am sufficiently frightened, but whatever your condition—humanly speaking, whether you are almost pure and innocent—when this confidant and preacher preaches for you, within you, then you will also feel what others perhaps feel with yet greater dread: you will feel a need to hide yourself. And even if you were told thousands and thousands of times that it was impossible to find this hiding place, you will still feel the need. Oh! But even if I were able to fly away to a desert island, where no one ever came or could ever come; oh, or if there were a refuge in which I could be so well concealed that not even the knowledge of my sin could find me; oh, or if there were a dividing line, no matter how narrow, between my sin and me; oh, or if there were a spot, no matter how tiny, on the other side of a yawning gulf, a spot on which I could stand while knowledge of my sin had to remain on the other side— Oh! If only there was forgiveness, a forgiveness that, instead of making me feel my guilt, the more truly took it from me along with having to be conscious of it; if only there was forgetfulness!

But this is how it really is. For love (Christ's love) hides a multitude of sins. See how everything is made new! What was vainly sought in paganism, sought and sought, and what was a barren striving under the dominion of the Law, was made possible by the gospel. At the altar, the Savior opens his arms precisely for the refugees who want to flee the consciousness of their sin, to flee from what is even worse than when one is persecuted: a troubled mind. He opens out his arms and says, "Come unto me": the fact that He opens out his arms already says, "Come," and the fact that, as He opens them out He says, "Come unto me," also says that love hides a multitude of sins.

Oh, believe Him! Could you believe that the one who opens His arms to embrace you with salvation, could you believe that He would be guilty of playing with words; could you believe that He would use a meaningless figure of speech; could you believe that He would deceive you and do so in the very moment when He says, "Come," in the very moment when you came and He held you in His embrace, so that it was as if you had been taken captive? Could you believe that there was no forgetting here, with the Holy One? No, you couldn't believe that, and if you did, then you wouldn't have come here. But blessed are they who quite literally believe that love (Christ's love) hides a multitude of sins. For a loving person, even the most loving, can lovingly judge tenderly, lovingly shut his eyes to your sins, but cannot shut your own eyes to them. Such a one can seek to attenuate your guilt, even in your own eyes, by speaking to you lovingly and sympathetically and to that extent hide them from you, but still only to a certain degree or in some way. Ah! But there is only one who can really hide them from you, literally hide them from you, so that they are as hidden as whatever lies at the bottom of the sea and what no one ever again gets to see; hidden in such a way that even if it had been as red as blood it would have become whiter than snow; hidden in the way that sin is changed into purity and you yourself might dare to believe that you had been justified and cleansed. He alone, the Lord Jesus Christ, whose love hides a multitude of sins, He alone can do this.

A human being has no authority and cannot order you to believe and, by thus ordering you, help you to believe. But if a certain authority is already a prerequisite of being able to teach, what authority—possibly even greater than the authority that commanded the stormy sea to be stilled—what authority must be needed to order those in despair, those who cannot and dare not forget the torments of repentance, those who are so crushed that they cannot and dare not prevent themselves staring at their own guilt? What authority must be needed to order them to shut their eyes, and what authority to then order them to open the eyes of faith and to see purity where before they saw guilt and sin? This is the divine authority that only He has, the Lord Jesus Christ, whose love covers a multitude of sins.

His love covers them quite literally. Imagine one person standing in front of another, so that the body of the one entirely covers the other in such a way that no one else can see the one who is hidden at their back: that is how Jesus Christ covers your sin with his *holy body*. Righteousness may be infuriated at it, but what more does it want? It makes satisfaction. And if, in agonies of repentance, you wanted to

help the righteousness that judged you from the outside by discover-
ing the guilt, there is satisfaction, an act of satisfaction, and one who
makes satisfaction, and who hides your guilt entirely, making it impossible to see it. This is impossible for righteousness and impossible,
too, for the spirit of repentance that is in you to do anything about,
for repentance, too, is unable to see when the righteousness to which
it appeals says, "I can see nothing."

He hides them quite literally. As when an anxious hen gathers her
chicks under her wings in the moment of danger and hides them, ready
to give up her life before denying them a hiding place and making it
impossible for the searching eye of the enemy to find them—that is how
He hides your sins. Just like that: for He, too, is anxious, infinitely anxious in love, and He is ready to give His life rather than to deny you your
safe refuge under His love. He is ready to give up His life—but, no, that
is why He gave up His life, in order to ensure that you have a hiding
place in His love. Moreover, it is not quite as in the case of the hen, or
is so only insofar as He is infinitely more anxious than she is when she
hides her chicks, and He is not like her in that He hides you by his death.
Oh, eternally safe, blessedly assured hiding place! For the chicks there
is still the risk that although they are hidden they are nevertheless still
in danger, and when their mother has done her utmost and laid down
her life for them, they will be robbed of their hiding place. But He, on
the other hand—indeed, if it was with His life that He concealed your
sin, then there would be the dangerous possibility that they would rob
Him of His life and you of your hiding place. But it is otherwise when it
is by His death that He conceals your sin. If it were necessary, if it hadn't
all been decided once and for all, He would rather give up His life once
more and make a hiding place for you by His death than rob you of your
hiding place. It is quite literally so: He hides your sin precisely because He
hides it with His death. Death may well get rid of the living but cannot
possibly get rid of the dead, and so it is impossible for you to be robbed of

your hiding place. Righteousness may be infuriated, but what more can it require than the death penalty? But this has been endured: His death is your hiding place. Infinite love! They speak about works of love, and many such can be named. But when we speak of a work of love or of *the* work of love, then there is only one work, and, wonderfully enough, you immediately know who is being talked about: it is Him, the Lord Jesus Christ, and his atoning death that hides a multitude of sins.

This is what is proclaimed at the altar. From the pulpit it is essentially His life that is proclaimed, but at the altar it is His death. He died once for the whole world and for our sins. His death is not repeated, but *this* is repeated: that He also died for you, you who, in His body and blood, receive the pledge that He also died for you, there, at the altar, where He gives *Himself* to you as a hiding place. Oh, sure hiding place for the sinner; oh, blessed hiding place, especially for those who have first learned what it means when conscience accuses and Law judges and righteousness hounds one with punishments. Then, weary to the point of despair, to find rest in the only hiding place that can be found! The most someone else is able to do for you, even the most loving, is to soften the blow, to excuse you, and to leave it to you to decide how to use what is offered—but no one can give you himself. Only Jesus Christ can do that, who gives Himself to you as a hiding place. He doesn't give you some reasons for having faith, nor a doctrine that He shares with you—no, He gives you Himself. As the night spreads itself out over all things and plunges them in concealment, so He gave Himself up and became the hiding place behind which lies a sinful world, a world He saved. Righteousness breaks against this hiding place, and not only is it made gentler, as when the sun's rays are broken up by colored glass—no!—it breaks powerlessly against this hiding place and can't break through it. He gave Himself up for the whole world to be a hiding place, for you, too, and for me.

And therefore, my Lord and Savior, you whose love hides a multitude of sins, when I feel my sin and the multitude of my sins as I should, and when heaven's righteousness is served only by the wrath that rests upon me and on my life, when there is only one person on earth I hate and despise, one person whom I would fly to the world's end to avoid, and that is myself—then I will not begin so as to begin in vain and in such a way as would only lead either deeper into despair or to madness, but I will flee at once to you, and you will not deny me the hiding place you have lovingly offered to all. You will tear me from the inquisitorial eye of righteousness and save me from that person and from the memories with which he torments me. You will help me to dare remain in my hiding place, forgotten by righteousness and by that person I despise, by my becoming changed: another, better person.

Devout listeners, this is the love that hides a multitude of sins that you are looking for today, seeking it at the altar. From the Church's servant you have received assurance as to the gracious forgiveness of your sins, and at the altar you receive the pledge thereof—and not only that. For you do not simply take this pledge in the way that you can be given a pledge by another human being to assure you of their feelings for you. No, you receive the pledge as a pledge that you receive Him Himself. As you receive the pledge, you receive Him Himself: in and with the visible sign He gives you Himself to hide your sins. He is the truth, not in such a way that you get to know from Him what the truth is and are then left to yourself but so as to remain in the truth only by remaining in Him. He is the way, not in such a manner that you get to know from Him which way you should be going and are then left to go your way on your own but so as to remain in the way only by remaining in Him. He is the life, not in such a way that you have life given you by Him and are then left to fend for yourself but so as to have life only by remaining in Him. It is in the same way that He is also your hiding place, for only by remaining in Him and only by living yourself into His life are you hidden and get the multitude of your sins hidden. That is why the Eucharist is called having Communion with him. It is not merely in remembrance of Him, not merely a pledge that you have Communion with Him, but it is Communion and it is this Communion that you are to strive to preserve in your daily life by more and more living yourself out of yourself and living into Him, into His love, the love that hides a multitude of sins.